DISARMAMENT UNDER INTERNATIONAL LAW

HUMAN DIMENSIONS IN FOREIGN POLICY, MILITARY STUDIES,
AND SECURITY STUDIES

Series editors: Stéphanie A.H. Bélanger, Pierre Jolicoeur, and Stéfanie
von Hlatky

Books published in the Human Dimensions in Foreign Policy, Military
Studies, and Security Studies series offer fresh perspectives on foreign
affairs and global governance. Titles in the series illuminate critical
issues of global security in the twenty-first century and emphasize the
human dimensions of war such as the health and well-being of soldiers,
the factors that influence operational effectiveness, the civil-military
relations and decisions on the use of force, as well as the ethical, moral,
and legal ramifications of ongoing conflicts and wars. Foreign policy is
also analyzed both in terms of its impact on human rights and the role
the public plays in shaping policy directions.

 With a strong focus on definitions of security, the series encourages
discussion of contemporary security challenges and welcomes works
that focus on issues including human security, violent conflict, terrorism,
military cooperation, and foreign and defence policy. This series is published in collaboration with Queen's University and the Royal Military
College of Canada with the Centre for International and Defence Policy,
the Canadian Institute for Military and Veteran Health Research, and
the Centre for Security, Armed Forces, and Society.

Disarmament under International Law

JOHN KIERULF

McGill-Queen's University Press
Montreal & Kingston • Chicago

© McGill-Queen's University Press 2017

ISBN 978-0-7735-4822-0 (cloth)
ISBN 978-0-7735-4823-7 (paper)
ISBN 978-0-7735-4847-3 (ePDF)
ISBN 978-0-7735-4848-0 (ePUB)

Legal deposit first quarter 2017
Bibliothèque nationale du Québec

Published simultaneously in the United Kingdom, Eire, and Europe in paperback by Djøf Publishing, Copenhagen.

Printed in Canada on acid-free paper that is 100% ancient forest free (100% post-consumer recycled), processed chlorine free.

McGill-Queen's University Press acknowledges the support of the Canada Council for the Arts for our publishing program. We also acknowledge the financial support of the Government of Canada through the Canada Book Fund for our publishing activities.

Library and Archives Canada Cataloguing in Publication

Kierulf, John, 1946–, author
    Disarmament under international law / John Kierulf.

(Human dimensions in foreign policy, military studies, and security studies; 4)
Includes bibliographical references and index.
Issued in print and electronic formats.
ISBN 978-0-7735-4822-0 (cloth). – ISBN 978-0-7735-4823-7 (paper). – ISBN 978-0-7735-4847-3 (ePDF). – ISBN 978-0-7735-4848-0 (ePUB)

    1. United Nations. 2. Disarmament. 3. Arms control.
4. Security, International. I. Title.

JZ5595.K53 2017   327.1'74   C2016-905362-8
                                           C2016-905363-6

This book was typeset by True to Type in 10.5/13 Sabon

Contents

Abbreviations

AAM	Air-to-air missiles
ABM	Anti-Ballistic Missile Treaty
APM	Anti-personnel mine
ATT	Arms Trade Treaty
BRIC	Brazil, Russia, India and China
BWC	Biological Weapons Convention
CBM	Confidence-building measures
CCD	Conference of the Committee on Disarmament
CCM	Convention on Cluster Munitions
CCW	Convention on Certain Conventional Weapons
CD	Conference on Disarmament
CFE	Conventional Armed Forces in Europe
CFSP	Common Foreign and Security Policy
CSBM	Confidence- and security-building measures
CSCE	Conference on Security and Co-operation in Europe
CSIS	Center for Strategic & International Studies
CTBT	Comprehensive Nuclear-Test-Ban Treaty
CTBTO	Comprehensive Nuclear-Test-Ban Treaty Organization
CWC	Chemical Weapons Convention
DIIS	Dansk Institut for Internationale Studier (Danish Institute for International Studies)
ECOWAS	Economic Community of West African States
EEAS	European External Action Service
EEZ	Exclusive Economic Zone
ENDC	Eighteen Nation Committee on Disarmament
ENISA	European Network and Information Security Agency

ENMOD	Convention on the Prohibition of Military or Any Other Hostile Use of Environmental Modification Techniques
EPAA	European Phased Adaptive Approach
EU	European Union
FMCT	Fissile Material Cut-Off Treaty
FSC	Forum for Security Co-operation
GDR	German Democratic Republic
G8	Group of seven major industrial countries, plus Russia
HCOC	Hague Code of Conduct
IAEA	International Atomic Energy Agency
IALANA	International Association of Lawyers Against Nuclear Arms
IANSA	International Action Network on Small Arms
ICAN	International Campaign to Abolish Nuclear Weapons
ICBL	International Campaign to Ban Landmines
ICBM	Intercontinental ballistic missile
ICC	International Criminal Court
ICJ	International Court of Justice
ICRC	International Committee of the Red Cross
ILA	International Law Association
ILC	International Law Commission
IMS	International monitoring system
INF	Intermediate-range nuclear forces
IRBM	Intermediate-range ballistic missile
ISU	Implementation Support Unit
JCG	Joint Consultative Group
MAD	Mutual assured destruction
MANPADS	Man-portable air defence systems
MBFR	Mutual and Balanced Force Reduction
MD	Missile defence
MIRV	Multiple independently targetable re-entry vehicle
MRBM	Medium-range ballistic missile
MTCR	Missile Technology Control Regime
NAM	Non-Aligned Movement
NAS	Nuclear-armed states
NATO	North Atlantic Treaty Organization
NGO	Non-governmental organization
NPT	Non-Proliferation Treaty (of Nuclear Weapons)
NRA	National Rifle Association

NSA	Negative Security Assurances
NSG	Nuclear Suppliers Group
NSP	Nuclear Security Project
NTI	Nuclear Threat Initiative
NWFZ	Nuclear-weapon-free zone
NWS	Nuclear-weapon states
OAS	Organization of American States
OPCW	Organization for the Prohibition of Chemical Weapons
OSCC	Open Skies Consultative Commission
OSCE	Organization for Security and Co-operation in Europe
PAROS	Prevention of an Arms Race in Outer Space
PIR	Russian Center for Policy Studies
PNET	Peaceful Nuclear Explosions Treaty
PSI	Proliferation Security Initiative
PTBT	Partial Test Ban Treaty
R2P	Responsibility to Protect
SALT	Strategic Arms Limitation Treaty
SALW	Small arms and light weapons
SAM	Surface-to-air missile
SAS	Small Arms Survey
SDI	Strategic Defence Initiative
SIPRI	Stockholm International Peace Research Institute
SLBM	Submarine-launched ballistic missile
SORT	Strategic Offensive Reductions Treaty
SRBM	Short-range ballistic missile
SSOD	Special Session on Disarmament
START	Strategic Arms Reduction Treaty
TBM	Tactical ballistic missile
TLE	Treaty limited equipment
TNCD	Ten Nation Committee on Disarmament
TNW	Tactical nuclear weapons
TTBT	Threshold Test Ban Treaty
UAV	Unmanned aerial vehicles
UN	United Nations
UNCLOS	United Nations Convention on the Law of the Sea
UNDC	United Nations Disarmament Commission
UNDP	United Nations Development Program
UNGA	United Nations General Assembly
UNIDIR	United Nations Institute for Disarmament Research

UNMOVIC	United Nations Monitoring, Verification and Inspection Commission
UNODA	United Nations Office for Disarmament Affairs
UNOG	United Nations Office at Geneva
UNOOSA	United Nations Office for Outer Space Affairs
UNSC	United Nations Security Council
UNSCOM	United Nations Special Commission
USCYBERCOM	United States Cyber Command
VERTIC	Verification Research, Training and Information Centre
WEOG	Western Europe and Other States Group
WHO	World Health Organization
WMD	Weapons of mass destruction
WMDFZ	Weapons of mass destruction–free zone
WP	Warsaw Pact

Preface

In the Old Testament Book of Isaiah (2:4), people are called to "beat their swords into plowshares and their spears into pruning hooks," in other words, a call for disarmament, a concept that has thus existed since the early Iron Age.

Disarmament, arms control, and non-proliferation are important components of security policy. Until now, these issues have mainly been dealt with in the literature on those subjects and by disarmament experts in the context of security policy. The threat from nuclear weapons during the Cold War and the threat of a devastating nuclear war in particular have been discussed in various books and articles, and at numerous conferences. The American and English literature on disarmament, arms control, and non-proliferation especially has dealt with these threats in a security policy and historical context. The United Nations, notably the United Nations Institute for Disarmament Research (UNIDIR), has published several books on specific topics about disarmament, arms control, and non-proliferation. One of the most comprehensive books in the field is Jozef Goldblat's *Arms Control – The New Guide to Negotiations and Agreements*. Issues of arms control, in particular the problem of the use of nuclear weapons, and of land mines, cluster bombs, and other conventional weapons, "which must be deemed to be excessively injurious or indiscriminate against the civilian population," are mainly described in the literature on the law of war – also called the international humanitarian law of armed conflict (*jus in bello*).

This book was originally written in Danish and published by Djøf Publishing in March 2014 under the title *Nedrustning i et folkeretligt perspektiv* (*Disarmament in a Perspective of International Law*). This new

English edition of the book, translated by the author, is not merely a strict translation of the original Danish text. *Disarmament under International Law* is an updated, revised, and expanded presentation of disarmament law, with new sections and paragraphs on disarmament developments and events that have occurred since the Danish book was published. The primary aim of this book is to introduce the reader to disarmament law, i.e., the rules as they are formulated in treaties and conventions as well as in customary international law, and to describe, explain, and discuss the system of international legal regulation of disarmament and arms control of both weapons of mass destruction and conventional weapons. It examines only the most important international accords, in the form of treaties, conventions, and agreements on disarmament, arms control, and non-proliferation, as part of international law.

My main objective in writing this book is to argue for stronger political action to take further steps toward disarmament, arms control, and non-proliferation concluding legally binding agreements. Their purpose is to promote the reduction of weapons and to strengthen arms control measures, especially for the most devastating weapons – nuclear weapons – which must be further reduced and ultimately abolished. Their use would be a gross violation of international humanitarian law.

The book is intended not only for experts in international law, researchers, students, and government officials who deal with these topics, but also for a broader audience of readers who want to know and understand more about current disarmament, arms control, and non-proliferation issues. The subject matter is technically complex, so the book is written in language that seeks to make the text understandable for readers with no previous knowledge in the field.

It is the author's wish that the book will contribute to raising awareness, understanding, and – most important – more public debate and political action on the problems of disarmament, arms control, and non-proliferation of both weapons of mass destruction and conventional weapons. I hope the book will also be used to educate and as a handbook for information on the most important disarmament and arms control issues. The interested reader who wants more information on the issues will find references to the texts of treaties and resolutions, literature, websites, and other source material in the appendices and footnotes.

I wish to express my gratitude to my former employer of forty years – the Danish Ministry of Foreign Affairs. My work in the foreign service has given me ample opportunity to participate in international negotiations and discussions in Vienna, Geneva, New York, and other cities on the drafting, interpretation, implementation, and compliance of disarmament and arms control agreements. That experience is the background and inspiration for writing this book.

I also wish to extend many thanks to the Danish Institute for International Studies for its support in publishing the original book in Danish and to McGill-Queen's University Press for publishing this new English version of the book. I am also very grateful to Associate Professor Anders Henriksen, University of Copenhagen, Faculty of Law, Centre for International Law, Conflict and Crisis, for his review, critical comments, and constructive suggestions for amendments and improvements in the original Danish edition. My sincere thanks to Wilfried Roloff, Djøf Publishing, Copenhagen, who facilitated my contacts with McGill-Queen's University Press, to Kathleen Fraser and Natalie Blachere, MQUP, and to Gillian Scobie, the copy editor, for their excellent work with the publication of my book.

Last – but most important – I wish to thank my wife Marly and our daughters for their inspiration, encouragement, and patience. Without their support, I would not have been able to realize my book projects.

Finally, I wish to dedicate this book to all the admirable people who are working tirelessly in civil society organizations and research institutes to promote disarmament and arms control. Their work is contributing to a safer world.

Charlottenlund, February 2016
John Kierulf

DISARMAMENT UNDER INTERNATIONAL LAW

Introduction

The book is divided into three parts:

PART ONE

Describes the background and context in international law (chapter 1); the historical development of disarmament and arms control agreements (chapter 2); the negotiation of agreements, including negotiating fora (chapter 3); and the interpretation, compliance, and enforcement of the agreements (chapter 4).

PART TWO

Contains the book's main substantive chapters on the existing disarmament, arms control, and non-proliferation agreements for both weapons of mass destruction and conventional weapons.

Chapters 5 to 10 discuss weapons of mass destruction, i.e., nuclear weapons, biological and chemical weapons and their means of delivery. Chapter 5 deals with nuclear weapons, including the Non-Proliferation Treaty (NPT), nuclear-test-ban treaties, nuclear-weapon-free zones, and the legality of nuclear weapons, including the International Court of Justice's advisory opinion. Other sections in chapter 5 include NATO's nuclear weapons policy, the prohibition on the use of nuclear weapons, and first use of nuclear weapons. The chapter ends with a discussion of the relationship between the use of nuclear weapons and human rights and of the humanitarian impact of nuclear weapons. Chapters 6 and 7 cover the two other main categories of weapons of mass destruction, biological weapons and chemical weapons. Chapter 8 discusses other types of weapons of mass destruction, including cyberwarfare. Chapter 9 deals with weapons of mass destruction in outer space. Finally, chapter 10 reviews delivery systems for weapons of mass destruction, i.e., missiles, unmanned aerial vehicles (drones), and missile defence.

The section on conventional weapons is divided into two main parts: heavy conventional weapons; and small arms and light weapons, inhumane conventional weapons, anti-personnel mines, and cluster bombs.

Chapter 11, on heavy conventional weapons, focuses on the Treaty on Conventional Armed Forces in Europe (CFE), the Vienna Document on Confidence- and Security-Building Measures, and the Treaty on Open Skies.

Chapter 12 discusses small arms and light weapons and reviews the regulation of inhumane conventional weapons, anti-personnel mines, and cluster bombs.

Chapter 13 covers arms trade, export control regimes, and world military expenditure.

PART THREE

Chapter 14 contains recommendations for further development of international law for disarmament, arms control, and non-proliferation.

The book ends with an epilogue on the threat of nuclear weapons and the necessity of nuclear disarmament and non-proliferation.

Notes are found at the end of the text after the appendices.

The appendices include:

- List of key disarmament, arms control and non-proliferation treaties, conventions, and agreements
- Classification of disarmament, arms control and non-proliferation treaties, conventions, and agreements

DEFINITIONS

To clarify the meaning of some of the general terms used in this book, some of the basic concepts are defined below. The definitions of the various types of weapons and agreements are stated in the respective chapters.

Disarmament

Disarmament, often used as a generic term for disarmament, arms control, and non-proliferation, is the reduction or quantitative limitation and destruction of military forces and inventories of weapons and military equipment to stop rearmament and an arms race, and reduce the number of military forces and weapon inventories.

Reduction of weapons refers to reducing the number of maximum permitted weapons and equipment.

Disarmament can be either

- unilateral: an independent national measure made by a single state;
- bilateral: an agreement between two states parties;
- multilateral: an agreement between several states parties

The reduction may be

- forced, for example by the victor in connection with a ceasefire or peace agreement;
- voluntary, on a state's own initiative (moratorium);
- agreed on between two or more states in a treaty or convention.

Disarmament may be limited either as

- quantitative reduction: the size of military forces or number of weapons is decreased;
- qualitative reduction: certain types of weapons are eliminated (i.e., completely prohibited).

Disarmament agreements may be further limited geographically to include only certain areas, e.g., nuclear-weapon-free zones.

Total disarmament means the complete elimination of weapons or of certain types of weapons, by prohibiting their production, storage, deployment, and use.

The opposite of disarmament is rearmament, or military build-up, or increasing military forces and inventories of weapons and military equipment.

Arms Control

International agreements on measures to limit the effect and capacity of weapons, and the testing, production, storage, deployment, transfer, and use of weapons. Arms control measures are found in many international treaties and conventions, and are introduced when embargoes are adopted against states taking part in an armed conflict. The concept of arms control is also used nationally with measures taken to regulate citizens' right to possess firearms.

In the English – and particularly in American – literature, the term "arms control" is often used as a generic term for both disarmament and arms control. The United Nations Charter uses the term "Regulation of Armaments" for arms control (see Articles 11 and 47 of the Charter).

Non-proliferation

The term "non-proliferation" is most commonly used in connection with efforts to prevent the spread of nuclear weapons (see the Non-Proliferation Treaty). There are two kinds of proliferation:

- horizontal proliferation: preventing the spread of weapons and weapons materials and technologies to states that have not previously possessed them or to other so-called non-state actors, e.g., terrorist organizations, insurgent movements, and criminal gangs or individuals; and
- vertical proliferation: the increase in the number, quality, or destructive capacity of existing weapons.

Non-vertical proliferation means eliminating or reducing the numbers of weapons through prohibitions or restrictions.

Disarmament law

The rules and norms of international law that apply to disarmament, arms control, and non-proliferation. The rules, which are generally enshrined in treaties and conventions or applied in the norms of customary international law, may contain provisions on prohibitions, or regulate the reduction, limitation, control, and destruction of weapons.

Verification

Testing or examining another state party to see if it is complying with its obligations under a disarmament, arms control, or non-proliferation agreement. According to certain agreements, verification may be carried out by inspecting the territory of another state party (on-site inspection) to determine if the other state has implemented and continues to comply with the agreement.

Customary International Law

A course of action that has been followed as a common and uniform practice without exception over a long period of time by the members of a society – or a large majority of its members. They are motivated by the conviction that they have a legal obligation to carry out the action or respect the omission, i.e., from a sense of legal necessity – *opinio juris* (see chapter 1 on the background of customary law in international law (ICJ (International Court of Justice) Article 38.1.b)).

Jus cogens

A legal principle or norm that cannot be waived – not even by a treaty – and that cannot be violated. This fundamental principle of international law is set out in Article 53 of the Vienna Convention of 1969 on the Law of Treaties. According to Article 53, *jus cogens* has to be accepted and recognized by all states as a norm from which no derogation is permitted. It can only be changed through a new standard of common international law. Article 2.4 of the United Nations Charter provides that "all Members shall refrain in their international relations from the threat or use of force against the territorial integrity or political independence of any state, or in any other manner inconsistent with the Purposes of the United Nations." This is considered to be a *jus cogens* norm in international law.

The prohibition of the use of force as an absolute *jus cogens* norm applies only to the use of aggressive force, i.e., the threat or use of force by an illegal attack (war of aggression), compared with the inherent right of individual or collective self-defence if an armed attack occurs against a member of the United Nations. This would be considered defensive war (see Article 51 of the Charter of the United Nations).

Which norms can be considered to fall within the category of *jus cogens* is a controversial issue in international law. In recent years, the United Nations International Law Commission has highlighted the following examples as the most frequently quoted *jus cogens* norms: the prohibitions of aggression, slavery and slave trade, genocide, racial discrimination, apartheid, torture, and the basic rules of international humanitarian law applicable to armed conflicts.

PART ONE

Background, Context, History, Negotiation, Interpretation, Compliance, and Enforcement of Agreements

1

Background and Context
in International Law

BACKGROUND

International law is usually defined as the legal rules, norms, and customs governing the relationship of autonomous states and associations of states. It is different than the law applicable in the various nation states, i.e., internal or domestic law. States are the subjects of international law; individuals, of domestic law.

The primary source of law in international law is the treaties and conventions that contain the legal rules that regulate the subject matter of the treaty or convention in question. The sources of international law also include judgments and advisory opinions from the ICJ.[1] In addition to the written law enshrined in treaties and conventions, international law theory also recognizes that binding customary law, i.e., general rules by which all states are bound, may be created as part of international law.

Article 38 of the Statute of the ICJ states that the Court, which decides disputes that are submitted to it in accordance with international law, shall apply:

- international conventions to establish rules expressly recognized by the contesting states;
- international custom, as evidence of a general practice accepted as law;
- the general principles of law recognized by civilized nations;
- judicial decisions and the teachings of the most highly qualified legal experts of various nations, as subsidiary means for the determination of rules of law, subject to the provisions of Article 59.

In contrast to national laws that apply to all citizens of the state, a specific feature of written international law is that treaties and conventions only apply to the states that have signed and ratified the treaty or convention in question or agreed to it (so-called states parties). This is also indirectly implied in the withdrawal provisions found in most treaties and conventions in which a state party has the right to withdraw from the agreement if it no longer wants to be legally bound by the treaty or convention. This may occur when the state decides that extraordinary events, related to the subject matter of the agreement, have jeopardized its most vital interests, for example if another state party has grossly violated the agreement. A treaty or convention is ratified by a state when the state, after signing the agreement, issues its final declaration of commitment to be bound by the agreement. The ratification consists of a written statement signed by the head of state, who usually only signs the so-called instrument of ratification after the national parliament has given its consent.

The reason international law cannot be imposed on all states in the world is that states are sovereign, thus autonomous, subjects of international law and cannot be forced to be bound by certain treaties and conventions which they do not want to sign and ratify or adhere to (i.e., become a state party). That is why a majority of United Nations member states cannot decide, by a simple or qualified majority, to declare, for example, all nuclear weapons, cluster bombs, and antipersonnel mines illegal and destroyed through disarmament. Because they need to protect and defend their sovereignty and territorial integrity, states reserve their right to produce or acquire and possess – and eventually use – the weapons that they consider necessary to avert armed attacks in self-defence and to maintain a deterrent capability so they can acquire or maintain an international position of power.

Like international law in other areas, disarmament law is limited in the sense that it is not formulated by any global legislative authority with binding effect for all states. Nor can disarmament law be executed or enforced against any state that is not a party to the disarmament agreement in question. The only exception to this international legal order is the United Nations Security Council's ability to adopt legally binding resolutions to maintain or restore international peace and security according to Article 42 of the Charter of the United Nations. Resolutions adopted by the United Nations General Assembly, often referred to as "soft law," are not legally binding on the United Nations member states, but only political recommendations. In many cases, these include *de lege ferenda* recommendations, i.e., what the law should be, on how the member states that have proposed and voted for the resolution want a particular conflict resolved or a particular legal regime imposed for a particular area.

International legal theory distinguishes between the international law regulating states' behaviour in times of peace (*jus pacis* (the law of peace)), and the law that applies to armed conflict (*jus in bello* (the law of war)). Disarmament measures that are in accordance with disarmament law in the first place apply in peacetime. Disarmament and arms control agreements are also applicable during armed conflicts.

The law of war that applies to armed conflicts (extensive and continuous fighting) is traditionally divided in two categories, with the following Latin terms:

Jus ad bellum – or the law concerning war – comprises rules on

- the prevention of war,
- the regulation of conditions under which states may resort to war, or
- the use of armed force in general.

The prohibition on the use of force among states and the exceptions to it (self-defence and United Nations authorization for the use of force) are set out in the United Nations Charter.

Jus in bello – or the law of war or law of armed conflict – regulates and restricts the means of warfare – in particular weapons – and the methods of warfare that are lawful, i.e., that regulate the conduct of the parties engaged in an armed conflict. *Jus in bello* is synonymous with international humanitarian law, which seeks to minimize the suffering in armed conflicts, notably by protecting and assisting all victims of armed conflict to the greatest possible extent.

JUS AD BELLUM

The fundamental rule, as enshrined in the Article 2 of the Charter of the United Nations, is that the use of force or the threat of the use of force in international relations between states is prohibited. Paragraph 3 of Article 2 stipulates, "All Members shall settle their international disputes by peaceful means in such a manner that international peace and security, and justice, are not endangered." Paragraph 4 contains a general rule, which prohibits member states from using or threatening to use armed force against any state's territorial integrity or political independence, or in any other manner inconsistent with the purposes of the United Nations.

The law about war includes the rules designed to prevent armed conflict, including prohibiting the use of armed force. There are only two exceptions to this general prohibition against the use of force, i.e., situations where a state is entitled to use military force outside its territory:

1 the right of individual or collective self-defence if an armed attack occurs (Article 51), or
2 the decision by the United Nations Security Council to use force by air, sea, or land forces in order to maintain or restore international peace and security. Such action may include demonstrations, blockades, and other operations by air, sea, or land forces of Members of the United Nations (Article 42).

The right to self-defence can be exercised individually by a single state, or collectively by several states, for example by NATO (North Atlantic Treaty Organization) member countries. Thus, only the UN (United Nations) Security Council can authorize the use of military force or other sanctions, such as commercial, financial, or arms and travel embargoes and restrictions. A decision in the Security Council requires that a majority of Security Council members vote in favour of the specific use of force, and that none of the five permanent members of the Council vote against (exercise their right to veto decisions).

It is implicit in the wording of Articles 51 and 42 that armed force only be used in self-defence, that is, what is needed to maintain or restore international peace and security. Self-defence must be reasonably proportional to the attack that triggers the right to self-defence. International customary law also recognizes that self-defence can be exercised before the attack is initiated if the attack is imminent. In that case, the preventive counterattack is carried out in self-defence under international law to prevent the attack before it starts. But the right to self-defence does not in itself legitimize a first attack.

Recent theories of international law have put forward the view that new customary international law has been created in recent years to allow so-called humanitarian intervention – using military force even without a mandate from the United Nations Security Council – both against other countries and in a state's internal conflicts to stop civil war or prevent genocide and massive violations of human rights, according to the "Responsibility to Protect" (R2P) concept.

Jus ad bellum also includes provisions on disarmament, arms control, and non-proliferation. The purpose of these rules is to prevent war, limit the risk of armed conflicts, and promote détente (relaxation of political tensions) by reducing weapons stocks, controlling existing weapons, and preventing the proliferation of weapons, especially weapons of mass destruction, as well as providing openness and transparency in military matters through confidence-building measures (CBMs) which are intended to reduce fear, suspicion, and misinterpretation. CBMs are designed to prevent unwanted escalations of hostilities and build mutual trust through openness by exchanges of information on military matters, for example exercises. However, as explained in the following chapters, the right to possess and use weapons is not unlimited. Disarmament and arms control law have imposed many limitations on the numbers, types, and capacities of weapons that states may have in their inventories (numerical and material limitations), and where they may be used (geographical limitations).

JUS IN BELLO

Jus in bello – or international humanitarian law – comprises the international laws of war that are applied in armed conflicts. The purpose of these rules is to regulate the warring parties' (combatants) actions and conduct in connection with and during combat operations to limit the harmful effects of armed conflicts and protect the victims of war, including civilians affected by war. International humanitarian law protects persons who are not or are no longer participating in hostilities and restricts the means and methods of warfare. It is also known as the law of war or the law of armed conflict.

International humanitarian law prohibits all means and methods of warfare that

- fail to discriminate between those taking part in the fighting and civilians not taking part in the hostilities,
- cause superfluous injury or unnecessary suffering, or
- cause severe or long-term damage to the environment.

The basic rules of war are:

- the rule of distinction, which prohibits the use of weapons that cannot distinguish between military and civilian targets;
- the rule of proportionality, which prohibits the use of weapons whose effects are disproportionate to achieving a specific, legitimate military target; and
- the rule of necessity, which provides that a state may only use the level of force in a military operation necessary to achieve its military objective.

Based on these rules, several treaties and conventions have banned the use of many weapons, including exploding bullets, biological and chemical weapons, blinding laser weapons, anti-personnel mines, and cluster bombs. It is generally recognized – even among states with nuclear weapons – that international humanitarian law applies to the use of nuclear weapons. The International Court of Justice also stated in its Advisory Opinion on the Legality of the Threat or Use of Nuclear Weapons that such use is subject to international humanitarian law. The Court ruled that nuclear weapons "would generally be contrary to the rules of international law applicable in armed conflict, and in particular the principles and rules of humanitarian law," except in marginal cases under extraordinary circumstances involving the very survival of a state. But even in such cases, a state's right of self-defence is always subject to international humanitarian law, as stated in chapter 5.

Jus in bello includes, first, the humanitarian rules for the protection of victims of armed conflicts, which must be observed during the armed conflict, both for enemy forces and for civilians. The main provisions of international humanitarian law during armed conflict are laid down in the four Geneva Conventions of 12 August 1949 and Protocols I and II of 8 June 1977 additional to the Geneva Conventions relating to the protection of victims of armed conflicts. The Geneva Conventions have become universal, with 196 states parties to the convention. Additional Protocol I has 174 states parties, Additional Protocol II 168 states parties. Iran, Pakistan, and the United States have signed both protocols, but have not yet ratified them.

These basic rules protecting the victims of war comprise protecting the wounded and sick in armed forces; improving the condition of the wounded, sick, and shipwrecked members of armed forces; the treatment of prisoners of war; and protecting civilian persons in time of war.[2] A detailed discussion of international humanitarian law during armed conflict falls outside the scope of this book. However, chapter 12, on small conventional weapons, includes a description of so-called inhumane conventional weapons. These are regulated in the United Nations Weapons Convention of 1980 on Certain Conventional Weapons and its Protocols on, among others, anti-personnel mines and cluster bombs. Chapter 5 also contains views about the question as to whether the use of nuclear weapons may be considered a violation of the fundamental principles of international humanitarian law.

Second, *jus in bello* includes rules on the methods and means (i.e., weapons) that may be used in warfare. These rules are found in the so-called Hague Conventions of 1907 (see chapter 2 on historical development).

CONTEXT IN INTERNATIONAL LAW

Just as a community founded on the rule of law is based on the nation state's existing legislation and case law, international relations between states should also be regulated by legal rules in international, legally binding treaties, and conventions. This is particularly true for disarmament law, which has great importance for state security and thus for states' survival as independent countries.

Disarmament law includes rules on prohibitions of certain types of weapons, reductions in weapons inventories, regulations of weapons, control of the use of weapons, and prevention of the spread of weapons, particularly weapons of mass destruction.

Economic development and social prosperity depend on both internal and international peace and security. Other factors are obviously also important for economic development and prosperity. International peace and security cannot be achieved and maintained without binding rules of international law on the regulation and control of weapons. As a result, disarmament, arms control, and non-proliferation are necessary to maintain international peace and security. Disarmament measures must always serve national security interests, if they are to be credible and sustainable. Otherwise the rule of law for disarmament cannot be expected to be implemented. Disarmament and arms control in international law is a prerequisite for ensuring peaceful internal conditions in individual countries and in the international relations between states. International peace and security should be based on legally binding treaties and not be dependent on power structures. The alternative is international lawlessness and tyranny, where the militarily strongest countries exert their power and exploit weaker countries by force or threat of force. International diplomatic cooperation to further develop the treaty regimes for disarmament, arms control, and non-proliferation should be strengthened and enhanced to ensure international peace and security, thus contributing to the conditions for global economic development and prosperity.

It is not clear when disarmament law was recognized as an independent part of international law. Since disarmament law mainly consists of treaties and conventions, which are international legal instruments, it seems obvious that disarmament treaties and conventions have always been part of international law.

On the initiative of Dr Julie Dahlitz, Australian National University, Canberra, and Professor Dr Detlev Dicke, dean of the faculty of law at the University of Fribourg, Switzerland, a symposium on disarmament law was held in Geneva in February and March of 1991. The symposium was attended by a number of prominent academics in international law. Representatives of the United Nations, the International Law Commission (ILC), and the International Atomic Energy Agency (IAEA) met in Geneva, as well as diplomats from the United Nations missions of thirty-six countries. Among the participants was Göran Lysén, professor of international law at Uppsala University, who had recently published *The International Regulation of Armaments: The Law of Disarmament*.

Treaty law was a major topic at the symposium, highlighting the importance of the Vienna Convention on the Law of Treaties. The discussions included agreements and declarations on disarmament and arms control that are not enshrined in treaties, but only formulated in political declarations and therefore only politically binding. Unilateral and multilateral declarations, including resolutions adopted by the United Nations General Assembly, were also discussed. These declarations are political recommendations to one or more states to undertake or refrain from taking a certain action or behaviour. Participants argued that such political expressions of states' common understanding – e.g., in resolutions adopted unanimously – may be considered *de lege ferenda*, i.e., "soft law," international standards that may evolve into binding international law if they reflect the current general international legal opinion in a particular area.

The Law of Disarmament, like other branches of international law, cannot be executed or enforced by means of force against any state, except in cases where the United Nations Security Council has adopted a resolution on coercive measures under UN Chapter VII, Article 42, for example in the form of trade or economic sanctions. The issue of verifying compliance with disarmament and arms control agreements was thoroughly discussed against this background during the seminar.

One of the key issues in several of the statements was the question of what status should be given to the international law on disarmament and arms control.[3] None of the participants doubted that the international law on disarmament and arms control forms an integral part of international law or that disarmament law is in conformity with the general principles and rules of international law. The discussions also showed that there was a common understanding and general acceptance that disarmament law, with its distinguishing features, constitutes an independent, specialized branch of international law deserving of special study and attention. The participants also agreed that disarmament law is gaining in importance.

2

Historical Development of Disarmament and Arms Control

INTRODUCTION

Disarmament and arms control are not new phenomena. Ever since ancient times, efforts have been made to promote disarmament, for example when victors after a war disarmed their defeated opponents to prevent them from attacking again.

Disarmament and arms control efforts in the form of international agreements have been implemented mainly over the past 100 years or so. Contracting treaties and conventions on disarmament and arms control gained momentum after the Second World War, because of the development and use of the atomic bomb in 1945, and after the end of the Cold War in 1991, which created the conditions for progress in developing disarmament and arms control law. The large number of agreements that have been concluded during the past fifty years can also be attributed to the desire to implement the United Nations Charter's objectives and intentions for maintaining international peace and security, as stated in the introduction and Article 1 of the UN Charter on the purposes of the United Nations.

During the first decade after the dissolution of the former Soviet Union in 1991, the public's interest and commitment to disarmament efforts – especially nuclear weapons disarmament – declined significantly. The confrontation between the US and USSR and the threat of using nuclear weapons during the Cold War had ceased and there was no longer any imminent danger of a devastating nuclear war between the two former rival superpowers. During this time, the number of operational nuclear weapons was reduced significantly – from about 65,000 nuclear weapons in 1986 to 25,000 in the late 1990s. After the end of the Cold War, international security policy attention was increasingly targeting peacemaking and peacekeeping operations in regional ethnic conflicts in the Balkans and in Africa.

Since the terrorist attacks on New York and Washington on 11 September 2001, and the ensuing "war on terror," the question of how to prevent the proliferation of weapons of mass destruction, particularly of nuclear weapons, has received renewed interest in international politics. The efforts by North Korea and Iran to acquire the capability to manufacture nuclear weapons have increased concerns about the further spread of nuclear weapons.

THE HAGUE CONFERENCES

The first international regulation (i.e., limitation) of certain types of conventional weapons is contained in the Saint Petersburg Declaration, adopted in 1868. The Declaration prohibited the use of projectiles under 400 grams that either explode or are loaded with flammable substances and codified the customary principle, still valid today, that prohibits the use of weapons that cause unnecessary suffering.

The first real multilateral arms control agreements were concluded in the form of joint declarations adopted at the First International Peace Conference in The Hague in 1899. The declarations included prohibitions on projectiles with asphyxiating or toxic gases and the so-called dumdum bullets (bullets that are easily flattened, thus expanding their size, and effect, on impact). The Hague Peace Conference was called on the initiative of Russia to ensure peace by, among other things, limiting the overly large weapons stocks, which the then-great powers in Europe – especially Germany – were in the process of building up. It was not possible during the peace conference to adopt proposals for general disarmament measures or prohibitions of certain other types of weapons. This was due to a general resistance against inspections and monitoring compliance with the proposed provisions, which – according to many states participating in the conference – would have implied a violation of the fundamental principle of national sovereignty and inviolability.

At the second Peace Conference in The Hague in 1907, a number of conventions on the law of war were adopted. One of these was the Hague Convention IV of 18 October 1907: respecting the Laws and Customs of War on Land and its annex: Regulations Concerning the Laws and Customs of War on Land, i.e., rules for warfare on land. According to the Convention's Article 22, the right of belligerents to adopt the means of injuring the enemy is not unlimited. Article 23 prohibits the use of poison or poisoned weapons, and the use of arms, projectiles, or material calculated to cause unnecessary suffering.

Protocol I of 18 June 1977 Additional to the Geneva Conventions of 12 August 1949 reiterates, reaffirms, and expands the prohibitions in the War on Land Regulations relative to the Protection of Victims of International Armed Conflicts. The basic rules on the methods and means of warfare are laid down in Article 35, which states that the right of parties to an armed conflict to choose the methods and means of warfare is not unlimited. The Article also prohibits the use of weapons, projectiles, and the material and methods of warfare that cause superfluous injury or unnecessary suffering. It is, however, the understanding of the nuclear powers that the rules of warfare established by Protocol I do not regulate or prohibit the use of nuclear weapons.[1] Furthermore, Article 35 contains a prohibition on the use of methods or means of warfare that are intended, or may be expected, to cause widespread, long-term, and severe damage to the natural environment. This prohibition is applicable to nuclear weapons.

The outbreak of the First World War in 1914 put a temporary stop to further efforts to promote disarmament and arms control, and a third Hague Peace Conference was planned, but was never convened.

Although no major disarmament results were achieved at The Hague Conferences, they influenced later efforts to promote both international humanitarian law and disarmament and arms control. The Conferences set in motion a trend for establishing further rules of international law for the conduct of war, especially for prohibitions and restrictions on the use of certain types of conventional weapons.

THE LEAGUE OF NATIONS

The League of Nations was an organization of states established in 1919 on the initiative of US president Woodrow Wilson as part of the peace settlement after the First World War. The organization's main objective was to prevent war, eliminate the causes of conflicts, provide opportunities for the peaceful settlement of international disputes, and promote disarmament.

The Covenant of the League of Nations, which was part of the Versailles Peace Treaty of 28 June 1919 between the Allies and Germany, included a disarmament program for reducing countries' armed forces and weapons holdings, especially for the defeated Germany: the German armed forces could not exceed 100,000 men; the navy could only consist of a certain maximum number and size of naval vessels with no submarines; and there could be no German air force. However, Germany never fully achieved these numbers and in the 1930s, after the Nazi takeover in 1933, Germany openly violated the program by rebuilding its military forces far beyond the established limits. In 1935, Germany unilaterally terminated the limitations of its armed forces that had been established by the Treaty of Versailles.

On the initiative of the League of Nations, a series of meetings were initiated in 1925 in a commission to prepare a planned disarmament conference. As a result of the commission's work, a Protocol for the Prohibition of the Use in War of Asphyxiating, Poisonous or Other Gases, and of Bacteriological Methods of Warfare was signed in June 1925, the so-called 1925 Geneva Protocol. The protocol was adopted as a result of the massive loss of life suffered by the armies of both warring parties during the First World War as a result of the use of poison gases. The human losses and suffering caused by poison gas had evoked strong negative reactions and condemnations in the public.

The most notable agreement from the period between the two world wars was the Kellogg-Briand Pact (named after its main authors, the US secretary of state and French foreign minister, respectively). The pact (officially the General Treaty for the Renunciation of War as an Instrument of National Policy) was signed in Paris in August 1928 by Germany, France, and the United States, and later by most other states. In the treaty, the states solemnly declared that they condemned war as a means of solving international disagreements and that they renounced war as an instrument of national policy in their mutual relations. However, the treaty contained no provisions for giving up the right to self-defence or on the conditions for exercising self-defence. Nor did it establish any monitoring body to control compliance, or specify any sanctions in case any country violated its agreement. The Kellogg-Briand Pact thus contained no clear obligations under international law, but was rather a declaratory expression of some idealistic principles.

Under the auspices of the League of Nations, the first global conference on disarmament was held in Geneva in 1932 to discuss universally reducing and limiting all types of weapons. During the two-year-long conference, a draft convention was discussed on restricting armed forces, weapons stocks, and military spending; on prohibiting the use of chemical weapons, incendiary weapons, and bacteriological weapons; and on trading and producing weapons. The discussions firmly stressed the need for an effective international monitoring system to ensure that states complied with their obligations. Germany's withdrawal from both the Conference on Disarmament (in 1933) and from the League of Nations (in 1935) and its rearmament resulted in the collapse of attempts to reach agreement on the draft convention. At the beginning of 1936, the League of Nations decided to suspend the Conference on Disarmament. The Conference was never reconvened.

After the outbreak of the Second World War in 1939, the principal organs of the League of Nations were no longer convened. The League was formally dissolved in 1946 after being replaced by the United Nations.

THE UNITED NATIONS

The UN was established at the end of the United Nations conference in San Francisco, where the Charter of the United Nations was signed on 26 June 1945 and entered into force on 24 October 1945.

The introduction of the United Nations Charter declares that one of the main objectives of the world organization is "to save succeeding generations from the scourge of war." According to Article 1 of the Charter, the purpose of the UN is "to maintain international peace and security and to that end: to take effective collective measures for the prevention and removal of threats to the peace, and for the suppression of acts of aggression or other breaches of the peace." Article 2 establishes the principle that the Organization and its members, in pursuit of the purposes in Article 1, shall act in accordance with the seven principles listed in the Article, i.e., that "All Members shall refrain in their international relations from the threat or use of force against the territorial integrity or political independence of any state, or in any other manner inconsistent with the Purposes of the United Nations."

In light of the declared purpose and principles of the UN, it is surprising that the UN Charter only mentions "disarmament" and "arms control" ("regulation of armaments") in 3 out of the Pact's total of 111 articles, namely:

- Article 11, paragraph 1, on the General Assembly's functions and powers to consider and make recommendations for the general principles of cooperation to maintain international peace and security, including the principles governing disarmament and the regulation of armaments;
- Article 26, on the Security Council's responsibility for formulating plans to establish a system of regulating armaments to promote international peace and security that minimizes diverting the world's human and economic resources for armaments;
- Article 47, on establishing a military staff committee to advise and assist the Security Council on all questions about the Security Council's military requirements for maintaining international peace and security, including the regulation of armaments and possible disarmament.

Less than two months after the signing of the UN Charter, the United Nations became involved in disarmament issues, prompted by the first – and so far only – use in war of nuclear weapons: the United States' dropping of atomic bombs on the Japanese cities of Hiroshima, on 6 August, and Nagasaki, on 9 August 1945.

The first resolution adopted by the first United Nations General Assembly, held in London in January 1946, resolution 1 (I) of 24 January 1946 established a commission to deal with the problems raised by the discovery of atomic energy. The Commission's mandate was to make specific proposals on:

- disseminating to all countries the exchange of basic scientific information on nuclear energy for peaceful purposes;
- controlling atomic energy to the extent necessary to ensure its use for peaceful purposes only;
- eliminating atomic weapons and all other major weapons of mass destruction from national armaments;
- creating effective safeguards by using inspection and other methods to protect complying states against the hazards of violations and evasions.

The Danish nuclear physicist Niels Bohr, whose pioneering research on atomic structure and quantum physics theory was instrumental in the development of the first atomic bomb in 1945, under the American Manhattan Project, warned in an open letter to the United Nations, dated 9 June 1950, of the dangers of nuclear energy being used for military purposes. In the letter, Professor Bohr called for international cooperation on nuclear energy and recommended openness among nations and exchange of information about scientific nuclear research. Bohr proposed establishing internationally controlled nuclear facilities through a standing committee of experts so that all countries could share the benefits of the peaceful use of nuclear energy in an open world.

Thus, even before the first use of a nuclear weapon in 1945, a warning had been sounded about the dangers of nuclear weapons and the need for controlling their fissile materials.

THE COLD WAR

During the Cold War between the United States and the former Soviet Union, which lasted from 1947 until the fall of the Berlin Wall on 9 November 1989, the two superpowers built up their arsenals of nuclear weapons, initiating the nuclear arms race.

The political differences and frictions between East and West were already evident during the first United Nations General Assembly in January 1946. The reason for this was Iran's complaint to the Security Council about Russian pressure on Iran to obtain oil concessions. Harry Truman, the American president, presented his political doctrine (the Truman Doctrine) in March 1947, which provided support from the United States to free nations threatened by oppression to stem the tide of Communist expansion. In June 1947, the US had also introduced the Marshall Plan on the economic reconstruction of Europe with American support. The Soviet Union opposed both initiatives, thus ending the peaceful cooperation between the two biggest victors in the Second World War. This was the beginning of the partition of Europe into two spheres of political and military interests, and had great significance for the military build-up in Europe during the Cold War, including the formation of NATO in 1949 and the former Warsaw Pact in 1955. The Warsaw Pact was dissolved 1 July 1991.

Despite mutual distrust and rivalry between the two superpowers during the Cold War period, the US and the USSR succeeded in reaching agreement on the establishment in 1952 of the United Nations Disarmament Commission (succeeding the Atomic Energy Commission set up in 1946), and on the establishment in 1956 of the IAEA. Originally, the Agency's main task was to assist states in their research, development, and use of nuclear energy for peaceful purposes. During 1953 to 1957, several attempts were made to reach agreement on proposals from both western countries (France, the United Kingdom, the United States, and Canada) and from the Soviet Union about comprehensive disarmament programs to reduce weapons stocks and prohibit nuclear weapons. The first General Assembly resolution on regulating, limiting, and balanced reducing of all armed forces and of all weapons stocks (UNGA (UN General Assembly) resolution 715 (VIII)) was adopted in November 1953. The negotiations toward these goals intensified at a summit in Geneva in 1955, but the efforts ended without result because some members disagreed on the proposed inspection methods to control compliance with the agreed reductions.

In 1959, the Soviet Union presented a proposal for general and complete disarmament, to be achieved through a program aimed at eliminating all armed forces and armaments. The proposal required that

- all the world's military forces would be disbanded within four years,
- states should only be allowed to maintain police forces to maintain internal order and security,
- all weapons systems should be destroyed,
- new weapons should be prohibited, and
- an international monitoring body should supervise the implementation and observance of the plan.

The realization of the proposal would have required establishing an international police force to verify compliance with the disarmament obligations. The Russians, however, were opposed to such a police force. It soon became evident that the proposal was unrealistic and had been suggested only for propaganda purposes.

Disarmament, however, was on the agenda for the UN General Assembly in 1960, and after direct negotiations between the American and the Soviet delegations, agreement was reached during the General Assembly in 1961 to establish a new disarmament committee, replacing the Disarmament Commission established in 1952.

During the Cold War, only one major multilateral agreement on disarmament was concluded: the Antarctic Treaty of 1959, by which the Antarctic gained status as a demilitarized area to be used only for peaceful purposes and where any form of military activity, including nuclear tests, is banned.

Comment

The historical development of disarmament law shows that the efforts in the first half of the twentieth century were largely focused on preventing war, regulating the conduct of war through international humanitarian law, and prohibiting certain types of conventional weapons.

Since the attempts in the late 1950s to agree on comprehensive disarmament programs, disarmament and arms control negotiations have focused on disarmament, and the prohibition, limitation, and regulation of certain categories of weapons.

The détente that took place during the 1960s and 1970s resulted in a better climate of cooperation between the two superpowers, especially during 1969 to 1979. During these years, many important bilateral agreements between the United States and the USSR on nuclear weapons and their means of delivery (missiles) were concluded and several important multinational treaties on disarmament, arms control, and non-proliferation were also signed.

3

Negotiation of Agreements

INTRODUCTION

Since the 1970s, disarmament law has increasingly been developed and regulated in treaties and conventions. "Treaties" and "conventions" are synonyms. Both terms are used for international agreements between two (bilateral) or more (multilateral) states (or international organizations).

Previously, the customs that the states were following in practice in their international relations were the main source of law. In recent decades, states have realized that agreement embodied in writing in treaties and conventions is the best way to codify international case law and establish written international law, and also to create new law in hitherto unregulated or inadequately regulated areas. Besides the advantage of having fixed and formulated rules for the conduct of states, adhering to treaties and conventions makes states legally bound to abide by the rules. In addition, the rules for verifying compliance with the treaties and conventions incorporated in most recent agreements as an integral part of the accords are effective ways of monitoring compliance.

Many disarmament and arms control issues that have not yet been regulated in international agreements are the subject of political declarations, for example the numerous declarations on abolishing nuclear weapons. Such policy statements are typically made by the participants in meetings of international organizations, for example in the resolutions of the United Nations General Assembly. Resolutions adopted by the General Assembly are politically binding statements only, not legally binding international law. They often contain recommendations on establishing a specific legal regime in a particular area. Even in cases when a resolution is adopted by consensus, i.e., without a vote or unanimously, the states participating in the unanimous adoption are not legally bound by the resolution.

Many of the major treaties and conventions in areas other than disarmament and arms control have had, in most cases, a long negotiating history. In several cases, *de lege ferenda* considerations on how the legal situation should be, or so-called soft law, were first expressed in UN resolutions adopted by the General Assembly's Legal Committee (Sixth Committee) or in other political declarations not binding under international law. Eventually "soft law" can develop into "hard law" in the form of legally binding treaties or conventions. This is especially the case with General Assembly resolutions that have been adopted unanimously and therefore have a special normative importance. The desired legal situation in areas where there is general international agreement has thus been developed and formulated in treaties and conventions adopted at specially convened treaty conferences. One such example is the United Nations Law of the Sea Conference, which lasted for ten years and resulted in the adoption of the UN Convention on the Law of the Sea in 1982. In other cases, the preparatory work has been carried out in the International Law Commission.

It is a characteristic feature of many disarmament and arms control agreements that the text of the treaties and conventions is not as clear and precise as one could wish. This is partly due to the fact that many of the representatives of the states involved who have negotiated the agreements are in many cases not international lawyers and often do not have special training or experience in drafting treaty texts. In some cases, the definitions have been drafted by military experts who have little regard for clear treaty language. In addition, the content of the treaties is in most cases the result of lengthy negotiations that have resulted in compromises painstakingly drafted to obtain agreement on the text of the draft treaty. Finally, some treaty texts are deliberately unclear or ambiguous in their formulations. This is because it has not been possible to reach agreement on a clear formulation. The negotiators have therefore agreed on a compromise text with "constructive ambiguity." This allows the parties to have different interpretations of how the wording on controversial issues in the provisions will be understood and what the purpose of the rule is. This is, of course, one of the main weaknesses of many international treaties and conventions.

NEGOTIATING FORA
WITHIN THE UNITED NATIONS SYSTEM

United Nations Disarmament Commission

Early in the history of the United Nations it became obvious that there was a need for a special negotiating body on disarmament and arms control. In 1947, the Commission for Conventional Armaments was established by the UN Security Council with the same membership as the Council. In 1952, the General Assembly, with resolution 502 (VI), created the United Nations Disarmament Commission (UNDC), also under the Security Council. The UNDC was the successor to the Atomic Energy Commission and the Commission for Conventional Armaments. After having been inactive since 1965, the Disarmament Commission was restored in 1978 as a subsidiary organ of the Assembly at the First Special Session of the UN General Assembly devoted to disarmament. The reactivated UNDC considers and makes recommendations on disarmament and arms control issues. The agenda for the UNDC for 2015 to 2017 includes "Recommendations for achieving the objective of nuclear disarmament and non-proliferation of nuclear weapons" and "Practical confidence-building measures in the field of conventional weapons." The membership of the Disarmament Commission was expanded in 1958 to include all UN member states. It meets for three weeks every spring at UN Headquarters in New York.

Disarmament Committee

In order to comply with the request to governments in General Assembly resolution 1378 (XIV) of 1959 for general and complete disarmament, the Disarmament Committee was established in 1961 by resolution 1722. The Disarmament Committee – also called the Eighteen Nation Committee on Disarmament (ENDC) – consisted of eighteen member states, including the United States, the Soviet Union, some NATO members and former Warsaw Pact countries, and eight non-aligned countries, including Sweden. The Disarmament Committee was originally established in 1959 and included only ten member countries (the Ten Nation Committee on Disarmament (TNCD)). In 1969 the membership of the Disarmament Committee was expanded to include twenty-six member states and the name was changed to the Conference of the Committee on Disarmament (CCD). In 1975, five more members were added. Technically, the Disarmament Committee was not a UN body. It was established by an agreement between the United States and the Soviet Union and endorsed by the UN General Assembly resolutions. Between 1962 and 1978, important disarmament and non-proliferation agreements were negotiated and concluded by the Committee, among others, the NPT in 1968 and the Biological Weapons Convention (BWC) in 1972.

Conference on Disarmament

The current negotiating body is the Conference on Disarmament (CD), which was established in 1979 by a decision made at the first special session of the UN General Assembly on Disarmament Issues (SSOD I) in 1978.[1] The Conference on Disarmament was created because states understood how vital disarmament and arms control were to their security. For this reason, the disarmament negotiations in the CD are conducted behind closed doors with no media or public access.

The CD is located in Geneva. The Conference is the only permanent multilateral negotiating forum for negotiating and drafting international disarmament and arms control agreements. The CD is a lawmaking organ and has negotiated the Non-Proliferation Treaty, the Biological Weapons Convention, and the Chemical Weapons Convention, among other agreements. The CD is not a proper UN organ, but it submits reports to the General Assembly on its work and receives recommendations adopted in resolutions of the General Assembly on specific issues that the CD is asked to include in its agenda. The CD is financed from the regular UN budget, and the secretariat of the United Nations Office at Geneva also serves as the secretariat for the CD.

Originally, the CD consisted of forty member states from all over the world. The membership was increased in 1996 with twenty-three new member states, including Finland, Norway, Australia, and South Africa. In 1999, five more countries, including Ireland, became CD members. The CD currently has sixty-five members, including the five nuclear-weapon states recognized in the NPT – the United States, Russia, the United Kingdom, France, and China – as well as Israel, India, and Pakistan, most European Union (EU) member countries, Canada, Japan, Australia, New Zealand, Norway, Switzerland, Argentina, Brazil, Mexico, Cuba, South Africa, Egypt, Syria, North Korea, Iran, and Iraq, among others. Cyprus, Czech Republic, Denmark, Estonia, Greece, Latvia, Lithuania, Luxembourg, Malta, and Portugal are among the forty-two observer countries to the CD.

The Conference on Disarmament meets three times a year for sessions of approximately eight weeks. As well as being a negotiating forum for drafting international disarmament and arms control agreements, the CD is also an important forum for states to deliver general statements about current disarmament and security issues.

Unfortunately, there have not been any substantial negotiations in the CD on new disarmament agreements since August 1996, when negotiations on the Comprehensive Nuclear-Test-Ban Treaty (CTBT) were completed. The reason for this inactivity is that some countries within the group of Non-Aligned countries (Non-Aligned Movement (NAM)) insist that the CD should address the issue of nuclear weapons disarmament. Several of the group's leading countries, with China as the most prominent advocate – supported by, among others, Russia – demand that the CD should start negotiations for the conclusion of a treaty banning weapons in outer space, to prevent an arms race in outer space. The other nuclear-weapon states are against negotiating a treaty on the disarmament of nuclear weapons, and the United States opposes a treaty banning weapons in outer space, because of American plans to further develop and deploy a missile defence system (MD) guided by satellites in space. At the same time, the western nuclear-weapon states, the EU countries, and most of the other members of the CD wish to initiate negotiations on a treaty banning the production of fissile material for use in nuclear weapons – a so-called Fissile Material Cut-Off Treaty (FMCT). Until now, Pakistan has blocked the opening of negotiations in the CD on FMCT, which Pakistan considers affects only itself.[2] Decisions in CD can only be made when there is a consensus. Thus, a single member's veto can break a consensus.

*The General Assembly's First Committee
on Disarmament and International Security*

In addition to the discussions in the Conference on Disarmament, arms control, disarmament, and non-proliferation are also discussed in a committee under the UN General Assembly – the First Committee on Disarmament and International Security. All UN member states in the General Assembly are members of the First Committee. The function of the Committee is to serve as a forum for political debate on disarmament, arms control, and non-proliferation issues, and as a body for adopting resolutions on these subjects. The Committee meets every fall for five weeks during the UN's annual General Assembly meetings at UN headquarters in New York. The resolutions adopted by the Committee are only politically binding, not legally binding recommendations. Therefore, the resolutions cannot be implemented by use of force, for example by sanctions. Sanctions can only be adopted by the UN Security Council.

Each year the First Committee adopts more than fifty resolutions during the fall General Assembly. All the draft resolutions are put to a vote twice: first in the First Committee, then in the Plenary of the General Assembly. The number of votes cast may differ in the First Committee and the Plenary, where more states participate in the voting. Most of the resolution texts are repeatedly presented every year or every second year with some updates and other changes. During the latest (70th) General Assembly in 2015, fifty-three resolutions and four decisions were adopted – twenty-three of them on nuclear weapons issues. Some of the most important and controversial resolutions adopted during the 70th and earlier General Assemblies that were put to a vote are mentioned in later chapters. Twenty-six uncontroversial resolutions were adopted without a vote.[3]

The member states of the General Assembly are arranged in five regional groups for various purposes, including presentation of candidates for elections to United Nations bodies, delivery of common statements, and coordination of voting on resolutions: African Group, Asia-Pacific Group, Eastern European States Group, Group of Latin American and Caribbean States, and Group of Western European and Other States. The Western Europe and Other States Group (WEOG) has twenty-eight members, including Australia, Canada, Israel, New Zealand, and Turkey. The United States is not a member of any regional group, but attends the meetings of WEOG as an observer and is considered a member of that group for voting purposes.

During the General Assembly sessions, the twenty-eight member states of the EU hold almost daily consultation meetings to exchange information and views on draft resolutions, to coordinate their voting intentions and – as far as possible – agree on common positions, as part of the EU's Common Foreign and Security Policy (CFSP). The meetings are chaired by a representative of the Delegation of the EU to the United Nations. The EU representatives also deliver common EU statements on behalf of all the EU member states.[4]

Similar coordination meetings are held between member states of the Non-Aligned Movement and NATO.

Special Sessions of the General Assembly on Disarmament Issues

Three Special Sessions of the General Assembly on Disarmament (SSODs) have taken place: in 1978, 1982, and 1988. Because members disagree on which topics should be included in the agenda for a possible fourth special session on disarmament issues, the Disarmament Commission has not been able to agree on a recommendation for the convening of a new, fourth SSOD. The nuclear-weapon states are against including nuclear weapons as an item on the agenda.

Separate negotiations under the auspices of the United Nations have also been conducted on, among others, Protocol V on Explosive Remnants of War of 2003, the 1980 Convention on Prohibitions or Restrictions on the Use of Certain Conventional Weapons, the Firearms Protocol of 2001, and the Arms Trade Treaty of 2013.

Review Conferences

Several treaties and conventions on disarmament, arms control, and non-proliferation provide for regular review or follow-up conferences between the states parties, for example the NPT review conferences every five years. At the review conference, the states parties concerned discuss how the agreement is being implemented and observed by the states, and if and how the agreement should be changed, updated, or expanded. Review conferences are thus a forum where every state party may raise questions if they suspect another state party is not complying or is breaching its treaty obligations.

NEGOTIATING FORA
OUTSIDE THE UNITED NATIONS SYSTEM

The most important multilateral negotiating forum outside the UN system in recent years has been the Conference on Security and Co-operation in Europe (CSCE). The Conference was established by the

Helsinki Final Act in 1975, and changed in 1994 to the Organization for Security and Co-operation in Europe (OSCE). Within the framework of the CSCE process, negotiations were conducted in Vienna during the years 1989 to 1990 on the Treaty on Conventional Armed Forces in Europe (the CFE treaty of 1990) between the member states of NATO and the former Warsaw Pact.

As a result of the inactivity of the Conference on Disarmament since 1996 in negotiating new disarmament agreements, multilateral negotiations on arms control have taken place outside the United Nations system in the so-called stand-alone negotiation processes. The most important negotiations outside the UN system have been the negotiation and conclusion of the Convention on the Prohibition of Anti-Personnel Mines (the Ottawa Convention of 1997), conducted in Ottawa on Canada's initiative and completed in Oslo, as well as the Convention on Cluster Munitions, negotiated in Oslo on Norway's initiative and concluded in Dublin.

A series of important bilateral negotiations between the United States and the Soviet Union/Russia on reductions and limitations of nuclear weapons have also taken place.

4

Interpretation, Compliance, and Enforcement of Agreements

INTERPRETATION OF AGREEMENTS

Introduction

In the principal work on the law of treaties, *The Vienna Convention on the Law of Treaties*, by Sir Ian Sinclair, the author notes that few topics in international law have given rise to such extensive controversy as the interpretation of treaties. The interpretation of disarmament and arms control treaties is further complicated because of the often highly technical content of these treaties. They may be difficult to understand even for international law scholars, who are usually not familiar with technical-military concepts and terminologies.

The purpose of the rules of treaty interpretation is to ensure that a given treaty or convention is uniformly interpreted and applied in the same way by all states parties to the Treaty. The rules of interpretation further ensure that treaties are implemented in accordance with the object and purpose of the treaty, as stated in Article 18 of the Vienna Convention on the obligation not to defeat the object and purpose of a treaty before it enters into force and thereby becomes law. Article 18 applies to states that have signed a treaty or expressed consent to be bound by the treaty, pending the formal entry into force of the treaty. In such situations, the state is obliged to refrain from acts that would be contrary to the objectives and purposes of the treaty.

Questions and disputes between states parties about treaty interpretation most often occur in connection with the application of treaties but also occur in cases of withdrawal from a treaty, or suspension of a treaty (Articles 54 and 57). The reason given by a state for its decision to withdraw or suspend is often the subject of disagreement: interpreting whether the cause is sufficient to justify the withdrawal or suspension. The decision, however, is the state's own. Many treaties contain provisions for states parties' right to withdrawal from a treaty "if it decides that extraordinary events, relating to the subject matter of the treaty, have jeopardized its supreme interests." There may also be doubts about the interpretation of a treaty that builds on and replaces an earlier treaty on the same subject, for example the Biological Weapons Convention of 1972 and the 1925 Geneva Protocol, see Article 59 of the Vienna Convention on terminating or suspending the operation of a treaty and Article 30 on applying successive treaties relating to the same subject matter.

Because of the complexity of many disarmament treaties, defining the main concepts in the treaty text makes it easier to interpret the treaties in accordance with their purpose. This provides clarity for interpreting and applying the treaty. Often treaties contain standard introductory phrases such as "for the purposes of this treaty the term ... means." or "within the framework of this treaty the following definitions shall apply." A different kind of contribution to treaty interpretation is given for many bilateral agreements, for example the Strategic Arms Limitation Treaty (SALT I and SALT II), and the Anti-Ballistic Missile Treaty (ABM), by having parties agree on specific interpretations. Such agreement may be expressed in statements or common understandings that the parties have agreed to in the course of the negotiating process.

Furthermore, reservations that a state party has had and which have been communicated in writing to the other treaty partners in connection with the ratification of or agreement to the treaty, may contain interpretative statements on how certain formulations or articles of the treaty shall be understood. The right to make reservations under certain circumstances is expressly stated in Article 19 of the Vienna Convention. According to this Article, a state may, when signing, ratifying, accepting, approving, or agreeing to a treaty, formulate a reservation unless the reservation is prohibited by the treaty, or the treaty provides only specified reservations, which do not include the reservation in question, to be made, or the reservation is incompatible with the object and purpose of the treaty.

A specific practice for the application of a treaty that has developed since its adoption can also create criteria or guidance for interpreting the treaty.

Vienna Convention on the Law of Treaties

The basic rules of treaty interpretation are found in the Vienna Convention on the Law of Treaties of 1969, which is based upon and codifies customary international law on treaty conclusion. The Vienna Convention, whose provisions are largely considered to reflect current customary international law, was drafted by the United Nations ILC and entered into force in 1980. As of January 2016, the Convention has 114 states parties, including China, Russia, and the United Kingdom. Forty-five countries have signed the Convention, but have not yet ratified it, including the United States, Iran, and Pakistan. France and India, among others, have not even signed the Convention.

"Ratification" means the international act whereby a state establishes, internationally its consent to be bound by a treaty (see the Convention's article 2, paragraph 1 (b)). A ratification is carried out when the ratification document (so-called ratification instrument), approved by the respective country's parliament and signed by its head of state, is handed over to the state or states or international organization acting as depositary(ies) for the treaty in question.

According to the Convention's Article 31 on the general rules of interpretation, a treaty shall be interpreted in good faith in accordance with the ordinary meaning to be given to the terms of the treaty in the context of the treaty and in light of the treaty's object and purpose. In addition to the treaty text, consideration should also be given to any agreement related to the treaty that was made between all the parties in connection with the conclusion of the treaty as well as any declarations and reservations that were made by one or more of the parties in connection with the conclusion of the treaty and accepted by the other parties as an instrument related to the treaty. Together with the context, the following shall also be taken into account: any later agreement between the parties regarding the interpretation of the treaty or the application of its provisions, any later practice in the application of the treaty that establishes the parties' agreement on its interpretation, and any relevant rules of international law applicable in the relations between the states parties. Finally, a special meaning shall be given to a term if it is established that the parties intended it that way.

According to Article 32, on supplementary means of interpretation, the preparatory work of the treaty and the circumstances of its conclusion may be taken into consideration

- to confirm the meaning resulting from the application of Article 31, or
- to determine the meaning when the interpretation, according to Article 31, is ambiguous or obscure, or leads to a result that is manifestly absurd or unreasonable.

The Vienna Convention applies to all kinds of disarmament and arms control treaties and conventions, whether they are concluded bilaterally between two states, multilaterally within the framework of an international organization, or regionally between countries within a specific geographic region.

The Convention is not retroactive and therefore only applies to treaties that have been concluded by states after the entry into force of the Convention with regard to such states.

Treaties concluded between states and international organizations or between international organizations are subject to the rules of the Vienna Convention on the Law of Treaties Between States and International Organizations or Between International Organizations, of 1986, which has not yet entered into force. It has forty-three participants, including twelve international organizations, among them the UN, IAEA, and OPCW (Organization for the Prohibition of Chemical Weapons). Its rules are identical to the rules of the Vienna Convention of 1969.

COMPLIANCE OF AGREEMENTS

Introduction

Pacta sunt servanda is a basic legal principle that agreements must be observed. The principle applies generally in contract law, civil law, and international law and is enshrined in Article 26 of the Vienna Convention on the Law of Treaties: "Every treaty in force is binding upon the parties to it and must be performed by them in good faith."

When states conclude or agree to international treaties, they are expected to act in good faith and to comply with their treaty obligations. This applies to all treaties. With disarmament, arms control, and non-proliferation agreements, where vital national security interests are at stake, the parties to a treaty need to have special guarantees to ensure that the other states parties comply with the treaty and do not violate or circumvent their obligations under the treaty. Therefore, it is necessary to verify compliance with disarmament, arms control, and non-proliferation agreements to avoid international conflicts and to maintain international peace and security.

The issue of compliance – or non-compliance of states' treaty liabilities – arises when a state party suspects, makes allegations, or presents evidence of another state party's breach of a treaty. All recent disarmament and arms control treaties provide for procedures for violations of the treaty in the case of a state's non-compliance – so-called compliance rules. Some cases of non-compliance by a state party to fulfill its obligations occur because of misinterpreting the treaty in question. Therefore, it is essential that the procedure for treaty violations include provisions that can guide the parties in a dispute over a treaty violation to determine whether there is well-founded suspicion or allegation of infringement, whether a demonstrated violation is serious, and whether the violation is made accidentally or deliberately. This avoids developing into a major political problem that can undermine the treaty. In the worst case scenario, non-compliance can lead to a state party's withdrawal from the treaty, or a conflict arising between the parties. On the other hand, there must also be rules on how to act in case of serious infringements.

Control through Verification

Verification can be defined as controlling or investigating another state party's compliance with its obligations under a disarmament or arms control agreement.[1]

Trust and verification are important elements in the relations between states. The purpose of verification is to detect non-compliance, deter violations, and build confidence between states parties to a treaty and ensure that the treaty is implemented and complied with effectively and correctly by all participants. Verification thus contributes to strengthening international security. Controlling whether a state complies with a treaty to which it is a party can be done through verification.

Provisions on verification have become even more essential in recent disarmament and arms control treaties and conventions. In many cases, the basis for verification is the states parties' own declarations to monitor implementation and compliance. These declarations typically contain information on the states parties' weapons and weapon systems covered by the treaty. Provisions on verification – and thereby transparency – have increasingly been included in negotiations on new disarmament and arms control agreements. This is because it is of vital importance for the security of states, the enforcement of their sovereignty, and ultimately for their survival as independent states that they can be assured that the disarmament and arms control agreements to which they have agreed and become parties to are being observed by the other treaty partners. The rationale behind these provisions is Lenin's proverb: "Trust is good, but control is better" – or as President Reagan used to say: "Trust, but verify." It takes many years to re-establish a military defence capability that has been reduced or completely abandoned by a state in accordance with its obligations under disarmament or arms control agreements.

The basis for verification is the right to carry out effective monitoring or surveillance to collect sufficient and relevant factual information on which a legal analysis can be made of the information gathered on the other states parties' compliance with a treaty. In case of violation a political decision on whether a response from the other participating states is required and if so, how to respond. Transparency of information and willingness to openness, including in the notifications under disarmament and arms control agreements, are therefore of utmost importance for effective verification. The purpose of verification is achieved in three ways: the possibility of discovering non-compliance, the effect of deterrence of potential offenders, and the confidence building between states parties.

A recent example of the difficulties of carrying out effective verification when a state is trying to hide an activity that is suspected to be in violation of treaty obligations was the attempts by Iran to impede and in some cases obstruct IAEA inspectors' work to verify that Iran's nuclear program – as claimed by Iran – was exclusively for peaceful nuclear energy purposes.

States may have legitimate national security considerations that are not relevant for verifying compliance with a given treaty. Commercial information protected by copyright (e.g., patents) may also be covered by confidentiality and protected from verification.

According to some treaties, verification may be performed by on-site inspection, i.e., physical inspection in the territory of another treaty party, to determine whether another state party has implemented and continues to comply with the agreement. Some treaties make it possible to conduct inspections at very short notice.

Comment

Effective verification is dependent on the treaty parties' political, financial, and technical support. The more effective a verification system is, the greater the probability that the verification system will be able to detect violations and deter a state from violating a treaty.

An effective verification system can contribute a great deal to building confidence between states parties that the other treaty parties will comply with their obligations. This confidence can be crucial for a state to decide whether it wishes to become a party to a treaty. Only if there is a high degree of certainty that all parties will comply with the treaty, and that any violation will be discovered in time by means of the verification system and dealt with in an effective "compliance procedure," will a state be prepared to comply itself, for example, by abolishing or restricting certain types of weapons or capacity through disarmament or arms control measures. Adherence to a verification regime implies reciprocity, i.e., assurance that the regime is applied uniformly without discrimination to all treaty parties. Treaty parties participating in verifying compliance with a treaty allows them to own the treaty. This may have great importance for the credibility of verification, the implementation of the treaty, and for its continued effectiveness. An effective verification and compliance system can also contribute to promoting disarmament and non-proliferation and prevent outbreaks of international conflicts, as well as enhancing international confidence in the functioning of the international treaty regime for disarmament and arms control.

According to Hans Blix, the head of UNMOVIC (United Nations Monitoring, Verification and Inspection Commission), it became apparent after the 2003 Iraq war that the inspections and supervisions by the inspectors of the IAEA, UNSCOM (United Nations Special Commission), and UNMOVIC had been effective: they had resulted in the dismantling of Iraq's weapons of mass destruction (chemical and biological weapons and a planned nuclear weapons program), and had deterred Saddam Hussein from rearming. If the request by UNMOVIC and the majority of the members of the UN Security Council (including France) to continue the inspections in Iraq had been approved, the weapons inspectors would have been able to verify that there were no more weapons of mass destruction in Iraq. According to Dr Blix, UNMOVIC's experience showed that it was possible to build a professional and effective UN inspection system that was supported but not controlled by individual governments and therefore had international legitimacy. Such an international inspection regime also has the advantage, compared with national intelligence agencies, that the international inspectors carrying out on-site inspections can gain lawful and – in principle – unimpeded access to the facilities and activities to be verified.

United Nations Verification Principles

The need for an effective system of monitoring compliance with disarmament and arms control agreements through verification measures has been on the United Nations agenda since the creation of the UN. The issue received increased attention in 1959, when the General Assembly, in resolution 1378 (XIV), stated for the first time that the objective of UN efforts was to achieve "general and complete disarmament under effective international control." The question of "verification in all its aspects" was first the subject of a separate resolution in 1985 (resolution 40/152 O). Detailed principles of verification were formulated in the Final Document of the UN General Assembly's First Special Session on Disarmament in 1978.[2] The verification principles were later developed and adopted in the UNDC and endorsed in 1988 by the General Assembly (in resolution 43/81 B). The sixteen principles are set out in a report from a group of government experts, set up by the General Assembly.[3] Following are the main principles:

- Adequate and effective verification is an essential element of all arms limitation and disarmament agreements.
- Verification is not an aim in itself, but an essential element in the process of achieving arms limitation and disarmament agreements.
- Verification should promote the implementation of arms limitation and disarmament measures, build confidence among states, and ensure that agreements are being observed by all parties.
- Adequate and effective verification arrangements must be capable of providing, in a timely fashion, clear and convincing evidence of compliance or non-compliance. Continued confirmation of compliance is an important ingredient in building and maintaining confidence among the parties.
- Verifying compliance with the obligations imposed by an arms limitation and disarmament agreement is an activity conducted by

the parties to an arms limitation and disarmament agreement or by an organization at the request, and with the explicit consent of, the parties, and is an expression of the sovereign right of states to enter into such arrangements.

In 1993 and again in 2004, the General Assembly established new groups of experts to conduct further studies of verification.[4] Certain arms control agreements allow the UN secretary general an important role in verification. For example, the secretary general receives compliance reports from states parties to the Convention on Anti-Personnel Mines.

United Nations Verification Activities

The United Nations has also been involved in monitoring and verifying weapons programs and activities in specific countries, for example in Iraq with UNSCOM and UNMOVIC, the United Nations special commissions for monitoring, verification, and inspection.

UNSCOM was established by Security Council resolution 687 of 1991 to set out the conditions for the formal ceasefire between Iraq and the coalition of member states and Kuwait (after the Gulf War, which began in August 1990). The resolution called for the abolition under international monitoring of Iraq's weapons of mass destruction and ballistic missiles with a range greater than 150 kilometres. The purpose of UNSCOM was to implement the provisions of the resolution on non-nuclear weapons and assist the IAEA in the nuclear area. The first chairman of the Commission was the Swedish diplomat Ambassador Rolf Ekéus. In August 1998, Iraq stopped cooperating with UNSCOM, and in December 1998 ordered the weapons inspectors to leave the country. That same month, the United States and the United Kingdom bombed Iraq in the operation called "Desert Fox."

UNSCOM was replaced by UNMOVIC, established by resolution 1284 of 1999. Its first chairman was Dr Hans Blix (2000–03). The mandate for both Commissions was to verify whether Iraq was complying with its obligations under the Security Council resolutions to eliminate its weapons of mass destruction, and, through monitoring and verification, ensure that Iraq did not obtain these weapons again. The UNMOVIC weapons inspectors were pulled out of Iraq in March 2003 immediately before the coalition invaded the country on 20 March

2003. On the initiative of the US and the UK, the Commission was dissolved by resolution 1762, of 2007.

The United Nations also monitors compliance with arms embargoes and other sanctions against certain member states that have been imposed by the Security Council, and collects and distributes reports from member states on their compliance with a number of disarmament and arms control agreements, for example those mandated by resolution 1540 on the non-proliferation of weapons of mass destruction. But an integrated multilateral verification system within the United Nations or a global verification organization to monitor all disarmament and arms control agreements has not yet been established. Specialized verification regimes and organizations for each individual treaty are probably more effective and acceptable for states.

Treaty Provisions on Verification

Disarmament and arms control treaties contain very different rules on treaty compliance and verification. One of the first treaties to provide for the right to unrestricted access to inspection is the Antarctic Treaty of 1959 (see Article 7, para. 3). Some of the most detailed verification provisions are contained in the bilateral treaties between the United States and the Soviet Union/Russia on disarmament and arms control of their nuclear weapons and their means of delivery (see e.g., START and INF). These treaties contain detailed provisions on the establishment of special commissions for dealing with cases of treaty implementation and of violations, for example in the INF and the Treaty on Strategic Offensive Reductions of 2002. Several multilateral treaties contain provisions on the establishment of executive councils or other treaty bodies to monitor the implementation and compliance of the treaty, for example the IAEA, JCG (Joint Consultative Group) (CFE), OPCW, and the Comprehensive Nuclear-Test-Ban Treaty Organization (CTBTO) (CTBT's international monitoring system (IMS)). The BWC is an example of an important convention that does not contain substantive verification provisions. The treaty simply refers compliance questions about the BWC to the UN Security Council.

Verification can be carried out collectively by a group of states or individually by a single state. Several treaties establish the right of a state party to conduct its own monitoring and verification by means of so-called "national technical means," for example by the use of surveillance satellites, reconnaissance aircraft, or drones. Information that is available for the public, for example on the Internet, may of course also be used in the verification process.[5]

ENFORCEMENT OF AGREEMENTS

The purpose of the provisions on compliance and verification of treaties is to avoid conflicts between a treaty's states parties, through a direct dialogue between the parties on a peaceful settlement of the dispute. In the event that the matter cannot be resolved through dialogue, an investigation of whether there is an infringement can be undertaken. Many treaties allow for an inspection to be carried out on the spot when the treaty body has approved the inspection or not opposed its implementation. Normally, a state accused of a treaty violation does not refuse a request for inspection if the treaty body has approved it. In case of disagreement, whether there has been an infringement or a discussion is needed on how a proven breach is to be remedied, the matter would be decided at a conference between all states parties. When all possibilities for resolving the conflict within the treaty framework have been tested and exhausted, a matter of infringement may be submitted to the UN General Assembly, the Security Council, or both bodies, as a last resort.

In addition to the procedures for examining violations of the treaty and the verification provisions laid down in the various treaties, states can also use traditional diplomatic tools. These include, in particular, submitting diplomatic protests, recalling diplomatic representatives, interrupting diplomatic relations, cancelling planned official visits, interrupting aid or other forms of bilateral cooperation, and trade or economic sanctions. These responses to treaty violations can contribute to international pressure on the state that has violated a treaty to stop its violation.

Several multilateral treaties provide for various sanctions against a state that violates the treaty. The penalties may consist of excluding that state from the treaty, suspending the state's participation and cooperation in the treaty, or terminating the right to receive financial and technical assistance under the Treaty.

There are also treaty rules for settling disputes on the application or interpretation of treaties. The main rule is that states, as a first step, must consult with the intention of working together to find an early resolution of the dispute through negotiation or by other peaceful means chosen by the parties. If consultations between the parties do not resolve the dispute, the parties may apply to the relevant treaty monitoring body or to the Security Council if the treaty provides the power to do that, or if the offence constitutes a threat to international peace and security.

Comment

Although resolutions adopted by the UN General Assembly are only politically and not legally binding under international law, a resolution in which a state is condemned for a treaty violation may have political significance – in particular if the resolution has been adopted unanimously or by the overwhelming majority of UN member states. Decisions in resolutions adopted by the Security Council are binding on all UN member states and can be enforced by sanctions against the offending state. Eventually, the Security Council may authorize the use of armed force, i.e., Chapter VII measures in case of any threat to the peace, breach of the peace, or act of aggression. Chapter VII measures are rarely imposed because of permanent Security Council members' use of their veto. Before a decision on sanctions or use of force is made, the Security Council may deploy a mission to investigate the facts surrounding the suspected violation. The case may also be presented for the UN when the state party that has violated the treaty ignores or rejects the recommendations to comply with the treaty. In cases where the violation is of such a serious character that it may endanger international peace and security, the matter may be brought before the Security Council at any time.[6] The Security Council's most extensive involvement in matters of treaty violations concerning non-proliferation of weapons of mass destruction was the many resolutions adopted by the Council before the US-led invasion of Iraq in March 2003 – see S/RES/1441(2002).

Bringing Disputes before the International Court of Justice

The parties to a dispute may ultimately bring the case before the International Court of Justice. The seat of the Court is at the Peace Palace in The Hague (Netherlands). The International Court is one of the six principal organs of the UN bodies and the UN's principal judicial organ for settling disputes between states (see UN Charter, Article 92). The Court was established in 1945 by the Charter of the UN. The Statute of the ICJ is an integral part of the UN Charter. The Court is composed of fifteen judges who are elected for nine-year terms of office by the General Assembly and the Security Council.

The International Court of Justice acts as a world court and has two main functions: the Court passes judgments in legal disputes submitted to it by states (i.e., has jurisdiction in contentious cases), and gives advisory opinions on legal questions referred to it by United Nations organs and specialized agencies authorized to make such a request (advisory jurisdiction) (See also Articles 36 and 65 of the ICJ Statute). According to Article 96 of the Charter, the General Assembly or the Security Council may request the ICJ to give an advisory opinion on any legal question. ICJ's advisory opinions express the Court's views and are not legally binding under international law.

In exercising its jurisdiction in contentious cases, the International Court of Justice has to decide, in accordance with international law, legal disputes that are submitted to it by states. An international legal dispute can be defined as a disagreement on a question of law or fact, a conflict, or a clash of legal views or of interests. Only states may apply to and appear before the International Court of Justice (Article 34 of the Statute). International organizations, other collectivities, and private persons are not entitled to institute proceedings before the Court. The Court can only deal with a dispute when the states concerned have recognized the Court's jurisdiction. The court proceedings in disputes between states are thus voluntary. No state can be a party to proceedings before the Court unless it has in some way or other consented to it, i.e., has explicitly declared that the state recognizes as compulsory the jurisdiction of the Court to deliver judgment in intergovernmental disputes. The states parties to the Statute of the Court may "at any time declare that they recognize as compulsory *ipso facto* and without special agreement, in relation to any other state accepting the same obligation, the jurisdiction of the Court" (Article 36, para. 2 of the Statute). The competence of the Court thus depends on the consent of the states involved. Each state that has recognized the compulsory jurisdiction of the Court has, in principle, the right to bring any one or more other state(s) that has accepted the same obligation before the Court by filing an application instituting proceedings with the Court. Conversely, states are also obliged to appear before the Court should proceedings be begun against it by one or more such other states.[7]

As of January 2016, seventy-two states have submitted declarations to the effect that they recognize the jurisdiction of the Court as compulsory in relation to any other state that has undertaken the same obligation. Among the five permanent members of the Security Council (the nuclear-weapon states), only the United Kingdom has made such a declaration. India and Pakistan have also made Article 36 declarations. China, France, Russia, Israel, the United States, and North Korea have not made such declarations. The United States withdrew its acceptance of the Court's competence in 1984 after the ICJ judgment in the case "Nicaragua v. United States on Illegal Use of Force against the Nicaraguan Government."

Between May 1947 and January 2016, the International Court of Justice pronounced approximately 130 judgments and issued 26 advisory opinions. Thirteen cases are pending before the ICJ. Most of ICJ's judgments relate to issues of territorial or maritime boundaries. Only two of the judgments concern questions of disarmament and nonproliferation. The two cases against France were submitted simultaneously by Australia and by New Zealand in May 1973 because of the French nuclear tests on the islands of Mururoa and Fangataufa in the southeastern Pacific Ocean. Between 1966 and 1996, France conducted a total of 181 nuclear test explosions on the two islands, including 41 explosions in the atmosphere. The decisions in the two cases were delivered in December 1974. Nine out of the fifteen judges found that the Court no longer needed to rule in the case because France had stopped conducting nuclear tests in the atmosphere earlier in 1974. The subject matter of the case had thus disappeared after the plaintiffs' claim that the atmospheric nuclear tests had to be brought to an end because of the harmful effects on the environment by the radioactive fallout had been met.[8] In September 1995, the ICJ rejected New Zealand's request for a new examination of the situation.

Bringing Cases before the International Criminal Court

In cases where an individual or a group of people has violated one of the two existing treaties banning the use of Weapons of Mass Destruction (the BWC and the Convention on the Prohibition of the Development, Production, Stockpiling and Use of Chemical Weapons and on Their Destruction (CWC)) or the Convention on Certain Conventional Weapons (CCW), the International Criminal Court (ICC)[9] in The Hague may also be used. According to the Rome Statute of the ICC, the Court has jurisdiction to prosecute individuals according to Article 25 on individual criminal responsibility, which states: "The

Court shall have jurisdiction over natural persons pursuant to this Statute." The definition of war crimes in Article 8 explicitly mentions the use of poison or poisoned weapons, asphyxiating, poisonous, or other gases, but not the use of nuclear weapons, due to heavy resistance during the negotiation of the statute from the nuclear-weapon states. The deliberate use of nuclear weapons, directed intentionally against civilians in a city, could constitute a crime against humanity and a war crime, as defined in Articles 7 and 8 of the Rome Statute. War crimes also include employing bullets that expand or flatten easily in the human body, as well as using weapons, projectiles, and material and methods of warfare that can cause superfluous injury or unnecessary suffering or which are inherently indiscriminate in violation of the international law of armed conflict, if such weapons, projectiles, and material and methods of warfare are prohibited.

Disarmament, Arms Control, and Non-Proliferation Agreements

Part Two contains review and comments on the key disarmament and arms control agreements, including their main provisions, purpose, interpretation, implementation, compliance, and enforcement of the agreements. Most of these agreements are multilateral, i.e., agreements concluded between several states, either globally or as regional agreements. Several of the most important agreements on nuclear weapons and their means of delivery (missiles) are concluded bilaterally between the United States and the former Soviet Union and its successor state, Russia. However, a detailed review of the arms control agreements on reducing and regulating the strategic nuclear weapons and their means of delivery that have been concluded between the United States and the Soviet Union/Russia, falls outside the scope of this book.

Weapons of Mass Destruction

INTRODUCTION

Weapons of mass destruction (WMD) are normally defined as non-conventional weapons that have the capacity to cause massive, uncontrolled, and indiscriminate loss of life and major destruction. However, there is no authoritative definition in international law, either in treaties or in customary international law, of weapons of mass destruction. The term WMD is used for specific categories of weapons of mass destruction that include nuclear, biological, and chemical weapons and their delivery systems (missiles) when they are an integral part of the weapon system. Radiological weapons are also classified as WMD. The term was first used in 1937 in connection with the air bombardment of Guernica during the civil war in Spain. As opposed to precision weapons, i.e., radar or laser-guided bombs and missiles that can hit their targets with great accuracy, weapons of mass destruction may also hit civilians indiscriminately.

Chapter 5 reviews and comments on the prohibitions and regulations of weapons of mass destruction in international law and includes the non-proliferation of nuclear weapons, test ban agreements, nuclear-weapon-free zones, and the question of the legality of the threat or use of nuclear weapons, including the Advisory Opinion of the International Court of Justice. The chapter also discusses the relationship between nuclear weapons and human rights.

Chapters 6 and 7 deal with biological and chemical weapons, respectively.

5

Nuclear Weapons

INTRODUCTION

A nuclear weapon is an explosive device that releases enormous amounts of energy, in the form of blast wave, heat radiation, and radioactive fallout, through either an uncontrolled nuclear fission chain reaction or combined nuclear fission and fusion reactions that result in a powerful explosion.

In nuclear fission (or splitting), the nucleus of an atom splits into two or more subatomic particles (neutrons and protons) which produce additional fissions. In this process, large amounts of energy and highly radioactive particles are released. Nuclear weapons based on fission are called atomic bombs or A-bombs. The first generation of nuclear weapons was the A-bomb. The nuclear fuel used in A-bombs is highly enriched uranium – U-235 uranium enriched to 90 per cent or more – or weapons grade plutonium (Pu 239). Approximately 52 kilograms of uranium 235 or 16 kilograms of plutonium 239 is the minimum amount of fissile material – the so-called "critical mass" – that is needed to achieve and maintain the fission chain reaction in a nuclear weapon.

Nuclear fusion is the fusing of two or more lighter atoms into a larger one. Nuclear weapons that use a combination of a primary nuclear fission reaction to compress and ignite a secondary nuclear fusion reaction to provide explosive power are called hydrogen bombs, H-bombs, or thermonuclear bombs.

The world's first atomic bomb was detonated at a nuclear test site in New Mexico by the United States in July 1945. On 6 August 1945, the first atomic bomb was used in war on the Japanese city of Hiroshima. The bomb had a yield of 13.6 kilotons – each kiloton equal to the explosive force of nearly one thousand tons of TNT. Three days later, the US dropped a second nuclear bomb, with a yield of 18 kilotons, on Nagasaki. The bombings resulted in the deaths of approximately 200,000 people, mainly civilians, from acute injuries sustained from the explosions. Since then nuclear weapons have not been used as military weapons, but only as a political and military deterrent.

The second generation of nuclear weapons – hydrogen bombs – was developed in 1952 and was tested for the first time in November 1952, on one of the Marshall Islands, by the United States, with a yield of 10.6 megatons – each megaton equal to the explosive force of over 900,000 tons of TNT. The Soviet Union tested its first H-bomb in August 1953. A thermonuclear bomb can be many thousands of times more powerful than pure fission atomic bombs. Today the principal part of the nuclear arsenals of the United States and Russia consists of thermonuclear bombs. China, France, and the United Kingdom also have such nuclear weapons.

In this book, the term "nuclear weapons" includes both atomic bombs and hydrogen bombs.

NUCLEAR WEAPONS ARSENALS

According to the latest estimates from the Stockholm International Peace Research Institute (SIPRI), as of January 2015 there was an estimated total of approximately 15,850 nuclear weapons in the world. Deployed warheads and stocks of nuclear weapons in each of the five nuclear-weapon states and the four nuclear-armed states[1] are estimated as follows:

	Deployed warheads*	Other warheads†	Total
United States	2,080	5,180	7,260
Russia	1,780	5,720	7,500
United Kingdom	150	65	215
France	290	10	300
China	0	260	260
India	0	90–110	90–110
Pakistan	0	100–120	100–120
Israel	0	80	80
North Korea	0	6–8	6–8
Total	4,300	11,550	15,850

* "Deployed warheads" include operational warheads installed on missiles or located on bases with operational forces, i.e., ready for use on short notice.
† "Other warheads" include nuclear weapons in reserve, awaiting dismantlement or requiring preparation (e.g., assembly or loading on launchers) before they become fully operational.
Source: SIPRI Yearbook 2015.

Of the total number of nuclear weapons, the United States and Russia maintain 14,760 (93 per cent of the total number) in their arsenals. The number of nuclear weapons deployed by the United States includes – in addition to approximately 1,900 strategic warheads[2] – about 180 non-strategic (tactical) nuclear weapons, deployed in Europe. Other warheads in the US nuclear arsenal include about 2,680 warheads held in reserve and 2,500 retired warheads awaiting dismantlement. It is estimated that the United States has a total of 500 tactical nuclear warheads, which are included in the above numbers.

It is estimated that Russia maintains a nuclear arsenal of approximately 4,380 nuclear warheads assigned to operational forces, of which 2,430 are strategic warheads. About 1,780 of the strategic warheads are deployed on ballistic missiles (more than half of the warheads are deployed on some 300 land-based ballistic missiles and approximately 400 warheads on 140 SLBMs (submarine-launched ballistic missiles)). Sixty warheads are deployed with 60 bomber aircraft. Nearly 700 bomber and submarine warheads are kept in storage. Russia also has approximately 2,000 tactical nuclear weapons – all kept in storage. There are 3,120 warheads that are retired or awaiting dismantlement.

All of Britain's 215 nuclear weapons are sea-based Trident SLBM and their associated warheads. The United Kingdom has four nuclear-powered ballistic missile submarines.

France's nuclear weapons consist of 300 warheads for 48 SLBM and 54 air-launched cruise missiles. France also has four nuclear-powered ballistic missile submarines.

China's nuclear warheads are believed to be kept in storage, not ready for immediate launch. An estimated 190 warheads are assigned to land-based ballistic missiles and aircraft.

Compared with January 2014, the total number of nuclear weapons in the world decreased by approximately 500 warheads. The total number of weapons decreased from January 2012 to January 2013 by 1,730 weapons and by about 950 from January 2013 to January 2014. The United States and Russia reduced their nuclear weapons from 2014–15 by 40 and 500 warheads, respectively, as a result of the Treaty on Measures for the Further Reduction and Limitation of Strategic Offensive Arms ("New START") and unilateral reductions. The United Kingdom reduced its nuclear weapons by ten nuclear warheads. China increased its arsenal by ten warheads. In France and in the nuclear-armed states, the numbers of nuclear warheads remained unchanged. However, all the nuclear-weapon states and nuclear-armed states are modernizing their nuclear forces and have thus demonstrated that they are determined to retain sizeable nuclear arsenals for the foreseeable future. It is generally assumed that Israel became a de facto nuclear-weapon state as early as 1973. Israel has neither officially confirmed nor denied that it possesses nuclear weapons but is universally believed to possess them. There is no authoritative confirmation that North Korea has operational nuclear weapons, but according to SIPRI's estimates, North Korea has produced sufficient quantities of plutonium to build six to eight nuclear weapons.

About thirty other countries are assumed to have the technological capacity to develop and produce nuclear weapons, Iran among them. It was estimated that Iran would have been able to test its first nuclear weapon within a few years – or perhaps earlier. This presumed Iranian ambition was brought to an end by the so-called Joint Comprehensive Plan of Action of 14 July 2015 on the future of Iran's nuclear program. According to the Arms Control Association, the Plan of Action – the comprehensive nuclear agreement between Iran and the P5+1 – i.e., the five permanent members of the Security Council: China, France, Russia, the United Kingdom, and the United States, and Germany – verifiably blocks Iran's pathways to nuclear weapons development and guards against a clandestine Iranian nuclear weapons program. When fully implemented, the agreement will be a net plus for non-proliferation and will enhance US and regional security.[3]

Iraq's efforts to obtain nuclear weapons capability were temporarily shut down by Israel's bombing of Iraq's nuclear facilities in 1981 and were completely phased out after the First Gulf War in 1991. In 2007, Israel bombed Syria's nuclear installations and thus brought Syria's attempts to develop nuclear weapons to an end.

South Africa is the only country to have built nuclear weapons and then voluntarily dismantled them and abandoned its nuclear weapons program. South Africa had pursued a nuclear weapons program from 1974 through 1990 as a deterrent to counter a perceived Soviet threat in the region. In the 1980s, South Africa built six nuclear weapons and had started building a seventh. Less than a decade after assembling its first nuclear weapon, South Africa voluntarily joined the Treaty on Non-Proliferation of Nuclear Weapons (NPT) as a non-nuclear-weapon state, and allowed international inspections of its former nuclear weapons program.

TREATIES BETWEEN THE UNITED STATES AND THE SOVIET UNION/RUSSIA ON REDUCTIONS OF NUCLEAR WEAPONS

The United States and the Soviet Union/Russia have signed a number of treaties with significant limitations on the numbers of their strategic nuclear weapons and their means of delivery: the SALT I and II (Interim Agreement and Treaty on Limitation of Strategic Offensive Arms), START I and II (Strategic Arms Reduction Treaties), and SORT (Treaty on Strategic Offensive Reductions) (see page 247). During the Cold War, when their arsenals were at their highest level, the two former superpowers possessed a total of an estimated 64,500 nuclear weapons in 1986. Since 1991, 80 per cent of the American and Russian nuclear weapons have been eliminated. The bilateral agreements have superseded each other and are therefore of mainly historical interest.

The most recent treaty between the United States and Russia on further reductions and limitations of their offensive strategic nuclear weapons is the Treaty on Measures for the Further Reduction and Limitation of Strategic Offensive Arms of 2010 (New START or Prague Treaty). The treaty entered into force on 5 February 2011 and will remain in force for ten years, until 5 February 2021, unless it is superseded earlier by a subsequent agreement on the reduction and limitation of strategic offensive arms. According to the treaty, each of the states must reduce the number of their deployed strategic ICBMs (intercontinental ballistic missiles), SLBMs, and heavy bombers to no more than 700 and the number of warheads on their deployed ICBMs, SLBMs, and heavy bombers to a maximum of 1,550 before 5 February 2018. The treaty replaces the previous agreements between the two countries on the reduction of nuclear weapons, the latest of which is the Treaty on Strategic Offensive Reductions of 2002 (SORT or Moscow Treaty), by which each state committed to reducing and limiting its strategic nuclear warheads, so that by 31 December 2012 the aggregate number of such warheads did not exceed 1,700 to 2,200 for each party.

In 1987, the United States and the Soviet Union concluded an important bilateral agreement on the elimination of their intermediate-range and shorter-range missiles: Treaty Between the United States of America and the Union of Soviet Socialist Republics on the Elimination of Their Intermediate-Range and Shorter-Range Missiles (INF). The treaty entered into force in 1988. The INF Treaty globally abolished an entire class of American and Soviet land-based intermediate-range and shorter-range missiles with ranges of between 500 and 5,500 kilometres, i.e., not only the missiles deployed in Europe, but all the missiles in the arsenals of the two countries in those ground-launched categories. As a result of the INF Treaty, a total of 859 US intermediate-range and shorter-range missiles (Pershing and ground-launched cruise missiles) and 1,752 Russian intermediate-range and shorter-range missiles (various types of SS-missiles) were dismantled and destroyed. The INF Treaty was a breakthrough for the control of nuclear weapons; the treaty was the first disarmament agreement that included a comprehensive regime for mutual on-site inspections, i.e., on the territories of both participating states.

Unfortunately, the INF Treaty has come under pressure from Russia, which is feeling increasingly limited by the treaty against the background of the Americans' continued modernization of their nuclear arsenal and development of a ballistic missile defence system. The United States is accusing Russia of having technically violated the INF by testing a new type of intermediate-range cruise missile for use at sea. The missile was tested from a ground-based launcher, which is not allowed under the treaty. Russia has threatened to withdraw from the treaty as a response to US moves. The two parties should resolve this issue within the framework of the treaty, in the Special Verification Commission.

Comment

Most of the American and Russian strategic nuclear weapons are deployed in missile silos in their respective national territories and onboard US and Russian nuclear submarines that constantly patrol the world's oceans.

However, American tactical nuclear weapons are still deployed in five European countries in northwestern and southeastern Europe, in

Belgium, Germany, Italy, the Netherlands, and Turkey. This continued presence in Europe of US tactical nuclear bombs is a concern. Tactical (or non-strategic) nuclear weapons have a much lower yield and shorter range than strategic nuclear weapons and are designed for use on the battlefield. Although the number of US tactical nuclear weapons in Europe has been greatly reduced, from approximately 7,300 nuclear warheads in 1971, there are still today approximately 184 nuclear aircraft-delivered B61 gravity bombs deployed at six US bases in the above five European countries. The newly developed version, B61-12, which has increased accuracy in hitting targets and greater capability in penetratting hardened targets, is scheduled for deployment in Europe by 2020. The existing nuclear bombs in the European countries are not operationally deployed, but stored separately from their aircraft delivery systems in underground vaults in protected shelters. However, the risk of accidents while handling the bombs during training and maintenance exercises, sabotage by terrorist attacks against the nuclear weapons bases, or theft can never be completely ruled out. Because of their small size and mobility, tactical nuclear bombs are particularly vulnerable to theft or risk of an unauthorized launch.

It no longer makes sense to maintain this tactical nuclear deterrence capability in Western Europe more than twenty-five years after the end of the Cold War – even in light of the conflict in the Ukraine and the resulting serious increase in tensions between the US/NATO and Russia. The US tactical nuclear weapons had no deterrent effect on Russia's decision to annex the Crimea and invade the eastern part of Ukraine. The deployment of tactical US nuclear weapons in Europe was originally motivated by the former massive Soviet predominance of conventional armed forces. With the dissolution of the Soviet Union in December 1991, the threat from Soviet conventional forces disappeared. Today, conventional NATO forces are technically superior to those of Russia. The tactical US nuclear weapons in Europe no longer have any real and additional military significance and deterrence effect beyond the one already provided by the American, British, and French nuclear arsenals – only a political and symbolic significance, as an expression of transatlantic American-European unity and of NATO's common defence solidarity. The continued deployment and modernization of these weapons in Europe is very costly: It is estimated by the Congressional Budget

Office at 7 billion dollars and by the Pentagon at 10 billion dollars over the next decade. Moreover, if the modernized B61-12s are deployed, Russia has threatened to deploy its tactical nuclear missiles in the Russian enclave of Kaliningrad in Eastern Europe. If the American tactical nuclear weapons were relocated from European bases to national storage facilities in the United States, the Russians would probably be more willing to initiate new talks with the US on possible further overall reductions of both American and Russian strategic nuclear weapons.

Proponents of maintaining the tactical US nuclear weapons in Europe, in particular the Central European NATO countries, such as Poland, the Czech Republic, and the Baltic states, argue that these weapons continue to have not only a symbolic meaning as an expression of defence solidarity but also demonstrate America's determination to guarantee the security of Europe. In this context, proponents refer to the continued advantage in the numbers of Russian tactical nuclear weapons and the expected increasing role of nuclear weapons in Russia's defence posture. Under the current circumstances in Ukraine and Russia's involvement in the conflict, withdrawing American tactical nuclear weapons from Europe would send a wrong signal and be perceived in Moscow as an expression of weakness.

The current threats to the security of Europe are mainly coming from Middle Eastern countries or extremist religious groups in the Middle East, such as Islamic State (IS). These threats can only be countered effectively by building a missile defence for Europe in the southeastern part of the continent. In case of increasing threats and escalating conflict, there will be sufficient time to transfer tactical nuclear weapons to Europe from reserve stocks in the United States. Alternatively, a smaller number of tactical nuclear weapons could be maintained in Turkey and Italy. In addition, the strategic nuclear weapons (SLBM) deployed onboard American and British submarines constitute an overwhelming deterrence force, which – unlike the tactical US nuclear weapons deployed in the five European countries – are constantly operational and may be launched at short notice.

At the request of the former German foreign minister, Guido Westerwelle, there have been increasing calls since 2009 to reconsider the role of the American tactical nuclear weapons in Europe, in particular from Belgium, Germany, and the Netherlands, with support from Norway and Luxembourg. A decision to continue – for political reasons – to have tactical US nuclear weapons deployed in Europe is also becoming more relevant and urgent in light of concrete plans in Germany, Belgium, the Netherlands, Italy, and Denmark to replace their current fighter aircraft (F-16 and Tornado), some of which are currently equipped to carry nuclear bombs ("dual-capable aircraft"). The question is whether the new fighter aircraft (presumably the US-built F-35 JSF) in these countries should be equipped to carry nuclear bombs, which would add considerably to the costs of the aircraft.

It seems to be the general view among all the NATO member states that any decision to remove the tactical nuclear weapons from Europe should be based on consensus.

Legal Considerations

From the point of view of international law, the deployment of US tactical nuclear weapons on the territories of the five above-mentioned European non-nuclear-weapon states must be considered a violation of Articles 1 and 2 of the Treaty on the Non-Proliferation of Nuclear Weapons (NPT) – if not of the treaty's letter – of its purpose and aim (see more about the NPT below). This is the case even though the United States has not transferred the nuclear weapons or the control over them to the host countries. Another consideration is that maintaining the presence of the tactical US nuclear weapons in Europe contradicts and undermines the stated aim of European countries to promote the disarmament of nuclear weapons. As long as US nuclear weapons are deployed in Europe, it is unrealistic to expect Russia to take steps to reduce its tactical nuclear weapons in Europe, i.e., in the western part of Russia. It would be in NATO's interest for Russia to reduce its tactical weapons.

In NATO's Strategic Concept, adopted at the NATO summit in Washington in April 1999, the tactical US nuclear weapons in Europe are given less importance than before. However, these weapons can only be reduced if Russia does the same. In this context it should be noted that the tactical US nuclear weapons previously deployed in Greece were withdrawn in 2001. In 1991, the US nuclear weapons in South

Korea and Japan were also withdrawn from these countries. Why not remove this relic of the Cold War from Europe, which today – in spite of the Ukraine conflict – must be considered less of a potential conflict area than the Korean peninsula and Japan?

NATO'S NUCLEAR WEAPONS POLICY

There are still a number of countries, including the member states of NATO that maintain a deterrence policy and strategy based on nuclear weapons. These countries also do not exclude the use of nuclear weapons in case they are attacked with conventional weapons. NATO's nuclear policy is laid down in NATO's "Strategic Concept for the Defence and Security of the Members of the North Atlantic Treaty Organization," adopted by the heads of state and government at the NATO Summit in Lisbon in November 2010. According to the Strategic Concept's paragraph 17, "Deterrence, based on an appropriate mix of nuclear and conventional capabilities, remains a core element of our overall strategy. The circumstances in which any use of nuclear weapons might have to be contemplated are extremely remote. As long as nuclear weapons exist, NATO will remain a nuclear alliance." Paragraph 19 further states: "We will ensure that NATO has the full range of capabilities necessary to deter and defend against any threat to the safety and security of our populations. Therefore, we will maintain an appropriate mix of nuclear and conventional forces." However, in paragraph 26, the Strategic Concept also expresses the Alliance's readiness to create the conditions for a world without nuclear weapons: "We are resolved to seek a safer world for all and to create the conditions for a world without nuclear weapons in accordance with the goals of the Nuclear Non-Proliferation Treaty, in a way that promotes international stability, and is based on the principle of undiminished security for all. With the changes in the security environment since the end of the Cold War, we have dramatically reduced the number of nuclear weapons stationed in Europe and our reliance on nuclear weapons in NATO strategy. We will seek to create the conditions for further reductions in the future." The main content of the Strategic Concept is repeated in Alliance's "Deterrence and Defence Posture Review," adopted at the Summit Meeting in Chicago in May 2012, which also contains the following text: "Nuclear weapons are a core component of NATO's overall capabilities for deterrence and defence alongside conventional and missile defence forces ... The circumstances in which any use of nuclear weapons might have to be contemplated are extremely remote. As long as nuclear weapons exist, NATO will remain a nuclear alliance." The last statement is repeated again in the "Wales Summit Declaration" of 5 September 2014, which also states that "Deterrence, based on an appropriate mix of nuclear, conventional, and missile defence capabilities, remains a core element of our overall strategy." The above statements confirm that NATO does not exclude the use of nuclear weapons.

NUCLEAR NON-PROLIFERATION TREATY

The most important global agreement on nuclear weapons reduction is the "Treaty on the Non-Proliferation of Nuclear Weapons" (NPT) of 1 July 1968. The treaty, which came into force in March 1970, and is considered to be the cornerstone of international efforts to prevent the spread of nuclear weapons, now has 191 states parties, i.e., the entire world community except Israel, India, and Pakistan (plus the new state of South Sudan, which has not yet joined the treaty). At a review conference in May 1995 to review the functioning of the treaty, the states parties decided to extend it indefinitely.

North Korea was a party to the NPT but in March 1993 the country announced that it was withdrawing from the NPT. In January 2003, North Korea cancelled its participation in the NPT effective the following day, and then declared that it possessed nuclear weapons. However, because of procedural errors, the validity of North Korea's withdrawal from the NPT was disputed. The withdrawal did not comply with the provisions of Article 10 on withdrawal and was therefore not recognized. It remains to be seen whether North Korea will continue its clandestine and controversial nuclear program in order to develop (more?) nuclear weapons and nuclear weapon delivery capabilities (missiles).

The NPT makes an important distinction between two categories of states: Nuclear-weapon states and non-nuclear-weapon states. The non-proliferation obligations for the nuclear-weapon states are laid down in Article 1 of the treaty: "Each nuclear-weapon state party to the Treaty undertakes not to transfer to any recipient whatsoever nuclear weapons or other nuclear explosive devices or control over such weapons or explosive devices directly, or indirectly; and not in any way to assist, encourage, or induce any non-nuclear-weapon state to manufacture or otherwise acquire nuclear weapons or other nuclear explosive devices, or control over such weapons or explosive devices."

The nuclear-weapon states parties are defined in Article 9, paragraph 3: "For the purposes of this Treaty, a nuclear-weapon state is one which has manufactured and exploded a nuclear weapon or other nuclear explosive device prior to 1 January 1967." Five states – China, France, Russia, the United Kingdom, and the United States – are in this category of nuclear weapons possessor states officially recognized by the NPT, and are generally referred to as the "nuclear-weapon states." These five states are also the permanent members of the United Nations Security Council. Thus, the NPT may be said to have established a monopoly or legitimate right to possess nuclear weapons for states that already had such weapons before 1 January 1967. Although the NPT legitimized the nuclear arsenals of the above-mentioned five states, it also established that the nuclear-weapon states were not supposed to build and maintain nuclear weapons in perpetuity, (see Article 6, below). Besides the three nuclear-weapon states, who are members of NATO, the twenty-five other NATO members are so-called "nuclear-umbrella states," i.e., countries protected by the nuclear weapons of the United States and the United Kingdom. Australia, Japan, and South Korea are also nuclear-umbrella states, in alliance with the United States.

All other states parties are non-nuclear-weapon states, which are not allowed to have nuclear weapons according to the NPT. Article 2 of the Treaty lays down the non-nuclear-weapon states' obligations not to possess, manufacture, or receive nuclear weapons: "Each non-nuclear-weapon state party to the Treaty undertakes not to receive the transfer from any transferor whatsoever of nuclear weapons or other nuclear explosive devices or of control over such weapons or explosive devices directly, or indirectly, not to manufacture or otherwise acquire nuclear weapons or other nuclear explosive devices, and not to seek or receive any assistance in the manufacture of nuclear weapons or other nuclear explosive devices."

The so-called nuclear-armed states are countries that are not parties to the NPT, and therefore not explicitly bound by the prohibition on nuclear weapons in Article 2. The three non-parties to the NPT and non-recognized nuclear-armed states are Israel, India, and Pakistan.

The NPT does not prohibit or limit the use of nuclear energy. According to Article 4, all the parties to the treaty have an inalienable right to develop research, production, and use of nuclear energy for peaceful purposes without discrimination and in conformity with Articles 1 and 2 of the treaty. Article 5 expands this right of access for all states to the peaceful use of nuclear energy, guaranteeing all participating non-nuclear-weapon states the potential benefits of any peaceful application of nuclear energy under appropriate international observation according to a special international agreement or agreements, through an appropriate international body. Such special international agreements have been concluded in the form of safeguards agreements with the International Atomic Energy Agency (IAEA).

As a condition of their agreement to adopting the NPT, the non-nuclear-weapon states demanded that the treaty should contain a provision for a general disarmament obligation that would apply to all parties. This was called the "grand bargain" of nuclear weapons possession and disarmament. In practice, of course, this obligation is only relevant for the nuclear-weapon states. Article 6 contains the following disarmament obligation: "Each of the parties to the Treaty undertakes to pursue negotiations in good faith on effective measures relating to cessation of the nuclear arms race at an early date and to nuclear disarmament, and on a treaty on general and complete disarmament under strict and effective international control."

This was the non-nuclear-weapon states' "price" for giving up the development or acquisition of nuclear weapons. In return, the nuclear-weapon states committed themselves to negotiate disarmament of nuclear weapons – with a view to the complete abolition of these weapons. This commitment was re-established in Decision 2 on Principles and Objectives for Nuclear Non-Proliferation and Disarmament, which was adopted at the NPT Review Conference in 1995 and in which the nuclear-weapon states reaffirmed their commitment under Article 6 to disarmament of their nuclear weapons. In the Final Documents of the 2000 NPT Review Conference, the five nuclear-weapon states again committed themselves to "An unequivocal undertaking by the nuclear-weapon states to accomplish the total elimination of their nuclear arsenals leading to nuclear disarmament, to which all states parties are committed under article VI."[4]

The NPT does not provide for a secretariat or an organization to monitor and ensure that the states parties comply with their obligations under the Treaty. This supervisory function is carried out by the IAEA in Vienna. NPT's Article 3 stipulates, for example, that each non-nuclear-weapon state party to the treaty undertakes to accept IAEA safeguards, as set forth in an agreement to be negotiated and concluded with the IAEA – a so-called safeguards agreement. According to the IAEA safeguards agreement, the Agency's inspectors may control that the participating states fulfill the obligations they have assumed under the Treaty with a view to preventing peaceful uses of nuclear energy from being diverted from nuclear power plants to the manufacture of nuclear weapons. All nuclear materials in all peaceful nuclear activities may be verified. Inspections of the civilian nuclear facilities include their fissile material (nuclear reactor fuel) for the production of nuclear energy. Nearly every state in the world (182 states) has concluded safeguards agreements with the IAEA, including Iran, North Korea, Israel, India, and Pakistan, and 127 states have concluded additional safeguards protocols with the IAEA. All the five nuclear-weapon states have concluded safeguards agreements and additional protocols with the IAEA to inspect their civilian nuclear facilities. The additional protocols supplement the states' safeguards agreements by granting the IAEA expanded rights of access to information and sites. The additional protocols aim to fill the gaps in the information reported under the safeguards agreements. By enabling the IAEA to obtain a much fuller picture of the states' nuclear programs, plans, nuclear material holdings, and trade, the additional protocols help to provide much greater assurance on the absence of undeclared nuclear material and activities. All the five recognized nuclear-weapon states, as well as India, have safeguards agreements and additional protocols in force with the IAEA for inspections of their civilian nuclear facilities, activities, and materials. Israel and Pakistan have only safeguards agreements. The military facilities of the nuclear-weapon states are not subject to IAEA inspections.

Article 3 further obliges each state party not to provide fissionable material, equipment, or material especially designed or prepared for the processing, use, or production of special fissionable material, to any non-nuclear-weapon state for peaceful purposes, unless the source or special fissionable material is subject to the safeguards required by the Article.

An NPT review conference is convened every five years to review the operation and implementation of the treaty, to ensure that the states parties comply with its provisions, and to ensure that its purposes are being realized (Article 8, paragraph 3).

The latest review conference was held in New York from 27 April to 22 May 2015. During the review conference the participants were deeply divided over whether the nuclear-weapon states have met their commitments under the NPT to reduce, and ultimately eliminate their nuclear arsenals. The nuclear-weapon states insisted on an incremental step-by-step approach for nuclear disarmament and rejected proposals from the non-aligned states to initiate negotiations on a convention to prohibit and eliminate nuclear weapons and to establish a standing body to monitor compliance with the NPT. It was also recommended by a great majority of non-nuclear-weapon states that the General Assembly should establish an open-ended working group to "identify and elaborate" effective disarmament measures, including a stand-alone agreement for achieving and maintaining a world free of nuclear weapons.[5] However, the proposal also recommended that the working group should proceed by consensus, which would have given the nuclear-weapon states the ability to block any progress.

In the end, it was not possible to obtain consensus on a final outcome document from the review conference. This was mainly because the United States, Egypt, and the other Arab states disagreed on the modalities for convening a conference to establish a zone free of weapons of mass destruction in the Middle East, which had been agreed upon by the 2010 NPT Review Conference. The conference was to have been convened in 2012 but it was never held because of resistance from Israel, which insists that regional security issues must also be addressed, along with weapons of mass destruction issues. Therefore, Israel could not agree to the proposed agenda for the Middle East conference. On the last day of the 2015 Conference, the United States, the United Kingdom, and Canada stated that they could not accept the provisions in the draft final document on convening a conference to advance a zone free of weapons of mass destruction in the Middle East.

The 70th General Assembly adopted resolution 70/38, Follow-up to nuclear disarmament obligations agreed to at the 1995, 2000, and 2010 Review Conferences of the Parties to the Treaty on the Non-Proliferation of Nuclear Weapons, by which the General Assembly "calls for practical steps, as agreed to at the 2000 Review Conference of the Parties to the Treaty on the Non-Proliferation of Nuclear Weapons, to be taken by all nuclear-weapon states, that would lead to nuclear disarmament in a way that promotes international stability and, based on the principle of undiminished security for all." Among the practical steps mentioned in the resolution are:

- further efforts by the nuclear-weapon states to reduce their nuclear arsenals unilaterally,
- further reduction of non-strategic nuclear weapons,
- concrete agreed measures to further reduce the operational status of nuclear weapons systems,
- a diminished role for nuclear weapons in security policies.

The resolution was adopted, with 121 votes in favour, 48 against, and 12 abstentions. France, Israel, Russia, the United Kingdom, the United States, and Canada voted against. China, India, Pakistan, and North Korea abstained.

GLOBAL PARTNERSHIP AGAINST THE SPREAD OF WEAPONS AND MATERIALS OF MASS DESTRUCTION

The terrorist attacks against the United States on 11 September 2001 strongly intensified international concerns about terrorist organizations getting hold of nuclear, biological, chemical, and radiological weapons, materials, and technology. This led to the launch by the former Group of Eight (G8) countries – Canada, France, Germany, Italy, Japan, Russia, the United Kingdom, and the United States – at their summit in Kananaskis, Alberta, in June 2002, of the "Global Partnership against the Spread of Weapons and Materials of Mass Destruction."[6] The purpose of this security initiative was to prevent both state actors (so-called "rogue states," i.e., irresponsible states that do not respect the rules of international law and norms) and non-state actors (terrorist organizations) from acquiring weapons and materials of mass destruction. Originally, the efforts under the Partnership were concentrated on the security and environmental threats from the huge numbers of weapons of mass destruction left in Russia after the end of the Cold War. Among the priority areas in Russia were the following tasks:

- destroying chemical weapons stockpiles,
- dismantling 192 decommissioned nuclear submarines,
- securing and disposing of fissile materials,
- re-employing former scientists in the weapons of mass destruction industry, and
- destroying and preventing the proliferation of biological weapons.

The United States made a commitment of $10 billion to contribute to Partnership activities in Russia. The other G-8 countries pledged to contribute an additional $8 billion during a ten-year period. Other countries pledged to contribute 160 million Euros. A total of thirteen other countries, the European Union, and the Nuclear Threat Initiative have contributed to the Global Partnership, which was extended in 2011 until 2012–22.

UNITED NATIONS SECURITY COUNCIL RESOLUTION 1540
ON NON-PROLIFERATION OF WEAPONS
OF MASS DESTRUCTION

In April 2004, the United Nations Security Council adopted resolution 1540, Non-proliferation of weapons of mass destruction. The resolution, adopted unanimously, expresses grave concern about the threat of terrorism and the risk that non-state actors could acquire, develop, traffic in, or use nuclear, chemical, and biological weapons and their means of delivery. In the resolution, the Security Council also expresses grave concern about the threat of illicit trafficking in nuclear, chemical, or biological weapons and their means of delivery, and related materials. This threat adds a new dimension to the issue of the proliferation of such weapons and also poses a threat to international peace and security. Acting under Chapter VII of the Charter of the United Nations, on what actions to take when there are threats to the peace, breaches of the peace, and acts of aggression, the Council "decides that all states shall refrain from providing any form of support to non-state actors that attempt to develop, acquire, manufacture, possess, transport, transfer, or use nuclear, chemical, or biological weapons and their means of delivery." The Council also decides that "all states, in accordance with their national procedures, shall adopt and enforce appropriate effective laws which prohibit any non-state actor" from engaging in any of the above activities, in particular for terrorist purposes.

Furthermore, "all states shall take and enforce effective measures to establish domestic controls to prevent the proliferation of nuclear, chemical, or biological weapons and their means of delivery."

To this end, all states shall "develop and maintain appropriate effective measures to account for and secure production, use, storage, or transport of such items" as well as physical protection and border controls. Law enforcement efforts shall be taken to "detect, deter, prevent, and combat the illicit trafficking and brokering in such items." States are called upon to report to the "1540 Committee," set up by the Security Council, on the steps they have taken or intend to take to implement the resolution. The Committee's mandate has been extended to 2021.

In several other resolutions, the Security Council, acting under Chapter VII of the Charter, has taken measures under Article 41 to impose sanctions ("measures not involving the use of armed force") "to be employed to give effect to its decisions." Many of these resolutions have imposed arms sales embargoes to prevent supplying, selling, or transferring in any way all types of conventional weapons covered by the United Nations Register of Conventional Arms. Member states have also been called upon to take all necessary measures to prevent transfers of materials and technology that could be used for nuclear weapon programs and missiles, e.g., to North Korea and Iran.[7]

At a historic meeting of the Security Council on 24 September 2009, attended by President Obama and thirteen other heads of state, the Security Council unanimously adopted resolution S/RES/1887 (2009), Maintenance of international peace and security: Nuclear non-proliferation and nuclear disarmament. The resolution contains a number of paragraphs on a wide range of steps for member states to take in order to, for example, stop the spread of nuclear weapons, ensure reductions in existing stocks of nuclear weapons, and controlling fissionable materials.

On 26 September 2013, the General Assembly held a high-level meeting on nuclear disarmament.[8] The 70th General Assembly adopted resolution 70/36, Measures to prevent terrorists from acquiring weapons of mass destruction, by which the General Assembly "calls upon all member states to support international efforts to prevent terrorists from acquiring weapons of mass destruction and their means of delivery," and further "urges all member states to take and strengthen national measures, as appropriate, to prevent terrorists from acquiring weapons of mass destruction, their means of delivery and materials and technologies related to their manufacture." The resolution was adopted without a vote.

STRENGTHENING NUCLEAR SECURITY

Since the 2001 terrorist attacks on the United States, the physical security of nuclear power plants and their vulnerability to deliberate acts of terrorism by aircraft crashing into nuclear reactors or through sabotage or theft of nuclear materials, has become an issue of increasing concern. Most existing nuclear power plants are not designed to withstand crashes from large aircraft. A successful attack on a nuclear plant could have devastating consequences, killing, sickening, or displacing large numbers of residents in the area surrounding the plant, and causing extensive long-term environmental damage. Cyberattacks on nuclear power plants could also have devastating consequences. Uranium enrichment plants or uranium mines and civilian research reactors are also vulnerable to attacks, which could lead to widespread radioactive contamination.

The foreword to the NTI (Nuclear Threat Initiative) report *Bridging the Military Nuclear Materials Gap*, November 2015,[9] states: "One of the greatest threats the world faces is the possibility that a terrorist group could acquire and detonate a nuclear weapon or device. A terrorist nuclear attack in any large city would likely kill hundreds of thousands of people, inflict billions of dollars in damage, and have profound effects on global security, the global economy, and our way of life. The effects of such an attack would no doubt transcend national boundaries, thus compelling a global response to a global threat."

According to this report, more than 1,800 metric tons of weapons-usable nuclear materials – highly enriched uranium and plutonium – remain stored today in hundreds of facilities, some of them poorly secured and vulnerable to theft, in twenty-four countries around the world. Recent security breaches and incidents at nuclear facilities show that governments must do more to secure these dangerous materials and keep them out of the hands of terrorists. There is still no effective global system for how all weapons-usable nuclear materials should be stored. The existing mechanisms apply almost exclusively to a small part of all these materials – the 17 per cent used for peaceful, civilian purposes. The remaining 83 per cent are military nuclear materials outside the scope of existing international security standards that must apply to all nuclear materials that could be used by terrorists to build a nuclear device. The report therefore recommends strengthening the security of military materials in order to secure all nuclear materials, including military materials, and facilities; strengthening tools to detect and prevent the trafficking of nuclear materials across borders; and strengthening international cooperation on intelligence and law enforcement.

Experience shows that nuclear power plants – and even military nuclear facilities – are, in general, not sufficiently protected against intrusion, sabotage, or attack. One of the most spectacular incidents, considered the biggest security breach in the history of US atomic installations, is the break-in at the nuclear weapons plant at Oak Ridge, Tennessee, where the United States keeps thousands of kilograms of highly enriched uranium and parts for nuclear weapons. In July 2012, Sister Megan Rice, an 82-year-old nun, and two other peace activists cut through three fences before reaching a storage bunker. Although the protesters set off alarms, they were able to spend nearly an hour and a half inside the restricted area before they were arrested for trespassing! There have been other security breaches at military facilities where American nuclear missile launch officers and British law enforcement personnel at a nuclear weapons site were found sleeping and not completing patrols. There have also been incidents of intrusion into and theft of fissile material from nuclear power plants.

Illicit trafficking and smuggling of radioactive nuclear materials continue at an alarming rate. Since 1993, the IAEA has registered approximately 2,000 cases of illicit or unauthorized trafficking of nuclear and other radioactive material. In at least eighteen cases there have been confirmed thefts or losses of weapons-usable nuclear material.[10] Moldova has experienced three incidents, in 2011, 2014, and in February 2015, when smugglers transported radioactive materials by train from Russia and tried to sell these materials.

Against the background of growing international attention to the global threat posed by nuclear terrorism, and at the initiative of President Obama, world leaders from forty-seven countries and three international organizations gathered for the first Nuclear Security Summit in Washington in April 2010. In the communiqué from the Washington Summit, the participating leaders expressed their commitment to ensuring the effective security of all nuclear materials under their control, to consolidate or reduce the use of weapons-usable materials in civilian applications, and to work cooperatively as an international community to advance nuclear security. Leaders reaffirmed states' fundamental responsibility to maintain effective security of all nuclear materials, including nuclear materials used in nuclear weapons and nuclear facilities under states' control, and to prevent non-state actors from obtaining the information or technology required to use such material for malicious purposes. A second Nuclear Security Summit was held in Seoul in March 2012, and a third in The Hague in March 2014. A comprehensive summit communiqué on a wide range of measures to address the threats of nuclear terrorism was issued from The Hague meeting.[11] The fourth and probably final Nuclear Security Summit was held in March–April 2016, in Washington, DC.

Because the Nuclear Security Summit process will came to an end after the 2016 summit in its current form, a small group of four experts, members of the Nuclear Security Governance Experts Group, a project of the Asian Institute for Policy Studies, the Partnership for Global Security, and the Stanley Foundation, drew up a draft of an International Convention on Nuclear Security, which was presented in Washington in March 2015.[12]

This Convention would establish basic principles and standards for nuclear security and create mechanisms for additional rules. The objective of the Convention is "to ensure effective security of nuclear and other radioactive materials by codifying a set of essential elements for national nuclear security regimes and establishing a mechanism for continuous review and improvement of the international nuclear security regime" (Article 1). "Nuclear security" is defined in the Convention as "the prevention and detection of, and response to, theft, sabotage, unauthorized access, illegal transfer or other malicious acts involving nuclear and other radioactive materials or their associated facilities and equipment" (Article 2). Article 3 determines the scope of the Convention, which "shall apply to all nuclear and other radioactive materials used for civil purposes and the facilities in which they are contained and, to the extent possible, to such materials and facilities used for non-civil purposes."[13]

Such a Convention would fill the dangerous gaps in the current inadequate nuclear security regime and create an effective and sustainable global nuclear security system to prevent nuclear terrorism. The Convention would supplement the Convention on Nuclear Safety,[14] of 1994, whose aim is to commit the (78) participating states operating nuclear power plants to maintain a high level of safety to avoid nuclear radiation accidents by setting international standards for the location, siting, design, construction, and operation of nuclear installations.

The Nuclear Security Convention would expand the Convention on the Physical Protection of Nuclear Material, signed in March 1980 (153 states parties) and the International Convention for the Suppression of Acts of Nuclear Terrorism of 2005. The Convention on Nuclear Terrorism has been ratified by 115 states, including all the nuclear-weapon states and India. Israel has signed, but not ratified the Convention. Pakistan, Iran, and North Korea have neither signed nor ratified it. According to the Convention, nuclear terrorism is

- unlawfully and intentionally possessing or using radioactive material or a nuclear device,
- causing damage to a nuclear facility and releasing radioactive material in order to cause death,
- causing serious bodily injury or substantial damage to property or to the environment.

The Convention exempts the use of nuclear weapons in armed conflicts between states from this definition.

PROLIFERATION SECURITY INITIATIVE

The Proliferation Security Initiative (PSI) was launched by the United States in May 2003 as an international effort to prevent and stop the spread of weapons of mass destruction. The purpose of the PSI is to stop illegal transfers of weapons of mass destruction and technology, related materials, and delivery systems for WMD. The PSI activities include planning, exercises, and operations. The effort, which is based on the rules in international law and national legislation, may include interception and boarding of ships, aircraft, trains, and trucks transporting weapons of mass destruction, as well as the inspection of goods in containers in ports and airports, thereby preventing the proliferation of WMD. Thus, the PSI also includes cooperation between custom and police authorities. Many countries with large merchant fleets registered under flags of convenience, including Liberia and Panama, have signed agreements with the United States on joint operations in connection with the boarding of ships under their flag.

The PSI is not a formal, legally binding regime or organization, but a pragmatic group of states that support activities at sea, in the air, and on land to prevent the spread of weapons of mass destruction. The basic principles of the PSI, were committed to by the participating states, and adopted in September 2003. They include commitments to establish a more coordinated and effective basis on which to impede and stop shipments of WMD, delivery systems, and related materials flowing to and from states and non-state actors. These commitments must be consistent with national legal authorities and relevant international law and frameworks, including the United Nations Security Council.[15]

All countries and international organizations can participate in the proliferation regime. A total of 105 countries have joined the Initiative. China, Iran, North Korea, Syria, India, Pakistan, and Indonesia, among other states, are not participating in the PSI. Several of the countries that are not participating in the cooperation under the Initiative claim that the stopping and boarding of ships on the high seas is a violation of freedom of navigation on the high seas (Article 87 of the Convention on the Law of the Sea). These countries have also criticized the PSI for being a US-led, illegal, and non-transparent initiative that is not based on United Nations resolutions, and whose purpose is to seize ships of third-party countries on the high seas.

TEST BAN TREATIES

Introduction

To be sure that a nuclear weapon works and can be used as a deterrent, tests of a newly developed nuclear weapon need to be carried out.

Since the first American nuclear test on 16 July 1945 in the Alamogordo desert in New Mexico until July 1996, the five recognized nuclear-weapon states have carried out a total of 2,047 nuclear tests.[16] The Soviet Union conducted its first test of an atomic bomb on 29 August 1949, thus initiating the nuclear weapons arms race between the United States and the Soviet Union. The United Kingdom, France, and China conducted their first test explosions of nuclear bombs in 1952, 1960, and 1964 respectively.

Between 1945 and 1992, the United States carried out a total of 1,032 nuclear tests. In November 1952, the United States became the first country to test a hydrogen bomb. The test explosion, which took place at the Bikini Atoll in the Marshall Islands, yielded 15 megatons – equivalent to 15 million tons of TNT – and was the largest nuclear weapon ever detonated by the United States. By comparison, the nuclear bomb dropped over Hiroshima and Nagasaki had a yield of approximately 15 and 20 kilotons respectively – equivalent to 15 and 20 thousand tons of TNT, respectively. The total energy yield of all explosives used in the Second World War, including the Hiroshima and Nagasaki bombs, is estimated to have been 3 megatons.

The Soviet Union/Russia conducted a total of 715 nuclear tests between 1949 and 1990. From 1952 to 1991, the United Kingdom made forty-five nuclear tests. France carried out 210 nuclear test explosions between 1960 and 1996, and China forty-five tests between 1964 and 1996. India conducted its first nuclear test in 1974. In May 1998, India carried out two more tests. Two weeks later, Pakistan tested a nuclear weapon for the first time.

North Korea conducted its first nuclear test in 2006, the second in 2009, and a third in February 2013. The United Nations Security

Council condemned the 2013 North Korean test in the strongest terms in resolution 2094 of 2013. On 6 January 2016, North Korea conducted its fourth nuclear test, claiming that it was the country's first test of a hydrogen bomb. However, experts are skeptical of North Korea's claim that it detonated a hydrogen bomb, because of the low yield of the tested bomb (estimated yield between 5 to 10 kilotons). This is comparable to the test in 2013 and much smaller than what is usually obtained with hydrogen bombs. Although the latest North Korean test gives rise to serious concern, it should be noted that North Korea has not yet tested an intercontinental ballistic missile capable of reaching North America and has not yet demonstrated its ability to produce a nuclear warhead small enough to be deployed on a ballistic missile.[17] The same day as the latest test, the Security Council issued a press statement (doc. SC/12191), in which "the members of the Security Council strongly condemned this test, which is a clear violation of Security Council resolutions 1718 (2006), 1874 (2009), 2087 (2013), and 2094 (2013) and of the non-proliferation regime, and therefore a clear threat to international peace and security continues to exist." The members of the Security Council also recalled that they had previously expressed their determination to take "further significant measures" in the event of another North Korean nuclear test, and "in line with this commitment and the gravity of this violation" would begin to work immediately on such measures in a new Security Council resolution.

It is not known whether Israel has carried out any tests – and if so, how many. There are some indications that Israel has cooperated with South Africa in testing nuclear devices before the South African military nuclear program was closed. Since the nuclear tests conducted by India and Pakistan in 1998, no states other than North Korea have carried out test explosions. The Soviet Union introduced a temporary and unilateral moratorium for its nuclear tests in 1991. France, the United States, and the United Kingdom imposed a moratorium on their tests during 1992. France, however, resumed its tests in the fall of 1995. After heavy international criticism, the French government announced in January 1996 that France would refrain from further tests. The latest Chinese nuclear test was carried out in 1996 after which China announced a temporary moratorium on its tests.

Partial Test Ban Treaties

The question of limiting nuclear tests was first taken up for discussion in the late 1950s, when the United States, the Soviet Union, and the United Kingdom began negotiations to ban nuclear tests in the atmosphere, in outer space, and under water. The result was the "Treaty Banning Nuclear Weapon Tests in the Atmosphere, in Outer Space and Under Water," of 1963 – the so-called Limited or Partial Test Ban Treaty, originally concluded by the three states and later agreed to by another 123 countries.

In 1974, the United States and the Soviet Union concluded the Treaty between the United States of America and the Union of Soviet Socialist Republics on the Limitation of Underground Nuclear Weapon Tests, of 1974 – the so-called Threshold Test Ban Treaty, limiting underground nuclear tests to an explosive yield of less than 150 kilotons.

The prohibition in the Threshold Test Ban Treaty was extended to include nuclear explosions for peaceful purposes in the Treaty between the United States of America and the Union of Soviet Socialist Republics on Underground Nuclear Explosions for Peaceful Purposes, of 1976 (Peaceful Nuclear Explosions Treaty (PNET)). Until 1996, underground nuclear tests with an explosive yield of less than 150 kilotons were still allowed, for the United States and Russia only.

Comprehensive Nuclear-Test-Ban Treaty

After forty years of efforts to ban all nuclear weapons testing, the CD in Geneva began its substantive negotiations on a comprehensive nuclear-test-ban treaty in January 1994. In August 1996 the CD concluded the negotiations on the test-ban treaty. The draft treaty was not adopted by the CD because of opposition from India. As the only country to block consensus, India stated that it could not go along with a consensus adoption of the draft treaty text because India had strong misgivings about the provision on entry into force of the Treaty. India also considered the Treaty's failure to include a commitment by the nuclear-weapon states to eliminate their nuclear weapons within a time-bound framework as unacceptable. With support from Iran, India even opposed transmitting the draft treaty text to the United Nations General Assembly for adoption. However, the other members of the CD decided to forward the draft treaty to the General Assembly. In September 1996, the General Assembly adopted a draft resolution for the adoption of the treaty, which was initiated by Australia and sponsored by 126 states, with an overwhelming majority of 158 votes in favour, 3 against (India, Libya and Bhutan), and 5 abstentions (Cuba, Lebanon, Mauritius, Syria, and Tanzania).[18]

As of 30 November 2015, 183 states had signed and 164 states had ratified the Comprehensive Nuclear-Test-Ban Treaty. The treaty will only enter into force 180 days after all forty-four states listed in Annex 2 to the treaty have ratified or acceded to the treaty (see Article 14 of the treaty on its entry into force). The forty-four states are countries that were members of the CD as of 18 June 1996, have formally participated in the work of the 1996 session of the Conference, and have nuclear power reactors or nuclear research reactors (i.e., devices used to initiate and control a sustained nuclear chain reaction). They are therefore considered to have the capability to produce nuclear weapons. By the end of 30 November 2015, three of the forty-four countries listed in Article 14 have not yet signed the CTBT: India, Pakistan, and North Korea. Thirty-six of the forty-four countries have ratified the CTBT, including France, Russia, and the United Kingdom. The following eight countries must ratify the treaty before it can enter into force: China, Egypt, India, Iran, Israel, North Korea, Pakistan, and the United States. The US Congress rejected American ratification of the CTBT in October 1999.

The purpose of the CTBT is to prevent non-nuclear-weapon states from developing nuclear weapons by conducting nuclear weapons tests, and to prevent the nuclear-weapon states from developing new types of nuclear weapons.

According to Article 1 on the parties' basic obligations, "each state party undertakes not to carry out any nuclear weapon test explosion or any other nuclear explosion, and to prohibit and prevent any such nuclear explosion at any place under its jurisdiction or control." Furthermore, "each state party undertakes to refrain from causing, encouraging, or in any way participating in the carrying out of any nuclear weapon test explosion or any other nuclear explosion."

To achieve the purpose of the Treaty, to ensure its provisions are implemented, including those for international verification of compliance with it, and to provide a forum for states to consult and cooperate with one another, the CTBTO is established according to Article 2. All states parties are required to be members of the organization.

The main task of the organization's Technical Secretariat is to verify whether the states parties are complying with the Treaty provisions. The verification regime is designed to detect any nuclear explosion conducted on Earth, whether it is underground, underwater, or in the atmosphere. This is done by receiving and analyzing data from the Secretariat's International Data Centre. All data are made available to all states parties.

The treaty's verification regime, established by Article 4 to verify compliance with the treaty, consists of the following elements:

- an international monitoring system,
- an international data centre,
- a global communications infrastructure,
- consultation and clarification,
- on-site inspections,
- confidence-building measures.

The International Monitoring System (IMS) consists of 321 monitoring stations and 16 laboratories all over the world. These 337 facilities monitor the Earth for any sign of a nuclear explosion. The IMS uses four complementary verification methods – seismic, hydroacoustic, infrasound, and radionuclide stations – for monitoring underground, in the oceans, and in the atmosphere, respectively. The monitoring system ensures that any nuclear explosions anywhere in the world will be detected and identified as a nuclear explosion – and not as an earthquake – regardless of whether the explosion is detonated underground, underwater, or in the atmosphere.

If it has not been possible to clarify a case of concern with negotiations through consultation and clarification, i.e., suspicion of a nuclear explosion, any state party may request that an on-site inspection be made to determine whether a nuclear test has been carried out. Any state party that suspects or has evidence that a nuclear test explosion has been carried out may also request a special session of the Conference of the States Parties to be convened, provided that a majority of states supports this request (Article 2 B). In cases where damage to the object and purpose of the Treaty may result from non-compliance with the basic obligations of the Treaty, the Conference may recommend that states take collective measures in conformity with international law. The Conference may also bring the issue to the attention of the United Nations (Article 5).

In 2015, the 70th General Assembly adopted resolution 70/73, Comprehensive Nuclear-Test-Ban Treaty (CTBT), by which the Assembly "urges all states not to carry out nuclear-weapon test explosions or any other nuclear explosions, to maintain their moratoriums in this regard and to refrain from acts that would defeat the object and purpose of the Treaty." The Assembly further "urges all states that have not yet signed the Treaty, in particular those whose ratification is needed for its entry into force, to sign and ratify it as soon as possible." The resolution was adopted, with 181 states in favour, 1 against (North Korea), and 3 abstentions (India, Mauritius, and Syria).

Comment

Technological advances have made it possible to maintain nuclear weapons and ensure that they continue to function without tests having to be conducted. Through computer simulation it is also possible – at least for the United States – to develop new types of nuclear weapons without testing them through test explosions. It seems then that there are no compelling arguments for not joining the CTBT.

Although the CTBT has not yet formally entered into force, the International Monitoring System was already established in 1996, and has been made fully operational. Thus, it is no longer possible for any state to conduct a nuclear test explosion anywhere without being discovered.

Against the background of almost global adherence to the CTBT by the overwhelming majority of states – 183 signatories and 164 ratifications – the total prohibition of nuclear test explosions must be considered as an emerging part of international customary law.[19]

NUCLEAR-WEAPON-FREE ZONES

Introduction

During the past fifty years, non-proliferation and disarmament of nuclear weapons have been promoted by treaties for specific geographical regions in which the testing, possession, and stationing of nuclear weapons are prohibited – so-called Nuclear-Weapon-Free Zones (NWFZs). These treaties have prohibited the testing, manufacture, acquisition, receipt, storage, installation, deployment, possession, control over, stationing, transport, and use of nuclear weapons in the regions covered by the treaties. These prohibitions cover five continents – Latin America, the South Pacific, Southeast Asia, Africa, and Central Asia – where all nuclear weapons and nuclear-weapon-related activities are prohibited – and the Antarctic. The nuclear-weapon-free zones thus contribute to strengthening the international non-proliferation regime by limiting the geographical spread (horizontal proliferation) of nuclear weapons while promoting nuclear weapons disarmament, and thereby constituting an important contribution toward the ultimate goal of a world free of nuclear weapons.

The countries within the nuclear-weapon-free zones may continue to use nuclear energy for peaceful purposes. To verify that their programs for nuclear energy are exclusively for civilian purposes, the states in the zones must conclude comprehensive safeguards agreements with the IAEA, which controls states' nuclear facilities. To ensure that the countries covered by the nuclear-weapon-free zones comply with their obligations, an international verification and control system has been established.

The Disarmament Commission's report on NWFZs[20] from 1999 contains detailed information on the purpose and principles of the establishment of nuclear-weapon-free zones. The report states that the establishment of NWFZs must be based on voluntary agreements between the states of the region concerned. To achieve the aim of NWFZs, the agreements must include the following three elements:

1 States in the zone must not possess nuclear weapons.
2 No state shall deploy nuclear weapons within the zone.
3 No state can threaten to use nuclear weapons against any state within the zone.

Legal Basis in International Law

The international legal basis for establishing nuclear-weapon-free zones is laid down in Article 52 of the Charter of the United Nations. This article states that regional arrangements or agencies for maintaining international peace and security are allowed, provided that they are consistent with the purposes and principles of the United Nations.

The concept for NWFZs is further defined in Article 7 of the Nuclear Non-Proliferation Treaty, which states that "nothing in this Treaty affects the right of any group of states to conclude regional treaties in order to assure the total absence of nuclear weapons in their respective territories." This right was confirmed in 1975 by the United Nations General Assembly resolution 3472 B, which contains a definition of a NWFZ: A nuclear-weapon-free zone is any zone, recognized by the General Assembly of the United Nations, that any group of states has freely established with a treaty or convention; where the statute of the total absence of nuclear weapons, including the procedure for delimiting the zone, is defined; and where an international system of verification and control has been established to guarantee states comply with that statute. The nuclear-weapon-free zones include the territories of all the participating states, as well as their territorial sea, internal waters, and surrounding waters.

The General Assembly's resolution on NWFZ also defines the nuclear-weapon states' principal obligations for nuclear-weapon-free zones: that all nuclear-weapon states undertake or reaffirm, in legally binding treaties or conventions, their obligation

- to respect the total absence of nuclear weapons in all parts of the zone,
- to refrain from contributing in any way to acts in zone territories that violate the treaty or convention for the zone,
- to refrain from using or threatening to use nuclear weapons against the states included in the zone.

Security Assurances for Non-Nuclear-Weapon States

By agreeing to the NPT, the non-nuclear-weapon states renounced nuclear weapons. In return, the non-nuclear-weapon states have insisted on obtaining security guarantees from the nuclear-weapon states that they will not be subject to attacks with nuclear weapons. The NPT, however, does not guarantee protection for the non-nuclear-weapon states against attacks with nuclear weapons. The non-use obligations by the nuclear-weapon states to refrain from using or threatening to use nuclear weapons against non-nuclear-weapon states are called "Negative Security Assurances" (NSA) and consist in not using nuclear weapons against countries that do not have nuclear weapons.

In 1968, the Security Council adopted resolution 255, which welcomed the intention expressed by some nuclear-weapon states that they would provide or support immediate assistance, in accordance with the Charter, to any non-nuclear-weapon state party to the NPT that was a victim of an act or threat of aggression in which nuclear weapons were used. These states were the former Soviet Union, the United Kingdom, and the United States. At that time, China and France were not parties to the NPT and the resolution was therefore not relevant to them.

However, these security guarantees were found to be inadequate because that assistance would only be granted in case of an attack or threat of an attack from nuclear weapons. The non-nuclear-weapon states demanded formal negative security assurances, i.e., formal guarantees that nuclear weapons would not be used against them. Many proposals for unconditional and legally binding negative security assurances were presented during the following years but none of the proposals received general support – especially not from the nuclear-weapon states. Agreement was reached in the Security Council only a few days before the opening of the NPT Review Conference in 1995 on a resolution (984) that assured non-nuclear-weapon states that were parties to the NPT that nuclear weapons would not be used against them. However, the statements and the resolution did not provide complete negative security assurances. The statements made by France, Russia, the United Kingdom, and the United States only confirmed that none of these states would use their nuclear weapons against non-nuclear-weapon parties to the NPT, and had a number of exceptions: in case of an invasion or any other attack on their territories, on their armed forces or other troops, their allies, or a state to which they had a security commitment, and only when the invasion or attack was carried out or sustained by a non-nuclear-weapon state allied with a nuclear-weapon state.

In the case of Russia, the statement was a step backwards compared with earlier Russian commitments not to be the first country to use nuclear weapons. Only China made an unconditional declaration not to use or threaten to use nuclear weapons against non-nuclear-weapon states or NWFZs at any time or under any circumstance.

The 70th General Assembly adopted resolution 70/25, Conclusion of effective international arrangements to assure non-nuclear-weapon states against the use or threat of use of nuclear weapons. The resolution "reaffirms the urgent need to reach an early agreement on effective international arrangements to assure non-nuclear-weapon states against the use or threat of use of nuclear weapons" and "appeals to all states, especially the nuclear-weapon states, to work actively towards an early agreement on a common approach and, in particular, on a common formula that could be included in an international instrument of a legally binding character." The resolution was adopted by 127 votes in favour, none against, and 55 abstentions. China, India, Pakistan, and North Korea voted in favour. France, Israel, Russia, the United Kingdom, the United States, and Canada abstained, together with all the other western countries.

TREATIES ON NUCLEAR-WEAPON-FREE ZONES

Existing Nuclear-Weapon-Free Zones

Multilateral treaties on NWFZs have so far been concluded for Latin America, the South Pacific, Southeast Asia, Africa, and Central Asia, which are now nuclear-weapon-free areas. A total of 115 countries, which contain 39 per cent of the world's population, in the five nuclear-weapon-free zones, are nuclear-weapon-free territories, including their territorial sea and airspace. The five existing NWFZs cover approximately 50 per cent of the world's land territory and 74 per cent of all land territories outside the nuclear-weapon states. Four of the five NWFZs have made the whole Southern Hemisphere a large nuclear-weapon-free zone.

The 70th General Assembly adopted resolution 70/45, Nuclear-weapon-free southern hemisphere and adjacent areas, reaffirming "its conviction of the important role of nuclear-weapon-free zones in strengthening the nuclear non-proliferation regime and in extending the areas of the world that are nuclear-weapon-free, and calls for greater progress towards the total elimination of all nuclear weapons." The resolution was adopted with 178 votes in favour, 4 against (France, Russia, the United Kingdom, and the United States), and 1 abstention (Israel).

LATIN AMERICA

Latin America was the first continent to declare itself free of nuclear weapons in the Treaty for the Prohibition of Nuclear Weapons in Latin America of 1967 ("Treaty of Tlatelolco"). "Tlatelolco" is the name of a pre-Columbian Aztec city that is now a neighborhood in Mexico City and the location of the Mexican Foreign Ministry, where the treaty was signed. The title of the treaty was amended in 1990 to add "and the Caribbean." The proposal to establish a regional Latin American agreement for the control of nuclear weapons was originally presented by Costa Rica in 1958. However, it was only after the Cuban missile crisis in 1962 and on the initiative of Brazil that the negotiations on the zone were initiated and broad regional support for the initiative was achieved.

The Treaty of Tlatelolco includes all the countries of Latin America and the Caribbean – a total of thirty-three states. The treaty took effect in 1968, but only came into force formally in 2002 after Cuba had agreed to the treaty, as the last country in the region.

The Treaty's zone of application is defined in Article 4, which specifies the co-ordinates for the extension of the zone. The zone includes not only the territorial seas of the states, but also their Exclusive Economic Zone (EEZ), which is the area beyond and adjacent to the territorial sea, stretching up to 200 nautical miles (370 kilometres) from the baselines from which the breadth of the territorial sea is measured.[21] The Law of the Sea Convention stipulates in Article 58 the rights and duties of other states in the Exclusive Economic Zone that all states enjoy the freedoms referred to in article 87 of navigation and overflight in the EEZ. Therefore, the nuclear-weapon states do not recognize that the Treaty can be invoked to prohibit or prevent nuclear-armed naval vessels from navigating through the EEZ. Such right of "innocent passage" is recognized even through the territorial sea (Article 17). The meaning of innocent passage is further regulated in Article 19, which states that "Passage is innocent so long as it is not prejudicial to the peace, good order or security of the coastal state." There is thus a legal conflict between the Treaty of Tlatelolco and the Law of the Sea Convention. The United States has not signed the Convention on the Law of the Sea.

In 1992, two Additional Protocols to the Treaty of Tlatelolco were signed: Protocol I obliges other non-Latin American states responsible for territories in the region (France, the Netherlands, the United Kingdom, and the United States), to ensure that the Treaty is implemented within their respective territories in the region. Protocol I was signed and ratified by all the four states. Protocol II commits the five nuclear-weapon states to comply with the provisions of the Treaty and not to use or threaten to use nuclear weapons against any of the states parties. Protocol II has been ratified by all five nuclear-weapon states.

SOUTH PACIFIC

The South Pacific was established as a NWFZ by the South Pacific Nuclear Weapon Free Zone Treaty, of 1985 ("Treaty of Rarotonga," named after the island where the treaty was adopted and opened for signature). The Treaty entered into force in 1986 and has thirteen states parties, including Australia, New Zealand, and a number of island states in the Pacific. It applies to the territories of the South Pacific states, including their territorial sea, but not to the ocean area of the South Pacific, nor does it prohibit the transport of nuclear weapons through the zone on foreign vessels. In addition to two protocols, similar to the ones attached to the Treaty of Tlatelolco, the Treaty of Rarotonga has a third protocol by which the nuclear-weapon states undertake not to test any nuclear weapons anywhere within the zone. The United States is the only country among the nuclear-weapon states that has not yet ratified any of the protocols.

SOUTHEAST ASIA

Southeast Asia became a nuclear-weapon-free zone by the Treaty on the Southeast Asia Nuclear Weapon-Free Zone, of 1995 (Treaty of Bangkok), which entered into force in 1997. The Treaty covers all ten states in the region, including Indonesia, Malaysia, Philippines, Thailand, and Vietnam. Besides the land territories of the states, the treaty also applies to their respective territorial seas, continental shelves, and Exclusive Economic Zones. The treaty explicitly states that nothing in the Treaty shall prejudice the rights or the exercise of these rights by any state under the provisions of the Convention on The Law of the Sea, in particular with regard to the rights of innocent passage or transit passage of ships and aircraft. None of the nuclear-weapon states has signed the Protocol to the Bangkok Treaty, which is open for signature only by them. By becoming states parties to the protocol, the nuclear-weapon states would undertake an obligation not to use or threaten to use nuclear weapons against any state party to the treaty or within the Southeast Asia zone.

AFRICA

Africa has also been established as a nuclear-weapon-free zone by the African Nuclear-Weapon-Free-Zone Treaty of 1996 (Treaty of Pelindaba, which is the name of the location where South Africa conducted its nuclear tests in the 1970s). The treaty has thirty-nine states parties and entered into force in 2009. Another eleven African countries have signed, but have not yet ratified the treaty. Similar to the Treaty of Rarotonga, the Treaty of Pelindaba acknowledges the supremacy of the freedom of the seas and does not prohibit nuclear weapons beyond territorial sea limits. Protocol I, on negative security assurances, and Protocol II, on banning nuclear tests, have been ratified by four of the nuclear-weapon states, but only signed and not yet ratified by the United States.

CENTRAL ASIA

Central Asia has become the latest nuclear-weapon-free zone with the Treaty on a Nuclear-Weapon-Free Zone in Central Asia (CANWFZ). The treaty was signed in 2006 in Kazakhstan at the former Soviet nuclear test station in Semipalatinsk and entered into force in 2009. The five states parties are Kazakhstan, Kyrgyzstan, Tajikistan, Turkmenistan, and Uzbekistan. The protocol on negative security assurances to the Central Asia Treaty has been ratified by China, France, Russia, and the United Kingdom.

Single Nuclear-Weapon-Free Zones

NEW ZEALAND

In 1987, the government of New Zealand adopted the New Zealand Nuclear Free Zone, Disarmament, and Arms Control Act, confirming the country's nuclear-weapon-free policy. The New Zealand Act, one of the strongest existing legal prohibitions against nuclear weapons, prohibits placing or transporting nuclear weapons on land or internal waters, including harbors, in New Zealand.[22] The Act also prohibits nuclear-powered ships from entering internal waters. None of the regional nuclear-weapon-free zones prohibit nuclear weapons from entering the zone, including harbor visits and landing. The New Zealand Nuclear Free Zone Act prohibits nuclear weapons only from entering internal waters or on land territory. It does not prohibit nuclear weapons from entering territorial waters (up to 22.2 kilometres from land) or the Exclusive Economic Zone (up to 370 kilometres). When it adopted the Act, the New Zealand government believed that prohibiting the transit of nuclear weapons through territorial waters would violate a naval state's right of innocent passage, and that prohibiting nuclear weapons in the Exclusive Economic Zone would violate a naval state's right to freedom of navigation. The United Nations Law of the Sea Convention affirms both these rights.

MONGOLIA

In 1992, Mongolia's president announced that Mongolia's territory would become a nuclear-weapon-free zone and a law to this effect was passed in 2000. Mongolia's self-declared nuclear-weapon-free status was recognized internationally through the adoption in 1998 of United Nations General Assembly resolution 53/77D, Mongolia's international security and nuclear-weapon-free status. In 2000, the General Assembly welcomed the joint statement of the five nuclear-weapon states providing security assurances to Mongolia (resolution 55/33S).

ANTARCTICA

In 1959, Antarctica was declared a demilitarized zone, to be used for peaceful purposes only, where any kind of military activity, including the establishment of military bases and fortifications, the carrying out of military maneuvers, as well as the testing of any type of weapons, is prohibited. The Antarctic Treaty was signed in 1959 by the seven states that had claimed sovereignty over areas of Antarctica and the five original signatories. The treaty explicitly states that "any nuclear explosions in Antarctica and the disposal there of radioactive waste material shall be prohibited." The treaty entered into force in 1961 and now includes fifty-one so-called contracting parties.

Proposals for Additional Nuclear-Weapon-Free Zones

A NUCLEAR-WEAPON-FREE ZONE IN CENTRAL AND EASTERN
EUROPE?

In 1990, Belarus submitted a proposal to establish a nuclear-weapon-free zone in Central and Eastern Europe. According to the proposal, the zone would extend from the Baltic Sea to the Black Sea and include Estonia, Latvia, Lithuania, Belarus, and Ukraine. The aim of the proposed zone was to prevent Russian nuclear weapons from being stationed in Belarus and Ukraine. However, the proposal was not supported by France, the United Kingdom, or the United States and, after NATO's expansion to the East, is no longer relevant.

A NUCLEAR-WEAPON-FREE ZONE IN SOUTH ASIA?

In 1975, Pakistan proposed establishing a nuclear-weapon-free zone in South Asia. According to this proposal, a South Asian NWFZ would include Bangladesh, Bhutan, India, Maldives, Nepal, Pakistan, and Sri Lanka. Because China was excluded from the zone, India (and Bhutan) opposed its creation.

India and Pakistan have possessed nuclear weapons since 1998. There are prolonged tensions between the two countries because of their territorial dispute over the Kashmir region and over terrorism. Both India and Pakistan continue to expand and modernize their nuclear weapons in their growing regional nuclear arms race competition. Against this background it seems unrealistic to establish a NWFZ in South Asia in the foreseeable future that would include the two countries. Besides, it is India's view that disarmament of nuclear weapons is a global issue that requires a comprehensive global solution, which should include all five recognized nuclear-weapon states. India is also concerned about China's nuclear weapons.

A NUCLEAR-WEAPON-FREE ZONE ON THE KOREAN PENINSULA?

In January 1992, North Korea and South Korea signed a Joint Declaration on the Denuclearization of the Korean Peninsula. Under the Declaration, North Korea and South Korea agreed not to test, manufacture, produce, receive, possess, store, deploy, or use nuclear weapons, to use nuclear energy solely for peaceful purposes, and not to possess facilities for nuclear reprocessing and uranium enrichment. The two countries would conduct inspections of locations chosen by the other state and mutually agreed upon by both sides. The Joint Nuclear Control Commission of the two countries was not able to reach an agreement on the reciprocal inspection regime and it has been stalled since 1993.

North Korea's tests of nuclear weapons in 2006, 2009, 2013, and on 6 January 2016 have made it unrealistic to foresee a NWFZ being established in Northeast Asia any time soon.

A NUCLEAR-WEAPON-FREE ZONE IN THE MIDDLE EAST?
The question of establishing a zone free of weapons of mass destruction (WMDFZ) in the Middle East – first and foremost, without nuclear weapons – has been the subject of discussions at the United Nations and in many other international forums for many years. Iran and Egypt originally proposed establishing a nuclear-weapon-free zone in the Middle East in 1974. Every year since then, the United Nations General Assembly has adopted a resolution recommending the establishment of a NWFZ in the Middle East (originally resolution 3263 (XXIX) of 1974). In 1995 the NPT Review Conference adopted a resolution on the Middle East urging all countries in the Middle East to take practical steps in the appropriate forums to make progress toward establishing an effective and verifiable zone free of weapons of mass destruction – nuclear, chemical, and biological – and their means of delivery.[23]

The main reason for the lack of progress in the efforts to establish a NWFZ or a WMD-free zone in the Middle East is Israel's possession of nuclear weapons. Israel has never officially confirmed nor denied that it has nuclear weapons, but it seems to be a fact that Israel certainly has the technological capability to produce nuclear weapons[24] and Israel is generally considered to be a nuclear-armed state. According to SIPRI, Israel is estimated to have eighty nuclear warheads. The country continues to refuse to join the NPT.

It is unrealistic to expect Israel to give up its nuclear weapons as long as its existence as an independent state is not recognized by Arab countries, and as long as Israel's existence is threatened with extinction, in particular by Iran. Israel's security policy is primarily based on conventional weapons superiority, with the use of nuclear deterrence only as a last resort. Israel's nuclear weapons should be viewed in conjunction with the possession by some Arab countries of other weapons of mass destruction, i.e., biological and chemical weapons, and the imbalance of the sizes of Israel's and the Arab countries' conventional forces. Despite numerous calls in the United Nations General Assembly's annual resolutions,[25] and in IAEA's resolutions, for Israel to join the NPT and thus conclude safeguards agreements with the IAEA, the Security Council has never forced Israel to comply with these resolutions, nor has it adopted sanctions against Israel because the United States would certainly veto such a resolution.

Iran's clandestine nuclear program, which was kept concealed for many years, despite repeated Iranian assurances that its nuclear program was solely for peaceful purposes (nuclear power for energy production). The program has been a matter of serious concern for Israel in particular, and also for the United States and Europe. Suspicion about Iran's earlier nuclear program has not advanced the possibilities of establishing a comprehensive NWFZ in the Middle East.

According to Israel, it will not be possible to make the Middle East a nuclear-weapon-free zone and verify the Middle Eastern countries' compliance with the provisions of the NWFZ agreement for the region, until significant progress has been achieved in the Middle East peace process. Such progress must include, among others, that all the Arab states recognize the existence of the state of Israel and stop threatening the use of military force against Israel. The main obstacle for establishing a NWFZ in the Middle East is the continuing tensions between Israel on the one hand and the Arab countries in the region and Iran on the other, and the resulting lack of trust between the parties to the conflict in the Middle East. In 1991 the United Nations published the report *Effective and Verifiable Measures Which Would Facilitate the Establishment of a NWFZ in the Middle East.*[26] The report recommended introducing confidence-building measures between the parties as a first step toward establishing such a zone, referring to the confidence-building measures established in Europe during the Cold War under the Helsinki Final Act in 1975. The abolition of the other types of weapons of mass destruction, especially chemical weapons, and of their means of delivery (missiles), is also a prerequisite for a NWFZ in the Middle East. All chemical and biological weapons in the region must obviously also be abolished before a zone free of all kinds of weapons of mass destruction can be established in the Middle East.

At the NPT Review Conference in 2010, it was decided that the United Nations secretary general, after consulting with the countries in the region, should convene a conference in 2012 with all states in the Middle East participating to discuss establishing a Middle East zone free of nuclear weapons and all other weapons of mass destruction. Finland offered to host the conference, which was to have been held in Helsinki in December 2012. Due to further setbacks in the negotiations on the peace process for the Middle East, the conference was not convened and has been indefinitely postponed.

In view of the above comments, it may be concluded that a NWFZ in the Middle East can only be achieved in a step-by-step process that will take several years, during which mutual confidence between all parties may be gradually built up, so that all countries in the region are convinced that their national security is not threatened, on the principle of the indivisibility of security. A precondition for this to happen is that Iran fulfill all its obligations under the P5+1 Joint Comprehensive Plan of Action (JCPOA) for Iran and, accordingly, allow IAEA inspectors full and unrestricted access to all nuclear facilities in the country to verify that the Iranian nuclear program is, as claimed, exclusively for peaceful purposes. Another prerequisite for establishing the zone is that the nuclear facilities in all countries, including Israel's nuclear reactor near the town of Dimona in the Negev Desert, and stocks of nuclear materials, are subject to security guarantees under the IAEA safeguards regime and thus subject to verification under IAEA inspections of nuclear facilities and activities. The process of establishing a NWFZ in the Middle East will only make progress if parallel progress in the overall peace process for the Middle East is made.

To facilitate this process, the geographic area of application of a NWFZ in the Middle East could initially be restricted to covering only a limited area consisting of the core countries of the Middle East, i.e., Israel, Jordan, Lebanon, Syria, Iraq, Egypt, Saudi Arabia, and the other smaller countries of the Arabian Peninsula. However, it seems unrealistic to imagine that Israel would be prepared to give up its nuclear weapons and engage in a limited NWFZ in the Middle East that does not include Iran unless the IAEA inspections of Iran's nuclear facilities can continue to provide assurances that the Iranian nuclear program is exclusively for peaceful purposes. In 1989 the IAEA defined the group of core countries in a NWFZ in the Middle East as the countries from Libya in the West to Iran in the East, and from Syria to the North to Yemen in the South.

The positive developments after Syria's adherence in 2013 to the Convention on the Prohibition of Chemical Weapons and the completed destruction of Syria's chemical weapons may, hopefully, turn out to be a first step toward the further disarmament of weapons of mass destruction in the Middle East, and thus in the long-term contribute to a lasting peace in the Middle East.[27] Of course, it is also a prerequisite for a NWFZ in the Middle East that the civil war in Syria and the fighting in Iraq stop.

A NUCLEAR-WEAPON-FREE ZONE IN THE ARCTIC?

The intensified global warming caused by climate changes in recent years have already caused substantial and increasing melting of the ice in the Arctic Ocean. This trend is expected to accelerate over the coming years. One of the consequences is that a growing area in the Arctic Ocean will become accessible to shipping through the polar shipping routes (Northwest and Northeast Passage) and for economic exploitation of the natural resources of the Arctic Ocean and the continental shelf areas, i.e., oil, gas, fish, and minerals, including the strategically important rare earth minerals.

The expected increase in navigation and exploitation of the natural resources in the Arctic should be regulated further in international agreements, so that the fragile environment in the Arctic will not be damaged by pollution, including oil spills. Three of the coastal states in the Arctic Ocean – Canada, Denmark, and Russia – have already adopted plans to increase their military presence and capabilities in the Arctic area to support their territorial claims on the continental shelf and fishing zones and ensure their economic exploitation of the natural resources of the area.

Similar to the regulation of Antarctica, a key priority for the international regulation of activities in the Arctic should be to avoid militarizing the Arctic. One of the first steps to take to prevent the presence of weapons of mass destruction, should be to establish a NWFZ in the Arctic. Experience shows that it usually takes years or decades to negotiate and reach agreement on establishing a NWFZ. A process to establish an Arctic NWFZ should start as soon as possible before maritime activities expand and the race for natural resources in the Arctic has made it impossible to establish the zone. In order to begin the process for establishing a NWFZ in the Arctic, a first step could be to initiate regional consultations between the Arctic states. Such consultations could result in agreement on a draft resolution to be adopted by the United Nations General Assembly. The Arctic countries that do not have nuclear weapons could take the lead in this process.

In August 2007, the Canadian Pugwash Group called for the establishment of a NWFZ in the Arctic. The participants in a Conference on an Arctic NWFZ, held in Copenhagen in August 2009, also appealed for the establishment of a NWFZ in the Arctic.[28]

A NWFZ in the Arctic should ideally include all areas north of the Arctic Circle (66.34 degrees north). The following states have territories north of the Arctic Circle: Canada, Denmark (Greenland), Finland, Iceland, Norway, Russia, Sweden, and the United States (Alaska). Five of these countries – Canada, Denmark, Norway, Russia, and the United States – are coastal states on the Arctic Ocean.

Most likely, it will be extremely difficult for the United States and Russia to agree to give up deployment of their nuclear weapons on their northern land territories and on board their warships, permanently sailing in the Arctic Ocean, especially on their nuclear-armed submarines. Therefore, a limited Arctic NWFZ could be established initially, to include Canada and the five Nordic countries. Later, when the security situation allows it, and possibly as part of a new bilateral agreement to reduce their strategic nuclear weapons, the United States and Russia could join the Arctic NWFZ by signing additional protocols on their agreement to the zone, possibly supplemented by bilateral agreements on their obligation not to place nuclear weapons in the zone.

Although it seems natural to request the Arctic Council to take the initiative to start negotiations on the establishment of a NWFZ in the Arctic, this will not be possible under the current mandate of the Arctic Council, because it does not include military security.

A nuclear-weapon-free zone in the Arctic will differ significantly in many ways from the five existing NWFZs. The largest part of an Arctic Zone will include the Arctic Ocean and only small areas of land territories. Another major difference is that the zone will include part of the territories of the two largest nuclear-weapon states: the US territory of Alaska and Russia's northern territories. Russia in particular is likely to be strongly opposed to an Arctic NWFZ, because a large number of Russia's strategic nuclear weapons are placed on board submarines based on the Kola Peninsula. It seems unlikely that Russia would be willing to give up its nuclear submarine base at Kola. Although the possibility of a military confrontation in the Arctic between the United States and the former Soviet Union came to an end after the Cold War, it is assumed that both American and Russian nuclear-armed submarines are permanently present in the Arctic Ocean, submerged under the ice. In addition, the zone will also include four other NATO member states: Canada, Denmark, Iceland, and Norway. Although these four countries do not possess nuclear weapons, and as far as the three Nordic countries are concerned, have maintained a nuclear weapons policy for many years that does not allow nuclear weapons on their territories in peacetime, these countries are bound by NATO's strategic nuclear deterrence strategy (see paragraphs 17–19 of NATO's Strategic Concept, adopted at the NATO Summit in Lisbon in November 2010). Therefore, those four NATO countries will probably have to make declarations to NATO that their land and sea areas within the NWFZ in the Arctic are not covered by NATO's Strategic Concept, i.e., those countries will under no circumstances – not even in time of war – receive or allow nuclear weapons to be deployed within the zone area. Such declarations of exceptions from the common Strategic Concept would have to be approved by all the other NATO member countries.

Although no country will be permitted to place nuclear weapons in an Arctic NWFZ, states cannot prohibit or limit innocent transit passage through their territorial waters and international straits (the Northwest Passage) in the Arctic Sea of naval vessels that may have nuclear weapons on board. The United Nations Convention on the Law of the Sea (UNCLOS) has enshrined, in Articles 87, 17, and 52, respectively, the freedom of the high seas for navigation and overflight and the right of innocent passage through the territorial seas and archipelago waters of other states. Seven of the Arctic countries are parties to UNCLOS. The United States has signed the Convention but has not yet ratified it. Since the Convention to a large extent codifies already existing maritime law and has been endorsed by most countries, its provisions are considered applicable customary maritime law.

Some activities concerning nuclear weapons in the Arctic have already been regulated in international law. The deployment of nuclear weapons (and other WMDs) and nuclear testing at any location, including the sea, are prohibited according to the following treaties: Treaty on the Prohibition of the Emplacement of Nuclear Weapons and Other Weapons of Mass Destruction on the Seabed and the Ocean Floor and in the Subsoil Thereof, of 1971, ratified by all eight Arctic states; and The Comprehensive Nuclear-Test-Ban Treaty, of 1996, prohibiting nuclear tests anywhere. The CTBT has not yet entered into force. Seven of the Arctic countries have both signed and ratified the CTBT. The United States has signed the treaty but not yet ratified it. All eight Arctic countries are parties to the earlier Treaty Banning Nuclear Weapon Tests in the Atmosphere, in Outer Space and Under Water, of 1963.

LEGALITY OF NUCLEAR WEAPONS

For many years it has been a much discussed question – not least within the framework of the United Nations – whether the threat or use of nuclear weapons is legal or illegal, and whether, if it is illegal, it constitutes a violation of international law.[29] The use of the two other categories of weapons of mass destruction – biological and chemical weapons – was outlawed by the Biological Weapons Convention and Chemical Weapons Conventions of 1972 and 1993, respectively. Why have nuclear weapons not been made illegal? Would it not be logical to ban all types of weapons of mass destruction? Biological and chemical weapons are no more deadly and destructive than nuclear weapons! It is also illogical and incomprehensible that indiscriminate conventional weapons, which cannot distinguish between legitimate military targets and civilians – such as anti-personnel mines and cluster bombs whose destruction power is diminutive compared with nuclear weapons – have been banned, and not nuclear weapons!

All five recognized nuclear-weapon states persist in their view that nuclear weapons continue to be lawful since these weapons have not – contrary to the case of biological and chemical weapons – been explicitly prohibited by an international legally binding agreement.

Advisory Opinion of the International Court of Justice
on the Legality of the Threat or Use of Nuclear Weapons

The above question on the legality of nuclear weapons was addressed in the Advisory Opinion of the ICJ of 8 July 1996, on the Legality of the Threat or Use of Nuclear Weapons.[30] The request for an advisory opinion was submitted to the Court, both by the World Health Organization (WHO) and the United Nations General Assembly, in accordance with Article 65 of the Statute of the ICJ (see also Article 96 of the Charter).

WHO'S REQUEST FOR AN ADVISORY OPINION OF THE ICJ

In 1993, the WHO asked the ICJ to give an advisory opinion on the following question: "In view of the health and environmental effects, would the use of nuclear weapons by a state in war or other armed conflict be a breach of its obligations under international law, including the WHO Constitution?" The purpose of the question was to clarify whether it is legal or not to use nuclear weapons.

The ICJ did not give the opinion requested because a majority (11) of the Court's judges did not find that WHO's request for an advisory opinion related to a legal question that arises "within the scope of the activities" of the WHO, see Article 96, paragraph 2 of the Charter. The WHO was therefore not entitled to request an advisory opinion. Three judges voted in favour of admitting WHO's request.

GENERAL ASSEMBLY'S REQUEST FOR AN ADVISORY OPINION OF THE ICJ

The United Nations General Assembly's question, which was submitted to the ICJ for an advisory opinion, was adopted in resolution 49/75 K, and sent to the Court by a letter in December 1994. The question was the following: "Is the threat or use of nuclear weapons in any circumstance permitted under international law?"

The answer to the question is contained in ICJ's Advisory Opinion on the Legality of the Threat or Use of Nuclear Weapons, of 8 July 1996. In its Opinion, the Court states that "it is imperative for the Court to take account of the unique characteristics of nuclear weapons," i.e., the radiation, "and in particular their destructive capacity, their capacity to cause untold human suffering, and their ability to cause damage to generations to come." Furthermore, the Court recalled that the Charter of the United Nations, in Article 2, paragraph 4, contains several provisions on the threat and use of force: "All members shall refrain in their international relations from the threat or use of force against the territorial integrity or political independence of any state, or in any other manner inconsistent with the purposes of the United Nations." The Article also refers to "the inherent right of individual or collective self-defence if an armed attack occurs against a member of the United Nations," recognized in Article 51 of the Charter. The other exception to the prohibition on the use of force is envisaged in Article 42, which authorizes the Security Council to decide on the collective use of force when necessary to maintain or restore international peace and security. These provisions do not refer to specific weapons. They apply to any use of force, regardless of the type of weapons employed. Thus, the Charter neither expressly prohibits, nor permits, the use of any specific weapon, including nuclear weapons.

In its Advisory Opinion, the ICJ replied to the question put by the General Assembly in the following manner:

- "There is in neither customary nor conventional international law any specific authorization of the threat or use of nuclear weapons" (unanimous reply).
- "There is in neither customary nor conventional international law any comprehensive and universal prohibition of the threat or use of nuclear weapons as such" (by eleven votes to three).
- "A threat or use of force by means of nuclear weapons that is contrary to Article 2, paragraph 4, of the United Nations Charter and that fails to meet all the requirements of Article 51, is unlawful" (unanimously).
- "A threat or use of nuclear weapons should also be compatible with the requirements of the international law applicable in armed conflict, particularly those of the principles and rules of international humanitarian law, as well as with specific obligations under treaties and other undertakings which expressly deal with nuclear weapons" (unanimously).
- "It follows from the above-mentioned requirements that the treat or use of nuclear weapons would generally be contrary to the rules of international law applicable in armed conflict, and in particular the principles and rules of humanitarian law. However, in view of the current state of international law, and of the elements of fact at its disposal, the Court cannot conclude definitively whether the treat or use of nuclear weapons would be lawful or unlawful in an extreme circumstance of self-defence, in which the very survival of a state would be at stake" (by seven votes to seven).

- "There exists an obligation to pursue in good faith and bring
  to a conclusion negotiations leading to nuclear disarmament
  in all its aspects under strict and effective international control"
  (unanimously).

In voting on the second last opinion, the positive vote in favour of this opinion by the Court's president was decisive for its adoption. All fourteen judges made either individual, explanatory declarations or expressed their dissenting votes in separate statements. This clearly shows the disagreement and different views among the judges about how the ICJ should reply to the question of the legality of the threat or use of nuclear weapons.[31]
The above replies may be summarized and simplified as follows:

- The threat or use of nuclear weapons is neither specifically authorized, nor expressly prohibited in international law.
- A threat or use of nuclear weapons which is not in legitimate self-defence under the UN Charter is unlawful.
- A threat or use of nuclear weapons shall respect international humanitarian law and relevant treaty obligations.
- The threat or use of nuclear weapons will generally be contrary to the rules and principles in armed conflict and humanitarian law.
- It cannot be concluded definitively whether the threat or use of nuclear weapons in extreme circumstance of self-defence, where the survival of a state is at stake, would be lawful or unlawful.

Every year since 1996, the United Nations General Assembly has adopted a resolution on the Advisory Opinion of the ICJ. The first resolution (51/45 M, of 1996) called upon all states to fulfill the obligation to pursue in good faith, and bring to a conclusion, negotiations leading to nuclear disarmament in all its aspects under strict and effective international control. This was to be done immediately by beginning multilateral negotiations in 1997, leading to an early conclusion of a nuclear weapons convention prohibiting the development, production, testing, deployment, stockpiling, transfer, threat, or use of nuclear weapons and providing for their elimination. The resolution was adopted with 115 votes in favour, including China, India, Pakistan, and North Korea, 22 votes against, including the four other nuclear-weapon states, and 32 abstentions, including Israel. The latest resolution on the follow-up to the Advisory Opinion is resolution 70/56, which was adopted in December 2015, with 137 votes in favour, 24 against, and 25 abstentions. France, Russia, the United Kingdom, the United States, and Israel, among other western countries, voted against the resolution. China, India, Pakistan, and North Korea voted in favour. The abstaining countries were also western, including Canada.

COMMENT

It is important to note the references in the ICJ Advisory Opinion to the principles and rules of international humanitarian law. These include the general principles of proportionality and prohibition of attacks that target civilians. Any use of nuclear weapons would violate these principles.

A growing number of non-nuclear-weapon states consider the threat or use of nuclear weapons to be contrary to international law and therefore unlawful. These weapons of mass destruction should, accordingly, be abolished by a treaty banning all nuclear weapons. The nuclear-weapon states maintain the opposite view. The different views expressed in the dissenting votes and declarations in the Opinion reflect this reality and show the continued international disagreement on the legality – or illegality – of nuclear weapons.

Marshall Islands' Lawsuit

Twenty years have now passed since the International Court of Justice gave its Advisory Opinion. Although progress has been made in reducing the numbers of nuclear weapons since 1996, this is, unfortunately, not the case as far as prohibiting nuclear weapons is concerned. The non-aligned and non-nuclear-weapon states are increasingly losing their patience with the nuclear-weapon states because they are not complying with the obligations to disarm in Article 6 of the NPT.

This is being demonstrated by the legal proceedings instituted by the Marshall Islands in the International Court of Justice against all nine nuclear-weapon and nuclear-armed states: the United States, the United Kingdom, France, Russia, China, India, Pakistan, Israel, and North Korea.

In April 2014, the Marshall Islands filed applications against these states, claiming that they have violated and failed to comply with their nuclear disarmament obligations under the NPT and customary international law. The Marshall Islands is asking the ICJ to deliver a binding judgment on the following claims:

1 breach of the obligation to pursue negotiations in good faith, leading to nuclear disarmament, by refusing to begin multilateral negotiations to that end and/or by implementing policies contrary to the objective of nuclear disarmament;
2 breach of the obligation to pursue negotiations in good faith on stopping the nuclear arms race at an early date;
3 breach of the obligation to perform the above obligations in good faith, including by planning to keep nuclear forces for decades into the future;
4 failure to perform obligations relating to nuclear disarmament and cessation of the nuclear arms race in good faith by effectively preventing the great majority of non-nuclear-weapon states from fulfilling their part of those obligations.

This island country in the Pacific Ocean was used by the United States as a test site for its nuclear tests. Between 1946 and 1958, the United States conducted sixty-seven atmospheric and underwater nuclear weapon test explosions over the Marshall Islands. Twenty-three of the tests were carried out on the Bikini Atoll, which was contaminated with radioactivity and left uninhabitable. It has been calculated that these tests had an equivalent explosive force greater than 1.5 Hiroshima-sized bombs being detonated daily for twelve years. The inhabitants of the Marshall Islands paid a heavy price in their health and well-being because of these destructive tests, the effects of which are still present.

However, the Marshall Islands is not asking for compensation for these atrocities. It is asking the ICJ and the US Court (see page 106) to declare that the nuclear-weapon states are in breach of their obligations under international law, in Article 6 of the NPT, and from the requirements under customary international law to eliminate their nuclear weapons. The Marshall Islands requests the ICJ and the US Court to call upon the nuclear-weapon states to begin negotiating in good faith to stop the nuclear arms race and achieve a world without nuclear weapons. The Marshall Islands is asking for a judgment of breach of obligations and an order to take, within one year of the judgment, all steps necessary to comply with those obligations. These steps include the pursuit of negotiations in good faith aimed at concluding a convention on nuclear disarmament in all its aspects under strict and effective international control.

The lawsuits argue that the nuclear disarmament obligations apply to all nine nuclear-armed states – including the four non-state parties to the NPT – as a matter of customary international law, and to the five nuclear-weapon states primarily according to their obligations under the NPT.

However, only three of the defendant states – the United Kingdom, India, and Pakistan – have accepted the compulsory jurisdiction of the ICJ.[32] The United States renounced its acceptance of compulsory jurisdiction in 1985 during the case before the ICJ on American involvement in paramilitary operations in Nicaragua. The Marshall Islands is calling on the other six states to accept the jurisdiction of the Court in these particular cases and to explain to the Court their positions on their nuclear disarmament obligations. China has notified the Court that it declines to accept the Court's jurisdiction in this case.

Hearings on the preliminary procedural issues of whether the cases against India, Pakistan, and the United Kingdom are suitable and admissible for adjudication are scheduled for the beginning of 2016. If the cases are accepted before the Court, the proceedings on their substantive merits could start in 2016 and probably last for two to three years.[33]

The Marshall Islands is also filing its case against the United States separately in the US Federal District Court in San Francisco. In February 2015 the US Court dismissed the case as non-justiciable. The Marshall Islands has appealed this decision.

Tactical Nuclear Weapons

Should tactical nuclear weapons be allowed under international humanitarian law? Tactical nuclear weapons have only low-yield explosive and limited short-range capacity, and are primarily intended for battlefield use against conventional enemy forces. The ICJ's Advisory Opinion does not address this question. The Court makes no distinction between strategic and tactical nuclear weapons. Even when tactical nuclear weapons are used in attacks targeted against concentrations of an enemy's conventional ground forces, there is always an uncontrollable risk and a high probability that the civilian population in the war zone will also be hit indiscriminately. This is of course the case in densely populated areas, such as Europe. The question is whether there are any sparsely populated areas where a nuclear war with tactical weapons could be fought without civilian casualties and destruction. Therefore, the use of tactical nuclear weapons – at least when used in densely populated areas – is usually considered to be a violation of international humanitarian law and consequently prohibited. Depending on the specific circumstances, it could be argued that the use of tactical nuclear weapons is not always illegal, for example when a nuclear weapon is fired at a high concentration of enemy ground forces in an uninhabited area, such as a desert, or against a surface warship or submarine on the high seas. In such exceptional cases, there will, presumably, be no civilian casualties. However, the extremely harmful impact of radiation on the combatants and the radioactive contamination of the environment would still raise questions of compatibility with international humanitarian law.

First Use of Nuclear Weapons

The use of nuclear weapons can be carried out either as a preemptive surprise attack – "first strike" – aimed at destroying an adversary before the enemy has initiated its attack, or as a response to the enemy's attack with conventional weapons – "first use." A first strike with nuclear weapons must be regarded as a violation of the fundamental principle in the Charter of the United Nations: that the use of force against any state is prohibited. A counterattack with nuclear weapons by a state that has been attacked in a first strike with either nuclear or conventional weapons could be regarded as legitimate self-defence under the Charter, if the majority of the citizens of the attacked state are in imminent danger of being wiped out and the whole existence of the state is threatened. But the right to self-defence is not unlimited. The fundamental principles of proportionality and excluding the targeting of civilians must also be respected in a retaliatory counterattack. Since the effects of a nuclear explosion cannot be targeted solely to hit military targets and spare the civilian population, the principle of prohibiting attacks on civilians cannot be respected in connection with the use of nuclear weapons, whether strategic or tactical.

Among the nuclear-weapon states, only China (since 1964) maintains a nuclear policy of "no first use," i.e., that China will not be the first to use nuclear weapons and will not under any circumstances use nuclear weapons against non-nuclear-weapon states. In 1998, India also declared that it would not be the first to use nuclear weapons. India modified its no-first-use policy in 2010, and the policy now only applies for non-nuclear-weapon states. North Korea announced a no-first-use policy in 2006.

In this context it should be noted that the Allied Forces' "carpet bombings" of German cities, the German bombings of London during the Second World War, and the United States' dropping of atomic bombs on Hiroshima and Nagasaki in 1945 must all be considered examples of clear violations of the prohibition of attacks against civilians.

PROHIBITION OF NUCLEAR WEAPONS

For decades there have been attempts to reach international agreement on the adoption of a legally binding prohibition on the use of nuclear weapons. Already in 1961, the United Nations General Assembly adopted resolution 1653 (XVI), Declaration on the prohibition of the use of nuclear and thermonuclear weapons, in which the General Assembly declared that

- The use of nuclear and thermonuclear weapons is contrary to the spirit, letter and aims of the United Nations and, as such, is a direct violation of the Charter of the United Nations,
- The use of nuclear and thermonuclear weapons would exceed even the scope of war and cause indiscriminate suffering and destruction to mankind and civilization. As such, it is contrary to the rules of international law and to the laws of humanity,
- Any state using nuclear and thermonuclear weapons should be considered as violating the Charter of the United Nations, as acting contrary to the laws of humanity, and as committing a crime against mankind and civilization.

The resolution also requested the secretary general to consult the governments of member states to find out their views on convening a special conference for signing a convention on prohibiting the use of nuclear and thermonuclear weapons for the purposes of war. The secretary general's consultations were not successful and the conference was not convened. The resolution was adopted with 55 votes in favour, 20 against, and 26 abstentions. The United States, France, and the United Kingdom, as well as nine other NATO member countries, voted against the resolution. The argument for this negative position was that a country that is attacked must decide for itself how to respond, using any weapon that is not expressly prohibited. Several resolutions calling for a ban on the use of nuclear weapons have since been adopted by the General Assembly. For example, resolution 33/71B of 1978 states that "the use of nuclear weapons will be a violation of the Charter of the United Nations and a crime against humanity. The use of nuclear weapons should therefore be prohibited, pending nuclear disarmament."

A draft convention on the prohibition of the development, production, testing, deployment, stockpiling, transfer, threat, or use of nuclear weapons and on their elimination entitled "Model Nuclear Weapons Convention" was already elaborated in 1997 by the Lawyers' Committee on Nuclear Policy, and forwarded to the General Assembly by Costa Rica. An updated draft of a nuclear weapons convention was submitted to the General Assembly in 2007.[34] Since 1945, the humanitarian civil society organizations, in particular the Red Cross, have called on the international community to adopt a ban on nuclear weapons.

The 70th General Assembly of the United Nations in 2015 adopted resolution 70/34, a follow-up to the 2013 high-level meeting of the General Assembly on nuclear disarmament. This called for the urgent commencement of negotiations in the Conference on Disarmament for the early conclusion of a comprehensive convention on nuclear weapons to prohibit their possession, development, production, acquisition, testing, stockpiling, transfer, use, or threat of use, and to provide for their destruction. The resolution also "recalls its decision to convene, no later than 2018, a United Nations high-level international conference on nuclear disarmament to review the progress made in this regard." The resolution was adopted with 140 votes in favour, 26 against, and 17 abstaining. China was the only nuclear-weapon state to vote in favour. India, Pakistan, Iran, and North Korea, among other non-aligned countries, also supported the resolution.

France, Russia, the United Kingdom, the United States, Israel, and Canada, among others, voted against.

By resolution 70/33, Taking forward multilateral nuclear disarmament negotiations, the General Assembly "reaffirms the urgency of securing substantive progress in multilateral nuclear disarmament negotiations, and to this end decides to convene an open-ended working group to substantively address concrete effective legal measures, legal provisions and norms that will need to be concluded to attain and maintain a world without nuclear weapons; and decides that the open-ended working group shall convene in Geneva, in 2016, as a subsidiary body of the General Assembly." The resolution was adopted with 138 votes in favour, 12 against, and 34 abstentions. Austria, Ireland, New Zealand, Sweden, Switzerland, and North Korea voted in favour. All five nuclear-weapon states, plus Israel, voted against. Among the abstaining countries were India, Pakistan, and Canada. Three sessions of the working group have been scheduled for 2016.

In resolution 70/62, the Convention on the Prohibition of the Use of Nuclear Weapons, of the same date, the General Assembly "reiterates its request to the Conference on Disarmament to begin negotiations to reach an agreement on an international convention prohibiting the use or threat of use of nuclear weapons under any circumstances." This resolution was adopted with 130 votes in favour, 48 against, and 8 abstentions. The voting pattern was similar to the vote on resolution 70/34, with the major exception that Russia abstained.

The 70th General Assembly also adopted the following resolutions on nuclear weapons: 70/37, Reducing nuclear danger, 70/40, United action with renewed determination toward the total elimination of nuclear weapons, 70/51, Towards a nuclear-weapon-free world: Accelerating the implementation of nuclear disarmament commitments, 70/52, Nuclear disarmament, and 70/57, Universal Declaration on the Achievement of a Nuclear-Weapon-Free World. All these resolutions were put to a vote. Only China, India, Pakistan, and North Korea voted in favour of any of these resolutions. The four other nuclear-weapon states – France, Russia, the United Kingdom, and the United States – and Israel voted against the resolutions or abstained.

Comment

Many international disarmament lawyers believe that there is no need to adopt an international convention prohibiting the use of nuclear weapons, since such a prohibition is already evident from the international humanitarian law of armed conflicts. The argument for this view is that a first preventive surprise attack with nuclear weapons (first strike with nuclear weapons) is already prohibited by the international legal principle enshrined in Article 2, paragraph 4 of the Charter of the United Nations, according to which "all members shall refrain in their international relations from the threat or use of force against the territorial integrity or political independence of any state."

Even in cases where the right to legitimate self-defence – as recognized in Article 51 – is invoked, this right to use military force is not unlimited. The restrictions of the right to self-defence are founded in the general rules of international humanitarian law, adopted in the Fourth Hague Convention of 1907, and further developed in the Additional Protocols to the Geneva Conventions. According to these rules, the means of belligerents to injure the enemy is not unlimited, and the use of weapons that cause unnecessary suffering or destruction of the enemy's property is prohibited, unless such destruction is absolutely necessary from a military point of view as part of the warfare. The prohibitions of such harmful weapons in the Hague Convention also apply to future weapons and thus also to nuclear weapons. When strategic nuclear weapons are used in war, it will be practically impossible to comply with the rules of international humanitarian law because of the indiscriminate effects of nuclear weapons on civilians.

Another question is whether the use of nuclear weapons would be contrary to the principle of *jus cogens*, i.e., a fundamental, overriding principle or norm of international law from which no derogation is ever permitted. The general negative attitude toward nuclear weapons in the overwhelming majority of countries supports this view. The nuclear-weapon states have another position on the issue of the illegality of nuclear weapons: they refer to the fact that these weapons are not explicitly forbidden in any internationally binding agreement and therefore cannot be considered unlawful.

Proponents of the need to prohibit nuclear weapons by legally binding treaty law have often expressed the view that nuclear weapons are the only weapons of mass destruction that have not been outlawed like biological and chemical weapons. Therefore, there exists a "legal gap" that must be filled to prohibit and eliminate nuclear weapons. This formulation was also used in the conclusions in the "Humanitarian Pledge," presented by Austria at the Vienna Conference on the Humanitarian Impact of Nuclear Weapons, in December 2014.

In a letter to the editor of Arms Control Today, entitled "Legal Gap or Compliance Gap," and reproduced in the Arms Control Association (ACA) October 2015 publication, the co-president of the International Association of Lawyers Against Nuclear Arms (IALANA) and the executive director of the Association's UN office make the following point: "If the use of nuclear weapons already is unlawful, how should the concept of a "legal gap" be understood? The deficiency should be seen as a compliance gap, the failure to eliminate nuclear weapons in accordance with Article VI of the nuclear Nonproliferation Treaty (NPT). That article requires the pursuit of negotiations in good faith of "effective measures ... relating to nuclear disarmament." The letter further states that "nuclear weapons simply cannot be used in compliance with fundamental principles of international law protecting civilians from the effects of warfare, protecting combatants from unnecessary suffering, and protecting the natural environment." It is the view of the authors of the letter that "a treaty prohibition on the use of nuclear weapons in any circumstance would codify the existing illegality of their use. That is the way law generally develops, from common law to statutory law, from custom to treaty. By joining such a treaty, nuclear-armed and nuclear-umbrella states would unequivocally accept the illegality of use. For these reasons, an explicit prohibition of use should be included in the legal measures negotiated to fill the compliance gap."[35]

It could also be argued that the development, production, modernization, possession, and stockpiling of nuclear weapons is still not explicitly prohibited under international law. Although international humanitarian law does not specifically prohibit nuclear weapons, their use is considered, by an overwhelming majority of countries, as restricted by the general rules and principles of international humanitarian law, which regulate conduct in armed conflicts. These rules also apply to the use of nuclear weapons. So the legal gap consists in explicitly prohibiting the mere existence of nuclear weapons.

A strong argument for prohibiting nuclear weapons by way of a treaty – not only by referring to customary international law – is that compliance with a nuclear weapons ban has to be verifiable. Therefore, provisions on verifying compliance with the prohibitions have to be established in a treaty to ensure that all states comply with their obligations. A nuclear-weapon inspection regime would have to be part of the treaty banning nuclear weapons.

Even if the United Nations Charter and the relevant conventions and principles of international humanitarian law are interpreted to contain a general prohibition of nuclear weapons, there is a clear need to establish a specific and comprehensive prohibition of nuclear weapons in a legally binding treaty – similar to the conventions on biological and chemical weapons. A nuclear ban treaty should provide for the verifiable, irreversible, and enforceable prohibition on the use, possession, and elimination of all nuclear weapons. Before such a treaty is attainable, a treaty banning first use and non-use against non-nuclear-weapon states (negative security assurance) – or any use, in a retaliatory attack, of nuclear weapons – could be a first step and a prerequisite for achieving the objectives in Article 6 of the Non-Proliferation Treaty on nuclear weapons disarmament and a treaty on general and complete disarmament under strict and effective international control, with the complete abolition of nuclear weapons as the ultimate goal.

Although the Non-Proliferation Treaty may be considered to have legitimized – temporarily and under certain conditions (see NPT's Article 6) – the five recognized nuclear-weapon states' possession of nuclear weapons, a later treaty banning nuclear weapons would take precedence over the NPT and make continued possession of such weapons unlawful, meaningless, and dangerous. Why keep nuclear weapons, which are incredibly costly to maintain, when their use and threat of use has been banned? The continued possession of nuclear weapons would be dangerous, since a nuclear-armed state could be tempted to use these weapons in war, especially if the enemy has a superior capability in conventional forces. Therefore, any future treaty on nuclear weapons must contain the same absolute prohibition as the conventions on biological and chemical weapons, i.e., prohibit the development, production, acquisition, retention, stockpiling, transfer, deployment, and use of nuclear weapons.

A comprehensive exposition of possible elements to be included in a treaty banning nuclear weapons is presented in the paper *A Treaty Banning Nuclear Weapons – Developing a legal framework for the prohibition and elimination of nuclear weapons*, published in May 2014, by the two non-governmental organizations Article 36 and Reaching Critical Will. The report concludes that "ridding the world of nuclear weapons ... is achievable, feasible, and practical ... Banning nuclear weapons is an urgent necessity."[36]

PROSPECTS FOR NUCLEAR DISARMAMENT AND PROHIBITION OF NUCLEAR WEAPONS

The prospects for reaching broad international agreement, including the nuclear-weapon states, to launch international negotiations on nuclear disarmament, leading to the adoption of a treaty on the total prohibition of all nuclear weapons, are not bright for the foreseeable future. This pessimistic assessment appears to be realistic – not least against the background of increased international tensions in recent years and the deteriorating security situation in Europe due to the conflict in Ukraine and the war in Syria. The ongoing modernization of nuclear weapons, in all the nuclear-weapon states (the five recognized states according to Article 9, paragraph 3 in the NPT – US, Russia, UK, France, and China) and the nuclear-armed states (the four other states that possess nuclear weapons – India, Pakistan, Israel, and North Korea), is a clear indication of the nuclear-weapon states' intentions to keep their nuclear weapons and make them even more effective. The security concerns of the nuclear-weapon states seem to overshadow the argument that nuclear weapons are no longer required to maintain a balance of power – or balance of terror – as was the case during the Cold War. Another obvious demonstration of the lack of will on the part of the nuclear-weapon states to initiate even preliminary negotiations on nuclear weapons disarmament is the repeated negative votes year after year on all the General Assembly resolutions calling for nuclear disarmament. Another sign of this negative attitude toward disarmament of nuclear weapons is the continued modernization of these weapons.

The possibilities for further reductions of the overwhelming American and Russian arsenals of nuclear weapons seemed bright a few years ago. President Obama's speech in Prague on 5 April 2009 and his administration's continuing efforts to further reduce the numbers of strategic nuclear weapons gave hope for optimism.

These brighter prospects were confirmed in Obama's speech in Berlin on 19 June 2013, in which the president announced that the United States was prepared to reduce the number of deployed strategic nuclear weapons by up to one third of the current ceiling of 1,550 nuclear weapons, contained in the New START Treaty. This offer reinforced the hope that it would be possible to reduce the numbers of American and Russian nuclear weapons to levels of approximately 1,000 nuclear weapons in each country. However, the initial Russian reaction to this proposal was not encouraging. According to the statements made by the Russian foreign minister, Sergej Lavrov, Russia would only be prepared to further reduce its nuclear weapons if negotiations on this issue also included missile defence, conventional arms, and space weapons. The American missile defence program is also an obstacle to further reductions of Russia's nuclear weapons.

At a historic summit meeting of the United Nations Security Council on 24 September 2009, presided over by President Obama, the Council unanimously adopted resolution 1887, in which the Council called upon "the parties to the NPT, pursuant to Article VI of the Treaty, to undertake to pursue negotiations in good faith on effective measures relating to nuclear arms reduction and disarmament, and on a Treaty on general and complete disarmament under strict and effective international control, and calls on all other States to join in this endeavor."

NUCLEAR WEAPONS AND HUMAN RIGHTS

United Nations Declaration and Conventions on Human Rights

The protection of human rights is not only regulated in national constitutions and laws, but has primarily been formulated in international declarations and treaties. The fundamental international framework for the protection of basic human rights is laid down in The Universal Declaration of Human Rights, which was adopted by the third United Nations General Assembly on 10 December 1948 by resolution 217 A (III). Forty-eight countries voted in favour of the Declaration, none against, and eight countries abstained, including South Africa, Saudi Arabia, and several communist states. The Declaration of Human Rights implements Article 1 in the United Nations Charter on the purposes of the UN. According to paragraph 3 of this Article, one of the purposes of the UN is "to achieve international cooperation in promoting and encouraging respect for human rights and for fundamental freedoms for all without distinction as to race, sex, language, or religion." Article 55 further calls for promoting universal respect for, and observance of, human rights and fundamental freedoms in order to create conditions of stability and well-being, which are necessary for peaceful and friendly relations among nations. In Article 56, "all members pledge themselves to take joint and separate action in cooperation with the Organization for the achievement of the purposes set forth in Article 55."

The Universal Declaration of Human Rights is not a legally binding international instrument. However, some of the most fundamental rights enumerated in the Universal Declaration, e.g., the prohibitions against slavery and torture, constitute part of customary international law. Some of the rights may even be qualified as part of *jus cogens*, and therefore binding for all states. The European Court of Human Rights has contributed to this recognition.

In the years following the Second World War, it became evident that there was a need to transform the ideals of the Universal Declaration into legally binding standards. This was done by adopting the International Covenant on Civil and Political Rights and the International Covenant on Economic, Social and Cultural Rights, both of 16 December 1966. The Conventions have been ratified by 168 and 164 countries, respectively, including all the nuclear-weapon states and nuclear-armed states, except China, which has only signed but not ratified the Covenant on Civil and Political Rights, and the United States, which has only signed the Covenant on Economic, Social and Cultural Rights. These two human rights conventions came into force in 1976.

The Universal Declaration and the two Covenants constitute the foundation of international human rights law. It was on the basis of The Universal Declaration that the European Convention for the

Protection of Human Rights and Fundamental Freedoms of 1950 was adopted.

VIOLATION OF THE RIGHT TO LIFE

The fundamental right to life is embodied in Article 3 of the Universal Declaration of Human Rights. The Article states that "everyone has the right to life, liberty and security of person." The right to life is repeated in Article 6 of the International Covenant on Civil and Political Rights: "Every human being has the inherent right to life." The right to life is the most basic and highest ranking of all human rights, since the enjoyment of an individual's life is a basic requirement for being able to enjoy all other human rights. The scope of the "right to life" in Article 6 was considered by the International Court of Justice in its Advisory Opinion on the Legality of the threat or use of nuclear weapons. Invoking Article 6, the ICJ held that "in principle, the right not arbitrarily to be deprived of one's life applies also in hostilities (see paragraph 25 of the Advisory Opinion).

A cynic may ask if the use of nuclear weapons is a more serious violation of the right to life than the use of other types of weapons. Does it make any difference whether a person is killed by a nuclear bomb or by a bullet from a firearm? There is, however, a significant difference. The effect of a bullet from a gun and other major conventional weapons is usually limited to a single victim or a limited number of victims in a small (or smaller) geographic area. A nuclear bomb, as well as the two other categories of weapons of mass destruction (biological and chemical weapons), are non-discriminatory, i.e., they hit both military targets and civilian persons indiscriminately. The deadly and destructive effects of WMD cannot be limited and controlled, either in magnitude, or in proliferation or duration. The deadly effect of the radioactive radiation from an atomic bomb explosion may be spread over a very large area and last for a very long time, destroying all life in the area and making it uninhabitable for many years.

In addition to violating the right to life, the use of nuclear weapons would also constitute a violation of the "inherent right of all peoples to enjoy and utilize fully and freely their natural wealth and resources," as referred to in Article 47 of the Covenant on Civil and Political Rights. A nuclear war would have long and global disastrous impacts on the environment and climate by creating a "nuclear winter" which would affect human life and health negatively for generations, and in the worst case could threaten the survival of all mankind.

When the intent of an attack with nuclear weapons is to kill members of a national, ethnic, racial, or religious group, the attack could also be a violation of Articles 2 and 3 of the Convention on the Prevention and Punishment of the Crime of Genocide, adopted by the United Nations General Assembly in 1948 in response to the atrocities committed during the Second World War. The Convention has 147 states parties, including all the nuclear-weapon states and nuclear-armed states.

VIOLATION OF THE RIGHT TO PEACE

It is already evident from the first sentence in the introduction to the United Nations Charter that one of the main purposes of the United Nations is "to save succeeding generations from the scourge of war." The preamble also includes the overall objective, "that armed force shall not be used, save in the common interest." Article 2, paragraph 4 of the Charter determines that "all members shall refrain in their international relations from the threat or use of force against the territorial integrity or political independence of any state, or in any other manner inconsistent with the purposes of the United Nations." The principle of peaceful resolution of conflicts is enshrined in Article 33 of chapter 6 on the pacific settlement of disputes.

One may conclude from these provisions that the Charter – at least indirectly – has established a right for the peoples of the world to live in peace. The right to peace is not established specifically, neither in the Universal Declaration of Human Rights nor in the two covenants implementing the Declaration. Article 28 of the Universal Declaration, however, declares that "everyone is entitled to a social and international order in which the rights and freedoms set forth in this Declaration can be fully realized." The realization of the rights and freedoms in the Universal Declaration thus requires a peaceful social and international order.

In the Declaration on the Right of Peoples to Peace, which was adopted by General Assembly resolution 39/11 in 1984, the General Assembly "solemnly proclaims that the peoples of our planet have a sacred right to peace," and that "the preservation of this right and the

promotion of its implementation constitute a fundamental obligation of each state." The Declaration also emphasizes that "ensuring the
exercise of the right of peoples to peace demands that the policies of
states be directed toward the elimination of the threat of war, particularly nuclear war." The resolution was adopted with 92 votes in
favour, none against, and 34 abstentions. China, the former Soviet
Union, India, and Pakistan voted in favour. The other three nuclear-
weapon states abstained.

United Nations Decisions
on Human Rights under Armed Conflicts

The requirement to respect human rights during armed conflicts was
established by General Assembly resolution 2444 (XXIII) on Respect
for Human Rights in Armed Conflicts, which was adopted unanimously in 1968. The resolution affirms three basic principles for all
governmental and other authorities responsible for action in armed
conflicts to observe. It was adopted by the 20th International Conference of the Red Cross in 1965 and states that:

- the right of the parties to a conflict to adopt means of injuring the
  enemy is not unlimited,
- it is prohibited to launch attacks against the civilian populations
  as such,
- distinction must be made at all times between persons taking part
  in the hostilities and members of the civilian population to the
  effect that the latter be spared as much as possible.

By adopting resolution 2444, the General Assembly has thus
declared that it is unacceptable to wage war against the civilian
population. The basic principles for protecting civilian populations
in armed conflicts were later confirmed in resolution 2675 (XXV)
of 1970, which was adopted with 109 (non-recorded) votes in
favour, none against, and 8 abstentions. By resolution 2674 of the
same year on respect for human rights in armed conflicts, the General Assembly considered that air bombardments of civilian populations and the use of chemical and biological weapons constitute
a flagrant violation of the Hague Convention of 1907, the Geneva
Protocol of 1925, and the Geneva Conventions of 1949. This reso-

lution was adopted with 77 votes in favour, including China, India, Pakistan and the former Soviet Union, 2 against, and 36 abstentions, among them France, the United Kingdom, the United States, and Israel.

Only one year after the United Nations was established there was considerable international focus on the horrifying effects of nuclear weapons after the nuclear bombings of Japan at the end of the Second World War. The General Assembly's first resolution 1 (I), adopted on 24 January 1946, on "Establishment of a Commission to Deal with the Problems Raised by the Discovery of Atomic Energy," contained a mandate for the Commission (later the IAEA), which included preparing a concrete proposal "for the elimination from national armaments of atomic weapons and of all other major weapons adaptable to mass destruction."

During the 1960s, the question of the effects of nuclear weapons on the enjoyment of fundamental human rights, including the right to life, was put on the United Nations agenda. In General Assembly resolution 1653 (XVI) of 1961, Declaration on the Prohibition of the Use of Nuclear and Thermonuclear Weapons, the General Assembly declared that "the use of nuclear and thermonuclear weapons is contrary to the spirit, letter and aims of the United Nations and, as such, a direct violation of the Charter of the United Nations" and that such use "would exceed even the scope of war and cause indiscriminate suffering and destruction to mankind and civilization and, as such, is contrary to the rules of international law and the law of humanity." The resolution further stated that "any state using nuclear and thermonuclear weapons, is to be considered as violating the Charter of the United Nations, as acting contrary to the laws of humanity and committing a crime against mankind and civilization." The resolution was adopted by 55 votes in favour, including India and the former Soviet Union, 20 votes against, including China, France, the United Kingdom and the United States, and 26 abstentions, including Israel and Pakistan. The resolution's message has been repeated in a number of later General Assembly resolutions from 1978 to 1981. In resolution 36/100 of 1981, Declaration on the Prevention of Nuclear Catastrophe, the General Assembly proclaimed that "states and statesmen that resort first to the use of nuclear weapons will be committing the gravest crime against humanity." The resolution was adopted with 82 votes in favour, including India, Pakistan, and the former Soviet Union, 19 against, including France, Israel, the United Kingdom, and the United States, and 41 abstentions.

In the General Comment No. 14, Article 6 (Right to Life) Nuclear Weapons and the Right to Life of 1984, the United Nations Human Rights Committee declared that "it is evident that the designing, testing, manufacture, possession and deployment of nuclear weapons are among the greatest threats to the right to life which confront mankind today" and "that the production, testing, possession, deployment and use of nuclear weapons should be prohibited and recognized as crimes against humanity."

The issue of protection of and respect for human rights in connection with the use of weapons of mass destruction and of other weapons that have indiscriminate effects or are excessively injurious was the subject of a report by the Sub-Commission on the Promotion and Protection of Human Rights.[37] The report concludes that the use of nuclear weapons (and other weapons of mass destruction) is a violation of international humanitarian law and of human rights because of the catastrophic effect of these weapons and their potential to wipe out all of humanity and destroy the world's ecosystem. According to the findings in the report, the use of nuclear weapons – because of their uncontrollable and harmful effects on the civilian population – can never fulfill the requirement of international humanitarian law about proportionality and will therefore be illegal under any circumstances.

Human Security

Human security is a relatively new concept, which has been promoted by former Canadian foreign minister Lloyd Axworthy. In 2002, Axworthy established the Human Security Centre at the University of British Columbia, today the Human Security Report Project, which is an independent research centre at Simon Fraser University in Vancouver, Canada.[38] Since 2005, the Centre has published reports on human security.

The concept was first the object of global attention in the United Nations Development Programme (UNDP) report *Human Development Report 1994, New Dimensions of Human Security*. The report introduced a concept for human security that relates security to human beings rather than to states (territories) and to development rather than to weapons. The concept focuses on threats to the security of humans (the individual) and populations, rather than threats against state security (defence of state borders from external military attacks or threats of attack). There is no international consensus on the definition or scope of the concept – whether the concept, in addition to threats arising from poverty, diseases, pollution, natural disasters, climate change etc., also includes military threats. However, the concept does acknowledge the interlinkages between security, development, and human rights. The definition of human security in the UNDP report includes both "freedom from want and freedom from fear." There seems to be general international agreement that the concept at a minimum includes "freedom from fear," i.e., freedom from violent conflict and fear of violence.[39]

Comment

The above examples of decisions adopted in United Nations resolutions, declaring the use of nuclear weapons to be "crimes against humanity," show that there is widespread international agreement among non-nuclear-weapon states that the use of nuclear weapons is a violation of fundamental human rights and of international humanitarian law, and therefore should be prohibited. However, such a clear conclusion cannot be drawn from the ICJ's Advisory Opinion, mentioned earlier. The nuclear-weapon states do not agree that the use of nuclear weapons in all circumstances would be incompatible with international law or that these weapons should be banned. Thus, the fundamental question of the legality or illegality of nuclear weapons continues to be disputed.

The new security concept, where human security is at the centre rather than national security, puts greater focus on efforts to increase the protection of civilian populations through further steps to promote disarmament, arms control, and non-proliferation, particularly of weapons of mass destruction. Still, in many developing countries, the interests of national – often fragile – security come first, rather than the interests of individual human security. It is likely that in many countries it will take many years before the priority of individual security is recognized and respected.

Humanitarian Impact of Nuclear Weapons

In recent years, a growing number of states and many civil society organizations have focused increasingly on the humanitarian consequences and risks of nuclear weapons. In the Final Document of the 2010 NPT Review Conference, "the Conference expresses its deep concern at the catastrophic humanitarian consequences of any use of nuclear weapons and reaffirms the need for all states at all times to comply with applicable international law, including international humanitarian law." This was an important innovation in the context of the NPT review conference, because compliance with international humanitarian law became an obligation for the states parties to the NPT.

"The Humanitarian Impact of Nuclear Weapons" has been the theme for three conferences. The first conference was held in Oslo, Norway, in March 2013, the second in Nayarit, Mexico, in February 2014, and the third in Vienna, Austria, in December 2014.

The facts presented during the first two conferences and the continued discussions during the Vienna Conference underlined the fact that the humanitarian consequences and risks associated with nuclear weapons are far higher and far graver than previously assumed, and that these issues should be at the centre of continued global efforts to promote nuclear disarmament and non-proliferation.

The different views expressed in the discussions were presented in the Chair's Report and Summary of Findings of the Conference. The summary contains eight substantive conclusions that have emerged in the humanitarian initiative of the past three years and from the international conferences in Oslo, Nayarit, and Vienna. The main conclusions are (in abbreviated form):

- "The impact of a nuclear weapon detonation, regardless of the cause, would not be constrained by national borders and could have regional and even global consequences, causing destruction, death, and displacement as well as profound and long-term damage to the environment, climate, human health and well-being, socioeconomic development and social order, and could even threaten the survival of humankind,
- "The scope, scale, and interrelationship of the humanitarian consequences caused by nuclear weapon detonation are catastrophic

and more complex than commonly understood. These consequences can be large scale and potentially irreversible,
- "As long as nuclear weapons exist, there remains the possibility of
a nuclear explosion. Even if the probability is low, given the catastrophic consequences of a nuclear weapon detonation the risk is
unacceptable. The risks of accidental, mistaken, unauthorized, or
intentional use of nuclear weapons are evident because of the vulnerability of nuclear command and control networks to human
error and cyberattacks, the maintaining of nuclear arsenals on
high levels of alert, forward deployment, and the modernization of
nuclear weapons. These risks increase over time. The dangers of
access to nuclear weapons and related materials by non-state
actors, particularly terrorist groups, persists,
- "Opportunities to reduce risk must be taken now, such as de-alert-
ing and reducing the role of nuclear weapons in security doctrines. The only insurance against the risk of a nuclear weapon
detonation is the total elimination of nuclear weapons.
- "It is clear that there is no comprehensive legal norm universally
prohibiting possession, transfer, production, and use. The new evidence that has emerged in the last two years about the humanitarian impact of nuclear weapons casts further doubt on whether
these weapons could ever be used in conformity with international humanitarian law."

In addition to the Chair's summary, Austria issued the "Austrian
Pledge," which goes beyond that summary. The pledge contains the
conclusions that Austria drew from the humanitarian arguments presented during the conferences. In the Pledge, Austria calls on

- all states parties to the NPT to renew their commitment to the
urgent and full implementation of existing obligations under Article 6, and, to this end, to identify and pursue effective measures to
fill the legal gap for the prohibition and elimination of nuclear
weapons,
- all nuclear-weapon and nuclear-armed states to take concrete interim measures to reduce the risk of nuclear weapon detonations,
including reducing the operational status of nuclear weapons and
moving nuclear weapons away from deployment into storage,
diminishing the role of nuclear weapons in military doctrines, and
rapid reductions of all types of nuclear weapons.[40]

The Pledge has been endorsed by 121 – mostly non-aligned – countries. None of the nuclear-weapon states or nuclear-armed states, or any of the other NATO member states, have endorsed the Pledge. Only three western countries have supported the Pledge: Ireland, Liechtenstein, and Malta.

At the Vienna Conference, the International Committee of the Red Cross (ICRC) issued a statement on the use of nuclear weapons and international humanitarian law. It confirmed that although international humanitarian law does not specifically prohibit nuclear weapons, their use is restricted by the general rules of this law regulating the conduct of hostilities, which apply to the use of all weapons in armed conflict. The International Red Cross and Red Crescent Movement's Council of Delegates in 2011 stated that "it is difficult to envisage how any use of nuclear weapons could be compatible with the requirements of international humanitarian law."[41] The view was further expressed in the statement that the new evidence that has emerged in the last two years about the humanitarian impact of nuclear weapons casts further doubt on whether these weapons could ever be used in accordance with the rules of customary international humanitarian law. In another statement to the Conference in Vienna, the president of the ICRC said that "there has been a fundamental change in the debate about nuclear weapons. After decades of focusing on nuclear weapons primarily in technical-military terms and as symbols of power, states have finally engaged in a long overdue discussion of what they would mean for people and the environment, indeed for humanity." The statement also referred to "the catastrophic humanitarian consequences that we are now well aware of are too serious to ignore. The only way to ensure the indefinite continuation of the non-use of nuclear weapons would be to enshrine the non-use and complete elimination of nuclear weapons in a legally binding international agreement."

The 70th General Assembly in 2015 adopted three new resolutions addressing the humanitarian consequences of nuclear explosions:

Resolution 70/48, Humanitarian pledge for the prohibition and elimination of nuclear weapons, in which the General Assembly "stresses the importance of having fact-based discussions and presenting findings and compelling evidence on the humanitarian impact of nuclear weapons in all relevant forums and within the United Nations framework, as they should be at the centre of all deliberations and the implementation of obligations and commitments with regard to nuclear disarmament" and "appeals to all states to follow the imperative of human security for all and to promote the protection of civilians against risks stemming from nuclear weapons."

Resolution 70/47, Humanitarian consequences of nuclear weapons

1 Stresses that it is in the interest of the very survival of humanity that nuclear weapons never be used again, under any circumstances;
2 Emphasizes that the only way to guarantee that nuclear weapons will never be used again is their total elimination;
3 Stresses that the catastrophic effects of a nuclear weapon detonation, whether by accident, miscalculation or design, cannot be adequately addressed; and
4 Expresses its firm belief that awareness of the catastrophic consequences of nuclear weapons must underpin all approaches and efforts towards nuclear disarmament.

Resolution 70/50, Ethical imperatives for a nuclear-weapon-free world, declares that

(a) The global threat posed by nuclear weapons must urgently be eliminated;
(b) Discussions, decisions and actions on nuclear weapons must focus on the effects of these weapons on human beings and the environment and must be guided by the unspeakable suffering and unacceptable harm that they cause;
(c) Nuclear weapons serve to undermine collective security, heighten the risk of nuclear catastrophe, aggravate international tension and make conflict more dangerous;
(d) The long-term plans for the modernization of nuclear weapons arsenals run contrary to commitments and obligations to nuclear disarmament and engender perceptions of the indefinite possession of these weapons;
(e) In a world where basic human needs have not yet been met, the vast resources allocated to the modernization of nuclear weapons arsenals could instead be redirected to meeting the Sustainable Development Goals;
(f) Given the humanitarian impact of nuclear weapons, it is inconceivable that any use of nuclear weapons, irrespective of the cause, would be compatible with the requirements of interna-

tional humanitarian law or international law, or the laws of morality, or the dictates of public conscience;

(g) Given their indiscriminate nature and potential to annihilate humanity, nuclear weapons are inherently immoral.

All three resolutions were adopted by an overwhelming majority – 139, 144, and 132 votes in favour, respectively. Among the western states, Austria, Ireland, and New Zealand voted in favour of all three resolutions. The nuclear-weapon states and the nuclear-armed states either voted against or abstained. Among them, only India voted in favour of 70/47. China, Pakistan, and North Korea abstained on all three resolutions.

6

Biological Weapons

INTRODUCTION

Warfare with biological weapons is the deliberate use of biological agents, i.e., infectious agents in the form of live microorganisms (bacteria, viruses, fungi, or parasites) or toxins (poisons) to cause disease, death, disability (paralysis), and other related harm to humans, animals (livestock), or plants (agricultural crops). Toxins are poisonous substances produced either biologically from certain types of bacteria from animals, plants, or microorganisms, or produced synthetically, and which can have harmful effects in a living organism.

Biological weapons cause epidemics of infectious diseases that affect everyone, including civilians. Among the best-known biological weapons is anthrax bacterium, which was used in the autumn of 2001 in a terrorist attack in the form of letters to the Senate office building in Washington and to the media in New York. Ricin and botulinum toxin are other biological weapons. The diseases that may be used as biological weapons and present the greatest biological danger are botulism, plague, cholera, typhoid, and smallpox.

The most effective way to use biological weapons is by spreading the microorganisms or toxins in the air, for example in bombs and missiles, or aerial spraying from aircraft equipped with spray tanks. They can also be spread through foodstuffs and the drinking water supply.

The spread of pathogenic microorganisms in biological warfare or terrorist attacks is now regarded as one of the most serious threats to national and regional security. According to expert estimates,[1] spreading 100 kilograms of anthrax bacteria in the air over Washington, DC, could cause between one and three million deaths. By comparison, an atomic bomb of one megaton dropped on the US capital would cause between about half a million to two million deaths. What makes biological weapons particularly dangerous and feared is the fact that they are relatively uncomplicated and inexpensive to manufacture, compared with other types of weapons of mass destruction. Therefore, these weapons can easily be made available to non-state individual actors, including terrorist organizations. Biological weapons can be produced in small bio laboratories that are hidden in civilian laboratories, for example in the biotechnology and pharmaceutical drug industry. Hundreds of laboratories in the world have stocks of anthrax bacteria which is used for research, diagnosing diseases, and developing vaccines. Biological weapons, however, are not resistant to effects from outside and they are unstable. Airborne biological weapons can be affected by weather conditions (wind and temperature) and are thus uncertain and unpredictable. There are also significant technical challenges to producing larger quantities of biological agents for use as biological weapons.

Unlike chemical weapons, biological weapons have never been used in large-scale warfare. However, the possibility of biological weapons being used by terrorist organizations is regarded with the utmost seriousness and as a real threat today – especially in the United States. In November 2009, President Obama announced a national strategy to counter the threat from biological weapons (National Security Council's National Strategy for Countering Biological Threats). The strategy deals with the challenges of the proliferation of biological weapons and protection against the misuse of science that can be used to manufacture and proliferate biological weapons.

PROTOCOL FOR THE PROHIBITION OF POISONOUS GAS AND OF BACTERIOLOGICAL METHODS OF WARFARE

Efforts to ban biological weapons go back to 1925, when the Protocol for the Prohibition of the Use in War of Asphyxiating, Poisonous or Other Gases, and of Bacteriological Methods of Warfare of 1925 was adopted. The protocol was signed in Geneva and is therefore often referred to as the Geneva Protocol or the 1925 Protocol. It entered into force in 1928, and has been ratified, or agreed to, by a total of 140 countries, including all five nuclear-weapon states, the four nuclear-armed states, and Egypt, Iran, Iraq, and Syria. The use of poison gas during the First World War, which caused many deaths and terrible suffering for the wounded victims, had caused public outrage and condemnation. After the war there was international agreement to ban the use of poison gas in war. The adoption of the protocol extended the already existing prohibition in the Annex to the Fourth Hague Convention on the use of poison or poisoned weapons to include prohibiting the use of bacteriological methods of warfare.

By resolution 2603A of 1969, the United Nations General Assembly recognized that the 1925 Geneva Protocol constituted a concrete expression of the generally recognized rules of international law, which prohibits the use of all biological and chemical means of warfare in international armed conflicts. The resolution declares any use of chemical and biological weapons in international armed conflicts as contrary to the generally recognized rules of international law. The resolution was adopted with 80 votes in favour, 3 against (United States, Australia, and Portugal), and 36 abstentions (mostly western countries).

Comment

A weakness of the Geneva Protocol is that the obligation not to use poison gas and bacteriological warfare agents applies only to war, and, from a restrictive interpretation, not to internal conflicts or civil wars. In addition, the ban only applies to use, not to the threat of use. The Protocol does not provide for mechanisms to verify that states are complying with the prohibition. Nevertheless, the Protocol is important because it declares that "this prohibition shall be universally accepted as a part of international law, binding alike the conscience and the practice of nations." As a result of the ban having been in force for eighty-eight years, and of the fact that the overwhelming majority of the world's states since 1925 have subsequently ratified or adhered to both the Biological Weapons Convention and the Chemical Weapons Convention, an international customary rule, or internationally recognized standard, has developed, prohibiting the use of poison gases and bacteriological weapons under all circumstances. Arms control agreements adopted in recent years do not distinguish between the use of weapons in war and the use of weapons in internal conflicts, since the main purpose of the agreements is to protect civilian populations. Therefore, an analogous conclusion can be drawn that the norm in the Geneva Protocol prohibiting the use of chemical and biological weapons can also be applied to internal conflicts. The states that have not yet agreed to the conventions banning chemical and biological weapons are in any case still bound by the prohibition in the Geneva Protocol.

BIOLOGICAL WEAPONS CONVENTION

In 1972, the prohibition in the Geneva Protocol of 1925 was completed by the Convention on the Prohibition of the Development, Production and Stockpiling of Bacteriological (Biological) and Toxin Weapons and on Their Destruction (BWC), opened for signature on 10 April 1972. The BWC contains a total ban on biological and toxin weapons, and thus is the first category of weapons that has been totally prohibited. By January 2016, the BWC had 173 states parties. The Convention entered into force in 1975. Israel is among the few countries that are not parties to the Convention. Israel has neither signed, nor adhered to the BWC. All the other nuclear-weapon states and nuclear-armed states have ratified or adhered to the BWC. Egypt and Syria (among others) have signed the Convention but have not yet ratified the agreement. It is considered likely that Egypt, Syria, Iran, Israel, China, and North Korea continue to have development research programs or perhaps continue to produce biological weapons.

The BWC Convention is a short framework convention consisting of only fifteen articles. The introduction to the BWC refers to the Geneva Protocol. The Convention prohibits states from developing, producing, stockpiling, acquiring, or retaining biological weapons, as well as production equipment and/or means of delivery. The BWC does not contain an express prohibition against the use of biological weapons, but the prohibition against use is implied in the reference to the Geneva Protocol.

Article 1 of the Convention contains the main prohibitions, by which each party to the Convention undertakes never under any circumstances to develop, produce, stockpile, or otherwise acquire or retain microbial or other biological agents or toxins of any origin or produced by any method, and of types and in quantities that have no justification for prophylactic, protective, or other peaceful purposes. Weapons, equipment, or means of delivery designed to use such agents or toxins for hostile purposes or in armed conflict are also forbidden. Under the Convention (Article 3), it is also prohibited to transfer to any recipient whatsoever, directly or indirectly, and not in any way to assist, encourage, or induce any state, group of states, or international organizations to manufacture or otherwise acquire any of the agents, toxins, weapons, equipment, or means of delivery specified in Article 1 of the Convention. According to Article 2, the parties must undertake to destroy, or divert to peaceful purposes, not later than nine months after the entry into force of the Convention, all agents, toxins, weapons, equipment, and means of delivery specified in Article 1. In Article 10, the parties undertake to facilitate, and have the right to participate in, the fullest possible exchange of equipment, materials, and scientific and technological information for the use of bacteriological (biological) agents and toxins for peaceful purposes. Furthermore, the parties in a position to do so shall also cooperate in contributing individually or together with other states or international organizations to further developing and applying scientific discoveries in the field of bacteriology (biology) for the prevention of disease, or for other peaceful purposes.

Efforts to strengthen the states' national implementation and compliance with the Convention and ensure non-proliferation of biological weapons are discussed at periodic review conferences of states parties every five years. Annual meetings of states at an expert level are also held to discuss specific actions to promote the objectives of the Convention.

UN Security Council resolution 1540 expanded the prohibitions in the BWC in 2004 to include non-state actors.

Comment

It should be noted that the Convention does not prohibit biodefence programs.

The strength of the BWC lies primarily in the Convention's absolute prohibition of biological weapons. However, the total ban in Article 1 of biological agents and toxins in types and quantities that have no peaceful purposes contains no further definitions of the meaning of biological activities for peaceful purposes that are permitted and those that are expressly prohibited by the BWC. This shortcoming leaves the Treaty open to different interpretations. Another major weakness of the Convention is the fact that the BWC does not contain any provisions on verifying compliance with the total ban, including rules on investigations of alleged violations of the Convention. Article 6, however, declares that a state party that suspects that another state party is acting in breach of the provisions of the Convention may lodge a complaint with the UN Security Council with a request to consider the case. This right to appeal to the Security Council to investigate any dispute, or any situation that might lead to international friction or give rise to a dispute between states, is already secured in Article 35 of the UN Charter.

Between 1995 and 2001, an ad hoc group on verification negotiated a draft protocol to the BWC. The purpose of the verification protocol was to establish a system of declarations and control mechanisms similar to that applied to chemical weapons. But negotiations on the protocol collapsed in 2001 when the US delegation suddenly announced that the United States no longer wished to participate in the negotiations on the draft protocol on verification of compliance with the BWC. The reason for this changed attitude was that, according to the American view, the verification protocol would not strengthen compliance with the Convention and could harm US national security and commercial interests. It is widely believed that the protection of confidential business data of American pharmaceutical companies and fear of industrial espionage against the biotechnology industry and pharmaceutical companies in the US was a decisive factor in withdrawing from the negotiations on the protocol, which then ceased. Instead, the US delegation proposed that individual states parties should take a number of national implementing measures to strengthen compliance with the Convention. At the BWC Review Conference in 1986, the states parties agreed to make annual exchanges of information on their activities in the biofield as part of confidence-building measures. But so far, only less than half of the parties to the Convention are participating in this exchange of information, and the decision on confidence-building measures is only politically binding.

Another major weakness of the BWC is that the Convention does not contain any provisions for creating an international BWC-organization to monitor, verify, and ensure compliance and national implementation of the BWC, such as the OPCW and the IAEA under the Chemical Weapons Convention and the NPT, respectively. However, in 2006 the United Nations Office for Disarmament Affairs (UNODA) created a support unit to implement the BWC (Implementation. Support Unit (ISU)), which receives and distributes information that states submit about their national implementing measures.

The main problem in the coming years to prevent the spread of technologies and know-how for the manufacture of biological weapons is to ensure that the export controls for products with dual application are strengthened. At the same time, the global availability of new scientific and technological progress in the biological field for peaceful purposes should be promoted (see Article 10 of the BWC).

7

Chemical Weapons

INTRODUCTION

Chemical weapons have been used since ancient times, for example poisoning drinking water in wells. Mustard gas, chlorine gas, and phosgene gas were used for the first time as a method of warfare on a large scale during the First World War by both the warring parties, resulting in approximately 91,000 dead and 1.2 million wounded. The first attack with chlorine gas was carried out by German forces in 1915, killing about 5,000 French soldiers. Germany also used mustard gas against British forces, who suffered more than 9,000 casualties. Later during the First World War, both France and Britain used chemical weapons against German soldiers. The horrors of chemical poison gases during the war provoked strong reactions in the public. Chemical weapons have since been regarded with abhorrence and have been condemned as particularly inhumane weapons, whose use is contrary to international humanitarian law.

Since it was already "forbidden to employ poison or poisoned weapons" in Article 23 of the Annex to Convention IV respecting the Laws and Customs of War on Land, which entered into force in 1910 and was ratified by all the warring parties, the use of chemical weapons in the First World War violated the customary international law codified by the Convention.

At the end of the war, Article 171 of the Treaty of Versailles of 1919 (the Treaty of Peace between the allied and associated powers and Germany) prohibited "the use of asphyxiating, poisonous or other gases and all analogous liquids, materials or devices being prohibited, their manufacture and importation are strictly forbidden in Germany."

During the years between the two world wars, chemical weapons were used in Abyssinia (now Ethiopia) by Italy in 1935–36 and by Japan against China between 1937 and 1945. During the Second World War, poison gas (Zyklon B or hydrogen cyanide) was used to murder millions of people – mainly Jews – in gas chambers in German extermination camps (e.g., Auschwitz-Birkenau, Treblinka, and Sobibór), but not on the battlefields of Europe – probably because of fear of retaliation. Chemical weapons continued to be produced on a large scale during the Second World War in a number of countries. During the Cold War, large quantities of chemical weapons were developed, produced, and stored – especially in the United States and the Soviet Union. During the 1970s and 1980s, about twenty-five other countries developed the capabilities to produce chemical weapons.

Chemical weapons were used by Egypt in Yemen from 1963 to 1967 and by Iraq during the war against Iran from 1980 to 1988. Both countries are parties to the 1925 Protocol prohibiting the use of poisonous gases. In 1988, the Iraqi government used chemical weapons (sarin and mustard gas) against its own Kurdish population in the town of Halabja in the northern part of Iraq. An estimated 5,000 to 8,000 people were killed by the poison gas attack. Sarin nerve gas was used by the Japanese sect Aum Shinrikyo against civilians in 1994, in the city of Matsumoto, and in 1995 in Tokyo's subway, killing thirteen people. In the late 1990s, Al-Qaeda had a development program for producing chemical weapons in the eastern part of Afghanistan. In the ongoing civil war in Syria, government forces have used poison gas (sarin nerve gas) several times against the civilian population, in December 2012 and in March and August 2013. According to US intelligence sources, 1,429 people, including 426 children, were killed by the poison gas attack in August 2013. During the Vietnam War, the United States used chemicals (toxic Dioxin) as defoliants and to destroy agricultural crops. Between 1962 and 1971, the US military sprayed nearly 20 million US gallons (75.7 million litres) of chemical herbicides and defoliants – called "Agent Orange" – in Vietnam, Eastern Laos, and parts of Cambodia, as part of the aerial defoliation program known as "Operation Ranch Hand." More than 20 per cent of South Vietnam's forests were sprayed at least once over the nine-year period. Millions of Vietnamese citizens – the government of Vietnam claims that the number is around 4 million – were exposed to Agent Orange. The majority of the victims – an estimated 3 million people – suffered illnesses because of it, including serious skin diseases, a variety of cancers, and deformed babies. The above figures include the children of people who were exposed. Many US veterans suffer increased rates of cancer, and nerve, digestive, skin, and respiratory disorders. At the time of the Vietnam War, there were no specific provisions on herbicidal warfare in international humanitarian law or customary law. In 1976, a draft convention on the subject, which had been prepared in a working group under the Conference of the Committee on Disarmament, was presented to the United Nations General Assembly. In 1976, the Assembly, by resolution 31/72, adopted the Convention on the Prohibition of Military or Any Other Hostile Use of Environmental Modification Techniques (the Environmental Modification Convention or ENMOD Convention). The resolution was adopted with 96 votes in favour, including the United States, 8 against, and 30 abstentions. The Convention was opened for signature and ratification in 1977 and entered into force in 1978. The Convention prohibits the military or other hostile use of environmental modification techniques that have widespread, long-lasting, or severe effects. Many states do not regard this as a complete ban on the use of herbicides and defoliants in warfare as the Convention requires a case-by-case consideration.

PROTOCOL FOR THE PROHIBITION OF POISONOUS GAS AND OF BACTERIOLOGICAL METHODS OF WARFARE

The prohibition of chemical weapons (poison gases) goes back to 1925, when the Protocol for the Prohibition of the Use in War of Asphyxiating, Poisonous or Other Gases, and of Bacteriological Methods of Warfare was adopted (see chapter 6 on biological weapons).

CHEMICAL WEAPONS CONVENTION

Negotiations on a comprehensive ban on chemical weapons began in 1980 at the UN Disarmament Conference and the draft convention was adopted by the Conference in 1992. In November 1992, the United Nations General Assembly adopted a resolution that recommended concluding a convention on the prohibition of chemical weapons on the basis of the negotiated draft convention. The resolution (47/39) was adopted without a vote.

The CWC was signed in 1993 by 130 countries. As of January 2016, the Convention had been ratified or adhered to by 192 countries.

Israel has signed the CWC, but has not yet ratified it. Three countries have neither signed nor adhered to the CWC: Egypt, North Korea, and South Sudan. The 192 countries represent 98 per cent of the world's population and also 98 per cent of the global chemical industry. The CWC entered into force in 1997.

Syria joined the CWC in September 2013 and issued a declaration promising to comply with the provisions, and to apply the Convention provisionally pending the formal entry into force for Syria (30 days after the agreement). Two days after the CWC entered into force for Syria, the first inspectors from the Organization for the Prohibition of Chemical Weapons arrived in the country. The Syrian production plants for the manufacture of chemical weapons were destroyed by 1 November. After some diplomatic wrangling and protracted negotiations between the United States and Syria's closest ally, Russia, the UN Security Council unanimously adopted resolution 2118 (2013), which obliged Syria to eliminate all its chemical weapons, including materials, production equipment, and facilities before the end of the first half of 2014. According to US intelligence sources, Syria had about 900 tons of chemical weapons: sarin, mustard gas, and VX.

Egypt has signed and ratified the Geneva Protocol of 1925, but has refused to agree to the CWC until all weapons of mass destruction (i.e., Israel's non-declared nuclear weapons) have been removed from the Middle East. North Korea, Iran, Iraq, and Libya are known to have had chemical weapons programs, and Iraq and Libya may still have some chemical weapons in stock. This constitutes a breach of their obligations under the CWC. Egypt, China, Ethiopia, Israel, Myanmar (Burma), Pakistan, and Russia are believed to continue to have stockpiles of chemical weapons and/or to continue research and manufacturing. Algeria, Cuba, and Sudan may have development programs for chemical weapons.

The Convention on the Prohibition of Chemical Weapons is a very comprehensive and detailed agreement, containing twenty-four articles and three appendices on chemicals, on implementation and verification, and on the protection of confidential information.

In its introduction, the CWC refers to the Geneva Protocol of 1925 and reaffirms the principles and objectives of and obligations assumed under the Geneva Protocol. The Geneva Protocol only prohibits the use of chemical weapons (toxic gases) in war, but not the development, production, and stockpiling of such weapons. Furthermore, the Geneva Protocol contains no provisions on sanctions in case of violations or on verification to ensure compliance. In addition, a number of parties to the Geneva Protocol have reservations about retaining the right to use chemical weapons against non-participating states and in retaliation in case they themselves are attacked with such weapons.

In Article 1 of the CWC, the states parties undertake a general obligation never, under any circumstances, to develop, produce, otherwise acquire, stockpile, or retain chemical weapons, or to transfer, directly or indirectly, chemical weapons to anyone. States are also prohibited from using chemical weapons, from engaging in any military preparations to use chemical weapons, or from assisting, encouraging, or inducing, in any way, anyone to engage in any prohibited activity under the Convention. Each state party also undertakes to destroy chemical weapons it owns or possesses, as well as all such weapons it has abandoned on the territory of another state, and any chemical weapons production facilities. States parties also undertake not to use riot control agents, for example tear gas, as a method of warfare. The basic obligations under Article 1 show the CWC's comprehensive character: prohibition on the use and preparation of use of chemical weapons and obligation to disarm and prevent proliferation of chemical weapons. However, the obligations in Article 1 are not intended to restrict the use of chemicals or trade in chemicals between states.

Article 2 contains definitions and criteria for chemical weapons and other terms used in the Convention. Chemical weapons are defined as toxic chemicals and their precursors, munitions, and devices, specifically designed to cause death or other harm through the toxic chemicals they release and any equipment specifically designed to be used with those munitions and devices. Toxic chemicals are defined as any chemical that can cause death, temporary incapacitation, or permanent harm to humans or animals through its chemical effect on life processes. The toxic chemicals are divided into three categories, according to their harmful effects and listed in three schedules in the Convention's annex on chemicals. The most commonly known toxic chemicals are nerve gases (VX and sarin), blister gases (mustard gas), and asphyxiant gases (chlorine).

Article 3 requires states parties to submit detailed declarations on their chemical weapons, for example, their precise location and quantity, including old and abandoned chemical weapons, and their production facilities.

According to Article 4, states parties shall destroy all their chemical weapons in accordance with the provisions of the Verification Annex, to begin no later than two years after the entry into force for that state party and finish destroying the weapons not later than ten years after. If a state is not able to ensure the destruction of all its chemical weapons in category I (high-risk toxic chemicals) within the ten-year destruction deadline, the period may be extended by up to five years (see part IV(A) of the verification annex).

Article 5 requires states parties to destroy all chemical weapon production facilities and related facilities and equipment, within ten years after entry into force.

Article 6 stipulates that states parties have the right, subject to the provisions of the Convention, to develop, produce, otherwise acquire, retain, transfer, and use toxic chemicals and their precursors for purposes not prohibited under the Convention. Activities (i.e., chemicals and facilities) not prohibited under the CWC must be declared and may be inspected and verified by the OPCW.

In accordance with Article 7, states parties shall take the necessary measures to implement their obligations under the Convention, including prohibiting any activity that is prohibited under the Convention, and enacting penal legislation regarding such activity. To fulfill its obligations under the Convention, each state party shall designate or establish a national authority to serve as the national focal point for effective contact with the OPCW and other states.

Article 8 deals with the establishment of the OPCW. The purpose of the Organization is to achieve the object and purpose of the Convention and to ensure that its provisions are implemented, including provisions concerning international verification of compliance with the Convention. OPCW's purpose is also to provide a forum for states to consult and cooperate with one another.

The headquarters of the Organization is in The Hague, the Netherlands. States parties meet for regular, annual conferences where any questions, matters, or issues within the scope of the Convention are considered. The Conference also oversees the implementation of and reviews compliance with the Convention, and promotes its object and purpose.

The Executive Council and the Technical Secretariat for the CWC were established by the same article. The Executive Council is the executive organ of the Organization and consists of forty-one members, elected for two years. The Technical Secretariat assists the Conference and the Executive Council and carries out the verification measures provided for in the Convention.

The Convention's verification annex contains comprehensive and detailed provisions for establishing an effective verification system through a very intrusive inspection regime. Its purpose is to build confidence between states parties so that they can be assured that the Convention's obligations are met by all the other parties, and to detect any violations of the Convention, for example chemical weapons being secretly developed and produced. States must declare if they possess chemical weapons, their facilities, and equipment for producing chemical weapons, as well as shipments and reception of such weapons and facilities. The verification rules also provide for plans, principles, and methods of destruction of chemical weapons, facilities, and production equipment, as well as rules for executing inspections. The CWC also regulates the conversion of chemical weapons production facilities to purposes that are not prohibited under the Convention, and provisions for declarations, inspection, handling, and destruction of old and abandoned chemical weapons. The verification annex also contains rules for activities not prohibited under the Convention, i.e., chemicals used for research, medical, pharmaceutical, agricultural, or other peaceful purposes.

Finally, the verification system contains provisions on inspections of declared facilities, inspections in case of suspicion of violation of the Convention, and inspections in cases of alleged use of chemical weapons. Article 9 of the Convention authorizes the right of each state party to request an on-site challenge inspection of any facility or location in the territory of any other state party to clarify and resolve any questions about possible non-compliance with the provisions of the Convention. The verification annex further regulates challenge inspections, according to Article 9. However, no state party has yet exercised this right to request an on-site challenge inspection. One of the reasons for this may be that the requesting state would need to provide convincing evidence of its suspicion of the alleged violation.

Article 11 on economic and technological development states that the provisions of the Convention shall be implemented in a way that avoids hampering the economic and technological development of states, and international cooperation in the chemical field for purposes not prohibited under the Convention. States thus continue to have the right to participate in the international exchange of scientific and technical information and of chemicals and equipment for the production, processing, or use of chemicals for purposes not prohibited under the Convention. States shall not maintain any restrictions that would restrict or prevent trade and the development and promotion of scientific and technological knowledge in the chemical field for industrial, agricultural, research, medical, pharmaceutical, or other peaceful purposes. Export controls of chemicals and equipment with dual use for both peaceful and military purposes are conducted by the Australia Group (see chapter 13).

In cases where a state's activities prohibited under the Convention may result in serious damage to the object and purpose of the Convention, the Conference of States Parties may recommend collective measures to states in conformity with international law (Article 12) on measures to redress a situation and to ensure compliance, including sanctions. In cases of particular gravity, the Conference shall bring the issue to the attention of the UN General Assembly and the Security Council.

Resolution 42/37C of 1987 gives the UN secretary general a mandate to investigate the possible use of chemical, biological, or toxic weapons that may constitute a violation of the 1925 Geneva Protocol.

Comment

The challenges for fully implementing the CWC and thus for completely eliminating all chemical weapons in the world by destroying them, consist, among other factors, in the fact that many chemical weapons in declared stocks – mainly in Russia and the United States – have not been destroyed within the time limits stipulated in the Convention. Neither Russia nor the US, which have by far the biggest stocks of chemical weapons – approximately 40,000 and 28,000 tons respectively – has been able to comply with the deadlines for the destruction of its chemical weapons stockpiles. In 2012, both countries had their destruction deadlines extended. Russia has destroyed about 85 per cent of its chemical weapons, equivalent to 33,800 tons, and is expected to have destroyed the remaining 6,200 tons of chemical weapons only by the end of 2020. By April 2012, the United States had destroyed 90 per cent (24,900 tons) of its chemical weapons. It is expected that the destruction of the remaining 2,800 tons will only be completed in 2023. The Russian destruction programs have received massive financial and technical assistance from the United States and from the EU (see chapter 5 on the G8's Global Partnership).

Albania, India, Iraq, Libya, and Syria have also made declarations on their stocks of chemical weapons – a total of approximately 3,600 tons. Albania, India, Libya, and Syria have completed their destruction programs. Iraq still has large stocks of chemical weapons, which were encapsulated in the 1990s and sealed by UN weapons inspectors (UNMOVIC).

Since the CWC entered into force, approximately 60,000 tonnes, or 90 per cent, of the world's declared stockpile of 65,800 tonnes of chemical agent have been verifiably destroyed. But the stocks of chemical weapons and the presumed continuation of chemical weapons programs in several countries, possibly also continuing in North Korea, which has not adhered to the CWC, give rise to concern. Insufficient OPCW verification and inspection activities are also causes for concern.

Although so far, chemical weapons have been used mainly by governments, the possible use of chemical weapons by so-called non-state actors, including terrorist organizations, represents the biggest actual threat, concern, and challenge. In view of the technical difficulties in producing – and especially storing and spreading – chemical weapons, the fear of new terrorist attacks with chemical weapons is now more focused on terrorist attacks on chemical production facilities and on the transportation of hazardous chemicals, especially after the catastrophic accident in 1984 at a chemical plant manufacturing pesticides in Bhopal, India, where more than 3,000 people died. That same year, an explosion at a facility for liquid gas storage in Mexico City killed more than 500 people. National governments should therefore strengthen their monitoring and ensure that chemical industry plants have sufficient security measures to counter possible terrorist attacks.

In his article "The Future of Chemical Weapons" (2009), Jonathan B. Tucker, the late American expert on biological and chemical weapons, points out that there are reasons to be worried about a possible future resurgence of a chemical weapons threat. According to Tucker's assessment, this is due to the globalization of the chemical industry and the emergence of new destabilizing technologies in the chemical field, which will make it easier to produce chemical weapons. The materials, equipment, and technical knowledge for manufacturing chemical weapons are far more easily accessible to states and non-state actors, including terrorist organizations, than for nuclear and biological weapons. After the greater part of the global declared stocks of chemical weapons has been destroyed, the challenge for the future complete implementation of the CWC is now to prevent chemical weapons from proliferating and to ensure protection against non-peaceful uses of chemicals, equipment, and dual use technologies, which can be used both for peaceful and military purposes.

Another serious problem affecting human health and the environment is the hundreds of thousands of chemical weapons that have been dumped into the sea or buried in the ground before dumping was banned by the CWC. According to the verification annex (Part IV (B)), old chemical weapons (produced before 1925) and abandoned chemical weapons (produced after 1 January 1925) on the territory of another state party must be destroyed. One of the greatest destruction projects is the destruction of the hundreds of thousands of chemical weapons left by Japan in China.

8

Other Types of Weapons
of Mass Destruction

RADIOLOGICAL WEAPONS

Radiological weapons are weapons containing radioactive material, for example low-enriched or depleted uranium (toxic, radioactive heavy metal) and are designed to spread the materials by using conventional explosives. No nuclear explosion occurs. A radiological weapon is not a nuclear bomb, but is often called the "poor man's atomic bomb," a "crude nuclear device," or a "dirty bomb." Depleted uranium is found in large quantities in many countries in the form of stocks of waste from the production of nuclear weapons and from spent nuclear fuel that has been used in civil nuclear power plants. Many of the storage facilities for spent nuclear fuel are not adequately guarded against theft or sabotage. Other radioactive substances are stored and used in large quantities in laboratories in the health sector and in industrial processes, for example in factories for food irradiation. These radioactive materials may be used to manufacture radiological weapons. The material for producing a radiological weapon is much easier to obtain, and manufacturing a radiological bomb far less technically complicated, and much cheaper, than building an atomic bomb.

Unlike nuclear weapons, the detonation of radiological weapons does not cause widespread material destruction. But the radioactive fallout may cause significant loss of life, can have large-scale psychological effects, and may create long-term pollution, which may expose many people to harmful radiation. Depending on the weather and wind conditions, a radiological bomb blast could create panic and fear in the population and economic chaos in the affected community. In the longer term, a radiological bomb blast could cause many deaths as a result of the carcinogenic dispersion and radiation of radioactive uranium particles. Radiological weapons are therefore effective psychological weapons, primarily causing fear and economic chaos. There is a potential risk and growing fear that terrorist organizations might try to obtain and use radiological weapons. Many scientists and military leaders assess the threat from radiological terrorism as real and increasing. In the past ten years, the IAEA has registered 175 cases of terrorists and criminals smuggling and attempting to illegally acquire radioactive nuclear materials.

In November 1995, Chechen terrorists tried to detonate a radiological bomb in a Moscow park. The attempt failed when the bomb did not detonate.

The same terror effect as the detonation of a radiological bomb could be obtained by committing an act of sabotage against a nuclear reactor in a civilian nuclear power plant, whereby large amounts of radioactive materials could be spread in the air. The most serious radiation accidents at nuclear power plants – the Three Mile Island accident in Pennsylvania, in March 1979, the Chernobyl disaster in Ukraine in April 1986, and the Fukushima nuclear disaster in Japan in March 2011 – have shown the disastrous effects of radioactive leaks.

CYBERWARFARE

Cyberwarfare in the electronic space ("cyberspace") is politically motivated hacking, i.e., unauthorized intrusion in a computer network, with the purpose of destroying a computer network or obtain information (espionage). Designating an activity as cyberwarfare or cyberterrorism only applies to cyberattacks carried out in situations of armed conflict, not cyber actions carried out for criminal purposes, for example credit card fraud, child pornography, which are called cybercrime.[1] Cyberwarfare is carried out by so-called computer hackers (also called "crackers") or cyberwarriors, i.e., computer experts who are able to break into computer security systems (by breaking password barriers) and gain unauthorized access to restricted, confidential, or secret data in other computers and networks. The purpose of illegal intrusion into other computer systems may also be to destroy data and programs by spreading computer viruses. Cyberattacks may be directed toward public administration authorities, private companies (industrial espionage), or individuals.

In his book *Cyber War: The Next Threat to National Security and What to Do about It*, Richard A. Clarke, the former presidential security adviser and anti-terrorism expert, defines cyberwarfare as the actions of a nation state to penetrate into another state's computers or computer network to cause damage or collapse. Today, weapons and warning systems in modern warfare and national defence are extremely dependent on computers, which are used for communication and as systems for targeting and guiding missiles, drones etc., using satellites. Computer attacks can cripple both military computer systems and networks, and disrupt or destroy the functioning of nuclear reactors. Electricity grids, waterworks, hospitals, government and civil telecommunications systems, transport infrastructure, and financial and banking sectors, can also be destroyed paralyzing vital functions of the society attacked. Thus, cyberattacks or threats of cyberattacks can have a serious impact on deterrence capabilities, and have destabilizing consequences. Such attacks should be taken very seriously, not least the threat of cyberattacks committed by terrorist organizations. What is even worse is the possibility – which is real today – that an individual or a non-state actor such as a terrorist organization could breach security codes, hack into nuclear missile control and command centres, and simulate or launch a nuclear attack, thus provoking a retaliatory attack.

One of the many difficult issues of cyberwarfare is to identify the attacker to determine who the enemy is, against whom a possible counterattack could be directed. Another problem is that cyberattacks are invisible. They are carried out without warning and terminated in seconds. Normally, the attack is only detected when it is over, and the damage has been done. Therefore, defence systems against cyberwarfare must be both offensive, to avert attacks before they are made, and defensive, to prevent intrusion and damage by means of effective antivirus systems. Both in contemporary conventional wars and in possible future cyberwars, the enemy's communication and information systems (radars and satellites) will be the primary targets.

In April 2009, the *Wall Street Journal* reported that hackers had managed to penetrate the Pentagon's computer system and steal information about the electronic systems in the new Joint Strike Fighter, the

F-35. The aircraft manufacturer denied this. However, against this background, the Pentagon established a new Cyber Command (USCYBER-COM) in May 2010 to defend US military computer networks and develop counterattack capabilities against other countries' networks. China, Russia, North Korea, Iran, and Israel are also preparing for possible cyberwarfare. More than 120 other countries have developed both defensive and offensive computer programs for cyberwarfare.

In June 2012, the press reported that in 2009 the United States had carried out a cyberattack with the Stuxnet computer worm against the centrifuges for uranium enrichment in the Iranian nuclear facility at Natanz. Since 2006, there have been a number of similar incidents, including Israel's cyberattack against Syrian anti-aircraft systems in 2007 before the bombing of Syria's secret nuclear reactor, cyberattacks directed against public computer networks in Estonia in 2007, against the infrastructure in Georgia in 2008, and against the Saudi oil company Aramco and Qatar's RasGas in August 2012.

The EU's response to the cybersecurity issues of the European Union has been to establish the European Network and Information Security Agency (ENISA). In order to strengthen cybersecurity in general, the UN General Assembly has adopted several resolutions, in particular resolution 64/211 in 2010, to recommend how states can promote the protection of important information structures and improve cybersecurity.

Recently, the question has been raised as to whether a large-scale, devastating cyberattack could be considered an attack of the same standing as an attack with weapons of mass destruction, which could justify self-defence – possibly with the use of other types of weapons of mass destruction (nuclear, biological, or chemical weapons) in a retaliatory attack (see UN Charter, Article 51). In other words, could a massive computer attack be considered *casus belli* (cause for war), i.e., an act that could justify military retaliation? On the one hand, it may be argued that cyberattacks can cause much damage and chaos by paralyzing a society and an economy's vital functions. On the other hand, a cyberattack is not in itself lethal, although it may well be the indirect cause of loss of life, for example by paralyzing a control communication system for air traffic. In American military strategy, cyberattacks are considered a new and growing threat to national security and as a *casus belli* like other acts of war.

UNIDIR's publication *Cyberwarfare and International Law* (UNIDIR Resources 2011) by Nils Melzer discusses under which conditions a cyberattack can be considered a threat, use of force, or armed attack that gives the attacked state the right to exercise self-defence, and if a cyberattack can be considered a threat to international peace and security or a breach of the peace. If so, it could trigger a decision by the United Nations Security Council to impose intervention (sanctions or the use of military force). According to Melzer, there is no international consensus as to when a cyberattack can be classified as an international threat that could trigger the use of force in accordance with the Charter of the United Nations.

9

Weapons of Mass Destruction
in Outer Space

SMALL ARMS AND LIGHT WEAPONS

Introduction

The space race began in the 1960s, when outer space became a new area for exploration, military conquest, and competition. The superpowers began to be interested in the possibilities of placing weapons in outer space. Against this background, the United Nations General Assembly adopted resolution 1962 (XVIII) of 1963 in which the General Assembly declared that in the exploration and use of outer space, states should be guided by the following principle: "The exploration and use of outer space shall be carried on for the benefit and in the interest of all mankind and outer space and celestial bodies cannot be the subject for national sovereignty claims." The resolution was adopted unanimously. The resolution does not define the delimitation between outer space and the limit of the Earth's atmosphere, and it has still not been possible to reach international agreement on a precise definition of the limit between states' airspace and outer space. The most common delimitation of outer space is the limit of space beyond 100 kilometres above the Earth's surface.

OUTER SPACE TREATY

The first attempt at an international regulation of exploration and exploitation of outer space is the Treaty on Principles Governing the Activities of States in the Exploration and Use of Outer Space, Including the Moon and Other Celestial Bodies (Outer Space Treaty), which is the basic treaty on outer space. The treaty was adopted by General Assembly resolution 2222 (XXI) in 1966, opened for signature in January 1967, and entered into force in October 1967. One hundred and four states, including the five nuclear-weapon states, have ratified the treaty.

In Articles 1 and 2, the Outer Space Treaty repeats the contents of the above UN resolution by stating that "the exploration and use of outer space, including the moon and other celestial bodies, shall be carried out for the benefit and in the interests of all countries, ... and shall be the province of all mankind," and that "there shall be freedom of scientific investigation in outer space ... Outer space, including the moon and other celestial bodies, is not subject to national appropriation by claim of sovereignty, by means of use or occupation or by any other means." Article 4 contains the substance of the arms control provisions, restricting activities in two ways: first, by containing an obligation "not to place in orbit around the Earth any objects carrying nuclear weapons or any other kind of weapons of mass destruction, install such weapons on celestial bodies, or station such weapons in outer space in any other manner," and second, by limiting the use by all states parties of the moon and other celestial bodies exclusively for peaceful purposes and expressly prohibiting the establishment of military bases, installations, and fortifications, the testing of any type of weapons, and the conduct of military maneuvers. The use of military personnel for scientific research or for any other peaceful purposes is not prohibited, nor is the use of any equipment or facility necessary for peaceful exploration of the moon and other celestial bodies.

The treaty does not define what is meant by weapons of mass destruction, but it was the understanding during the treaty negotiations that WMD – besides nuclear weapons – would also include chemical and biological weapons. It was also the understanding that "peaceful use" of outer space does not exclude passive military use, for example by placing military satellites in orbit for reconnaissance, surveillance, early warning, and communication. The treaty does not prohibit the launch or passage in outer space of ballistic missiles with nuclear warheads, or the deployment of weapons other than WMD in space, for example laser weapons. The moon and other celestial bodies shall be used exclusively for peaceful purposes.

MOON AGREEMENT

On the initiative of the Soviet Union, the Agreement Governing the Activities of States on the Moon and Other Celestial Bodies (Moon Agreement) was adopted by resolution 34/68 of the General Assembly in 1979. The Agreement entered into force in 1984. Only sixteen states have ratified the Agreement. None of the space exploration states have adhered to it. Among the nuclear-weapon states, only France has ratified the agreement. India has signed but not yet ratified the agreement.

The Moon Agreement expands the provisions of the Outer Space Treaty and confirms the demilitarization of the moon (and other planets). According to Article 3, the moon shall be used by all states exclusively for peaceful purposes. The Agreement prohibits any threat or use of force or any other hostile act or threat of hostile act on the moon. States shall not send nuclear weapons or any other kinds of weapons of mass destruction in orbit around the moon, or place or use such weapons on the moon. The Agreement does not prohibit placing conventional weapons in orbit around the moon.

REGISTRATION CONVENTION

A third agreement on outer space has also been concluded: The Convention on Registration of Objects Launched into Outer Space (Registration Convention). The Convention was adopted by resolution 3235 (XXIX) of the General Assembly in 1974, opened for signature in 1975, and entered into force in 1976. The Convention has sixty-two states parties, including all the five nuclear-weapon states. The Convention complements the Outer Space Treaty, but states have often ignored the important requirement that the launching state must register in the UN Register space objects that it has sent into orbit around the Earth or further out in outer space. Information about the military functions of satellites launched by states active in outer space is not required.

NEGOTIATION OF A NEW TREATY
TO PREVENT AN ARMS RACE IN OUTER SPACE

In recent years, both military and civilian activities in outer space have been increasing drastically. Today all countries use outer space for peaceful purposes, including telecommunication via satellites. In spite of this development, no international legal regulation of space activities has taken place since the Outer Space Treaty was adopted in 1967. A large number of UN member states have stated that additional international regulation of space activities is needed to secure the current peaceful and responsible use of space and to prevent an arms race in outer space, which could threaten international peace and security. Many countries find that the Outer Space Treaty does not go far enough to guarantee that there will be no arms race in space. The regime needs to be strengthened for the peaceful use of outer space. There seem to be three options to enhance safety in outer space:

- ideally, a treaty banning the placement of weapons in outer space; or
- initially, a politically binding code of conduct for space activities;
- if agreement on this cannot be achieved, a first step could be adopting a set of confidence-building measures, including exchanging information and verifying the space activities of all countries.

Since the early 1980s, there have been efforts and proposals presented in the Disarmament Conference in Geneva (CD) to agree on opening negotiations in the CD on a treaty to prevent an arms race in outer space (PAROS). In 2000, China suggested that negotiations should be started on a new, legally binding international agreement prohibiting the militarization of outer space. According to the proposal, the agreement should prohibit tests, deployment, and use of weapons in outer space without putting obstacles to the use of outer space for peaceful purposes. The proposal was followed up in 2002, when China, together with Russia, prepared a working paper with the elements of a treaty on the subject. In 2006, China and Russia presented a draft treaty text. However, the proposal was received with resistance, especially from the United States. The American view was that there was no need for such a treaty – partly because the US thought that space activities in the existing treaties were sufficiently regulated, partly because it did not think that an arms race was taking place in outer space, that on the contrary, states were cooperating in the exploration of space in civilian space programs (the International Space Station) since 2000. However, in 2012, the US announced that it could support a code of conduct for activities in outer space to achieve sustainability and security in space. It should be noted that outer space is already militarized in the sense that military satellites are placed in orbit for surveillance, reconnaissance, and communication purposes. So far, no space weapons have been placed in outer space.

Since 2000, the UN General Assembly has adopted a number of resolutions about missiles and on preventing an arms race in outer space. The UN Secretariat has a special office to promote international cooperation on the peaceful uses of outer space – the United Nations Office for Outer Space Affairs (UNOOSA). Furthermore, since 2002, UNIDIR has held annual conferences on security in space and has published the report *Outer Space and Global Security* (2003).

In 2008, the European Union presented a draft of a politically binding international code of conduct for outer space activities containing guidelines for the responsible use of outer space and for space activities to improve security in space. The EU adopted a revised version of the code of conduct in 2010 and suggested convening a diplomatic conference where interested states could subscribe to it. The EU's latest draft code was presented in 2013. The EU code calls for greater cooperation on promoting security in outer space, both for civilian and military activities. It includes rules on the safety of space activities so as to avoid collisions with space objects and space debris, as well as exchanging information on space activities. At a meeting in Vienna in 2012, the EU launched a multilateral diplomatic process for discussing and negotiating the EU's international code of conduct for activities in outer space. The negotiations on the EU Code continue.

The 70th General Assembly adopted two resolutions on outer space: resolution 70/26, Prevention of an arms race in outer space, adopted with 179 votes in favour, none against, and 2 abstentions (the United States and Israel), and resolution 70/27, No first placement of weapons in outer space, adopted with 129 votes in favour, including China, Russia, India, Pakistan, and North Korea, 4 against (the United States, Israel, Georgia, and Ukraine), and 46 abstentions (France, the United Kingdom, and Canada).

10

Delivery Systems
for Weapons of Mass Destruction

MISSILES

Introduction

Today, ballistic missiles are spreading to a rapidly growing number of countries in all regions of the world. Many countries believe that possessing even short-range missiles provides an additional guarantee of their security and sovereignty. This development has shown that the existing non-proliferation regimes for missiles – the Missile Technology Control Regime and the International Code of Conduct against Ballistic Missile Proliferation – have not been effective enough in preventing the proliferation of missiles and missile technology. Missile equipment and technology is widely available. The spread of missiles and missile technology is having an increasingly negative impact on regional and global security.

The problem of the proliferation of the means of delivery – mainly missiles and aircraft – for weapons of mass destruction is closely connected with the proliferation of the weapons of mass destruction themselves. Most missiles have a longer range than airplanes, and missiles can fly faster than airplanes. Missiles can also be guided even more precisely to their targets than bombs released from aircraft. The proliferation of long-range ballistic missiles and of cruise missiles therefore gives rise to particular concern. The delivery vehicles for nuclear weapons are mostly ballistic missiles and cruise missiles. The problem of controlling the proliferation of military missiles is complicated because of their dual uses as space rockets for launching civilian satellites or manned spacecraft, which can be converted and used to deliver weapons of mass destruction.

Missiles are military rockets that are powered by their own engines for propulsion during the flight. Missiles can be guided to their targets either by remote control, using radio signals, or by radar (e.g., anti-aircraft or air-to-air missiles), by auto guidance (e.g., anti-aircraft missiles, which follow the radiation from the target's heat exhaust), or by programming a certain course, e.g., for intercontinental ballistic missiles and cruise missiles.

Ballistic missiles are missiles that are powered and guided by rockets in the initial part of their flight (boost phase). After the fuel in the rocket motor has been used up, the ballistic missile follows an unpowered free-falling curved orbit trajectory – mostly above the atmosphere – that is determined by gravity and aerodynamic drag. A ballistic missile is only guided during the initial short boost phase, but minor corrections can be made by means of control motors. Ballistic missiles can be launched from land (from silos in fixed sites or mobile launchers on heavy trucks or rails), or from submarines, surface ships, or aircraft.

The development and use of missiles began during the Second World War with the German V-1, which was an aircraft without a pilot, and later the V-2, a ballistic missile first launched in October 1942, and used against Paris and London in September 1944. Approximately 21,000 V-1s were launched against the Allies during the war, causing more than 18,000 casualties in London alone. During the last two years of the Second World War, 4,000 V-2 missiles were launched, mainly against London.

Missiles are classified in categories according to their launch platform (surface, aircraft, or ships), range, and target. There are seven main types of missiles according to launch platform: surface-to-surface, surface-to-air (SAM to target aircraft), surface-to-sea (to target ships), air-to-air (AAM against aircraft), air-to-surface, sea-to-sea, and sea-to-surface. Surface-to-surface missiles can be both long-range strategic intercontinental ballistic missiles (ICBM) and small man-portable air defence systems (MANPADS).

The main types of ballistic missiles are:

- tactical short-range missiles with ranges up to 300 kilometres (TBM),

- short-range missiles with ranges up to 1,000 kilometres (SRBM),
- medium-range missiles with ranges between 1,000 and 3,000 kilometres (MRBM),
- intermediate-range missiles with ranges between 3,000 and 5,500 kilometres (IRBM),
- intercontinental (or long-range) strategic missiles with ranges of over 5,500 kilometres and up to 12,000 kilometres (ICBM),
- intercontinental missiles with multiple independently targetable re-entry vehicles (MIRV),
- submarine-launched missiles with ranges of over 5,500 kilometres (SLBM),
- cruise missiles with typical ranges between 100 and 500 kilometres, and
- anti-ballistic surface-to-air missiles (ABM) designed to defend against intercontinental missiles.

Intercontinental ballistic missiles are surface-to-surface long-range missiles that can be launched from underground silos on a continent or from submerged submarines many thousands of kilometres from the target, and hit their targets on another continent after approximately thirty minutes. They are primarily designed to deliver nuclear weapons. All five permanent members of the UN Security Council – the United States, Russia, the United Kingdom, France, and China – have intercontinental ballistic missiles. The US, Russia, and China have both land-based and submarine-launched intercontinental ballistic missiles capable of delivering nuclear weapons. The British and French missiles armed with nuclear weapons are deployed on-board submarines. France also has airborne nuclear weapons. Israel and India also have intercontinental ballistic missiles. North Korea and Iran already possess medium-range missiles. The Iranian medium-range missiles have a range of 2,000 kilometres. In order to hit targets in Israel and Saudi Arabia, Iran would need missiles with ranges of 2,400 kilometres. Iran is developing such missiles. Today, thirty countries possess ballistic missiles. However, nineteen of these countries only have missiles with ranges under 1,000 kilometres, and seventeen countries have missiles with a range of only about 300 kilometres or less. This means that only eleven countries – the nuclear-weapon states, the nuclear-armed states, and Iran and Saudi Arabia – have missiles with long-range capabilities (i.e., ranges of more than 1,000 kilometres). According to the UN secretary general's 2002 report, *The Issue of Missiles in All Its Aspects*, the total number of ballistic missiles in the world was estimated to be 120,000 missiles.

Cruise Missiles

Cruise missiles are guided, self-navigating missiles that fly at supersonic or high supersonic speeds at extremely low altitude (as low as 20 metres from the surface). Their trajectory can be programmed to follow ground contours by means of guidance technology known as terrain contour matching (TERCOM). It is therefore much more difficult to detect cruise missiles in radar tracking systems than other types of missiles. Though the range of cruise missiles is normally between 100 and 500 kilometres, some can fly up to 2,500 kilometres. Their accuracy is very high (better than 10 metres), and they can be launched from land, air, or sea, including from submarines. Cruise missiles can be equipped with both conventional warheads and with nuclear weapons. Eighteen countries manufacture their own cruise missiles, and they are included in the weapons arsenals of eighty-one countries. Cruise missiles are therefore considered to be at least as great a threat as ballistic missiles.

Comment

Both during the Cold War and in the years following, medium-range missiles and intercontinental missiles for delivering nuclear weapons were the subject of reductions and prohibitions in treaties concluded between the United States and the Soviet Union/Russia.

The proliferation of missiles and of missile technology is closely linked to the risk of the proliferation of nuclear weapons and is therefore a growing concern. Without missiles, nuclear weapons have significantly less potential to cause mass destruction because of the vulnerability of bomber aircraft. Despite this, it has not been possible to obtain international agreement on a multilateral accord to regulate missile development, testing, production, acquisition, transfer, deployment, and use. The existing measures to regulate missiles are voluntary and informal, and have not been agreed to in legally binding treaties.

In 1987, however, the United States and the Soviet Union concluded an important bilateral agreement on the total abolition of all their intermediate-range and shorter-range missiles in the Treaty Between the United States of America and the Union of Soviet Socialist Republics (USSR) on the Elimination of their Intermediate-Range and Shorter-Range Missiles (the INF Treaty), of 1987 (see chapter 5).

UNMANNED AERIAL VEHICLES

Unmanned aircraft or unmanned aerial vehicles (UAVs) – or drones, as they are most often called today – are pilotless aircraft that can be reused several times (as opposed to cruise missiles). Drones are either auto-piloted by preprogrammed computers onboard using Global Positioning System (GPS) or are remotely piloted by an operator, who flies the drone from the ground on a computer, using the image transmitted from a camera onboard.

Drones are normally associated with military use but they are also increasingly used for search and rescue, surveillance and traffic, and weather monitoring, among other things. Military drones are used for a variety of tasks, including reconnaissance, surveillance, intelligence, target designation with laser for other weapon systems, and strikes with missiles, including targeted killings, or personality strikes, of individuals, for example identified leaders of terrorist organizations. The military use of drones has increased significantly since 2001. The technological development has been led by the United States and Israel. In recent years drones have been used in increasing numbers, including in the invasion of Iraq in March 2003. Drones continue to be used on a large scale by the US military for attacks in the war against the Taliban in Afghanistan, against Al-Qaeda, and strikes against terrorists in Pakistan, Yemen, and Somalia. There are more than fifty different types and sizes of drones, which are produced in more than fifty-five countries. More than a dozen countries have drones in their arsenals, primarily the United States (7,500 drones in 2012), Russia, and China. Iran also possesses some drones. The numbers and technical data of drones in the three latter countries are unknown. Drones have only been used in military operations by the United States, the United Kingdom, and Israel.

Comment

The advantages of using drones instead of aircraft are mainly that most types of drones are less expensive to produce than aircraft, and can be used in high-risk operations without risking loss, injuries, or capture of pilots. According to NATO's Strategic Concept of Employment for Unmanned Aircraft Systems in NATO (2010), using drones can "lower the risk and raise the political acceptance and confidence that high-risk missions will be successful." Many supporters of using drones instead of aircraft have argued that strikes from armed drones are more accurate and therefore cause fewer civilian casualties, an argument that has been contested because of the many civilian casualties, especially in Pakistan. The capability of drones to attack an enemy without risks for one's own pilots may make it easier for political decisions on the use of armed force and launch of an attack. This may have resulted in the increased use of drone attacks and, consequently, of growing civilian casualties.

Besides discussions of the ethical implications of the use of drones, there is also an increased focus on the legal implications. The use of armed drones is no different from the use of other conventional weapon systems, which are legal under international law. Drones are thus not by their nature illegal. The relevant question is how drones are used in practice, i.e., if their use in specific strikes on concrete targets is in conformity with applicable international law on the use of force and international humanitarian law. The rules on the use of force – *jus ad bellum* (law concerning war, prevention of war, or regulation of conditions under which the use of armed force is lawful) – are contained in the United Nations Charter, Chapter I, Article 2, paragraph 4. The rules of international humanitarian law – *jus in bello* (law of war, regulation of warfare, or of the means of war that are lawful) – are mainly laid down in the Geneva Conventions of 1949 and Additional Protocols I and II of 1977.

There is, however, one type of drone attack that is controversial in relation to the law of war on lawful targets, which is regulated in Additional Protocol I to the Geneva Conventions of 1949 and relates to the protection of victims of international armed conflicts. The basic rule in Article 48 of Protocol I states that the parties to a conflict shall at all times distinguish between the civilian population and the combatants and, accordingly, direct their operations only against military objectives. Article 51 further stipulates that the civilian population as such, as well as individual civilians, shall not be the object of attack. Acts or threats of violence whose primary purpose is to spread terror among the civilian population are prohibited. The controversial drone attacks are the so-called "signature strikes" that the United States has carried out in Pakistan and Yemen against persons gathered in larger groups of suspected terrorists whose identity is unknown. It has therefore not been possible to check whether the attacked persons are combatants taking part in hostilities, members of the local civilian population, or individual civilians who enjoy general protection against dangers from military operations. American drone attacks in Pakistan alone have resulted in hundreds of civilian casualties in connection with the killings of only some twenty senior Al-Qaeda leaders, causing widespread international criticism and condemnation.

MISSILE TECHNOLOGY CONTROL REGIME AND THE INTERNATIONAL CODE OF CONDUCT AGAINST BALLISTIC MISSILE PROLIFERATION

The existing agreements on the international regulation of missiles are the Missile Technology Control Regime (MTCR) and the International Code of Conduct against Ballistic Missile Proliferation (Hague Code of Conduct (HCOC)).

The Missile Technology Control Regime is an informal and voluntary association of countries that share the goals of non-proliferation of unmanned delivery systems capable of delivering weapons of mass destruction, and that seek to coordinate national export licensing efforts aimed at preventing their proliferation. The MTCR is the only multilateral arrangement covering the transfer of missiles and related equipment, materials, and technology needed to deliver weapons of mass destruction. The central stated goal in MTCR's guidelines for principles to follow in carrying out transfers of missiles or missile technology is to limit the risk of proliferation of weapons of mass destruction by controlling transfers that could contribute to delivery systems. The guidelines are also intended to limit the risk of controlled items (listed in the annex to the guidelines) and technology falling into the hands of terrorist groups and individuals.

The Control Regime was established in April 1987 to impose restraint and to control exports to prevent the proliferation of missile equipment, material, and related technologies and of missiles and unmanned aircraft (including cruise missiles and drones) that can carry explosive charges of more than 500 kilograms and have a range of more than 300 kilometres. In 1993, the missile regime's guidelines were extended to include missiles capable of delivering not only nuclear but also biological and chemical warheads, regardless of their weight and missile range. Originally, the Regime included the following seven countries: Canada, France, Italy, Japan, Germany, the United Kingdom, and the United States. Today, the MTCR has thirty-four principally western member countries, including twenty-two European countries, plus Australia, New Zealand, Argentina, Brazil, South Korea, South Africa, Turkey, Russia, and Ukraine. The member states coordinate their export policies and export control for missiles and missile technology by using common guidelines to issue export licenses and are committed to controlling their exports of missiles and missile-related technology. The MTCR has no secretariat; the French Foreign Ministry acts as the point of contact.

The MTCR has several major shortcomings: the membership is relatively small and limited to mainly western countries, without the participation of those countries of international concern who are pursuing the most worrisome political and military aspirations, such as Iran, North Korea, and Syria. The Control Regime is only politically binding. It is not a legally binding treaty, and it has no organs to monitor compliance with the Regime. The MTCR cannot take action against countries that are not members of the Regime and which have their own national missile programs. Several member countries have repeatedly violated and continue to violate the Regime without suffering any consequences. There is a well-founded suspicion that Russia has supplied missile technology to both India and Iran, contrary to MTCR restrictions.

The Regime has thus been unable to prevent the explosive proliferation of missiles and missile technology. The proliferation of missiles and missile technology to a growing number of countries has shown that the current system of international constraints is both inefficient and insufficient. The restrictions under the Missile Technology Control Regime need to be significantly improved, especially MTCR controls on cruise missile transfers. One of the most urgent priorities is the need to strengthen the ground rules for determining the range and payload of highly advanced cruise missiles and other unmanned aerial vehicles (see also pages 216–17).

The International Code of Conduct against Ballistic Missile Proliferation was adopted in 2002 in The Hague as an arrangement to prevent the proliferation of ballistic missiles (this is why it is called the Hague Code of Conduct (HCOC)). The Code has 137 participating states. The Foreign Ministry of Austria serves as the main contact point and coordinates the information exchange within the HCOC framework.

The HCOC is the only multilateral normative instrument to verify the spread of ballistic missiles capable of carrying weapons of mass destruction, and to promote international transparency and confidence-building about the spread of ballistic missiles. The Code does not ban ballistic missiles, but it does call for restraint in their production, testing, and export. However, HCOC does not cover cruise missiles, and is not legally binding. By subscribing to the HCOC, members voluntarily commit themselves politically to provide pre-launch notifications on ballistic missile and space-launch vehicle launches and test flights. Subscribing states also commit themselves to submitting an annual declaration of their policies on ballistic missiles and space-launch vehicles. The objective of the HCOC is to promote trust between the participants through their notifications before missiles and spacecraft are launched. In the annual declarations, the participating countries report on their missile policy with information on the number and types of missiles and spacecraft they have launched.

The major shortcoming of the HCOC is that those countries with the most worrisome political and military aspirations – for example, China, India, Iran, North Korea, Pakistan, and Syria – have not joined it.

MISSILE DEFENCE

Since ancient times, the emergence of new threats when new weapons have been invented or deployed has been meet with countermeasures in the form of new defence capabilities. In recent years, the development and proliferation of missiles capable of delivering weapons of mass destruction from a growing number of countries has provoked the development of new missile defence systems – also called missile shield against missile attacks – especially by the United States. There are several examples of the relationship between the development of a missile capability by one country and efforts to obtain missile defence systems in another country. For example, Iran's development of missiles induces Israel to develop its own missile defence system, China's and Pakistan's missile capabilities provoked India to create its missile defence, China's plans to develop its own missile defence against American and Russian intercontinental ballistic missiles, and South Korea and Japan building up missile defence systems against threats from North Korean medium-range missiles.

Missile Defence (MD) is a weapon system intended for active defence against missile attacks, originally with intercontinental missiles armed with nuclear warheads. Today, the new missile defence systems are also directed against attacks with short-range missiles with conventional weapons. Missile defence systems consist of anti-missile missiles designed for shooting down hostile missiles during their trajectory in the atmosphere and of radar systems to detect the enemy missiles and provide guidance for the defence missiles. According to the United Nations Office for Disarmament Affairs, the United States has spent more than $110 billion between 1983 and 2008 to develop its missile defence system. Russia has deployed a missile defence system around Moscow. Israel and Japan have also developed missile defence systems.

In 1972, the United States and the Soviet Union concluded the ABM Treaty. The purpose of the ABM Treaty was to limit the two former superpowers' defence against strategic intercontinental ballistic missiles, thereby maintaining their deterrence doctrines. The limitation was that each party could only have two ABM systems, one around their capital and one defending an area of ICBM launch silos. At each location, a maximum of 100 anti-ballistic missiles could be deployed. In 1974, the parties signed a protocol amending the ABM Treaty so that each party could have only one ABM system. In June 2002, the United States decided to withdraw from the ABM Treaty so it could develop a new ballistic missile defence system that included land-based missile defence systems in California and Alaska.

During the Cold War, the United States planned to deploy weapons in the outer space – the so-called Strategic Defence Initiative (SDI) or Star Wars project. The American space weapons were supposed to counter an attack from the Soviet Union by using laser beam weapons to shoot down attacking Soviet ballistic missiles. The debate on the SDI project was initiated during the Reagan administration in 1983, but after the collapse of the Soviet Union in 1991, the United States declined to realize the project.

During the Bush administration, the United States planned to deploy ballistic missile defence interceptors in Eastern Europe. The American missile defence would consist of a missile-tracking radar located in the Czech Republic and ten land-based anti-missile interceptors, to be placed in Poland where the anti-ballistic missiles were supposed to defend the European NATO member countries against the growing missile threat from certain countries in the Middle East, especially from Iran. America's planned missile defence in Europe was met with strong opposition from Russia which considered the US's missile defence as turned against Russian strategic ballistic missiles. In September 2009, President Obama abandoned his predecessor's proposed missile defence in Eastern Europe. Instead, the US continued its development of the ship-based missile defence system ("Aegis") against short- and medium-range ballistic missiles. This system is now deployed on twenty-six US Navy cruisers and destroyers.

At the NATO Summit in 2010 in Lisbon, NATO and Russia agreed to cooperate on developing a missile defence system against ballistic missiles. In 2011, however, the Russian government announced that it would not continue to reduce its numbers of strategic or tactical nuclear weapons until the United States had given assurances that the planned US missile defence was not directed against Russia. At their summit in Chicago in May 2012, the NATO countries announced that the first phase of a joint NATO missile defence system to protect a limited geographical area in southeastern Europe, had been operational. Coverage of most of the other European countries would be in place in 2015, and for countries in Northern Europe only after 2018. The European part of the missile defence would be integrated under NATO's command. The first phase of the system consisted of radar located in Turkey and an American naval vessel armed with anti-missile missiles deployed in the eastern Mediterranean. Subsequently, an expanded missile defence system of interceptors would be located in Romania and Poland. Part of NATO's missile defence will be the US missile defence system in Europe, the so-called European Phased Adaptive Approach (EPAA), which was announced in 2009. A planned fourth and final phase of the EPAA, which would be implemented in 2020, aimed at the potential threat from Iranian intercontinental ballistic missiles, was abandoned in 2013.

Comment

The proliferation of missiles and missile technology to a fast-growing number of countries, including countries in the Middle East that are of concern to western countries – especially Iran – has advanced the development and expansion of American and NATO missile defence systems, and made the prospect of achieving broad international agreement on a new global, legally binding treaty on international regulation (non-proliferation) of missiles and missile technology even more remote. Today missiles constitute an essential component of both defensive and offensive weapons systems, including in the nuclear deterrence strategies. It is therefore probably unrealistic to expect that a global, legally binding regulation of the development and possession of missiles would be adopted. A possible first step could be to adopt limited regional agreements to limit missiles in certain regions as well as to adopt confidence-building measures, including exchange of information on existing missile systems and national missile development programs as well as planned space launches.

Conventional Weapons

Conventional weapons are defined as weapons that are not weapons of mass destruction. They are divided into two major categories: heavy conventional weapons, and small arms and light weapons (SALW). Heavy conventional weapons include tanks, armoured combat vehicles, artillery (guns, howitzers, mortars, and multiple rocket launchers with a calibre (the inside diameter of the barrel of the gun) of 100 millimetres and above, combat aircraft, attack helicopters, and warships. Small arms and light weapons are defined as any weapon (and its ammunition) in the categories of pistols, revolvers, rifles, submachine guns, machine guns, heavy machine guns, mortars, rocket launchers (portable anti-tank weapons and MANPADS) with a calibre of less than 100 millimetres, hand-grenades, anti-personnel mines (APM), and cluster munitions (bombs).

There has been less public awareness and focus on conventional weapons than on weapons of mass destruction. This may seem paradoxical in view of the fact that nuclear weapons have not been used for more than seventy years and biological and chemical weapons have only been used in a few cases over the past few decades. Conventional weapons are by far the most widespread weapons. Virtually all states have them and they are also the most used weapons. Small arms and light weapons especially are easy to access in many countries, and have been used in numerous international conflicts and civil wars by rebel groups. Small arms are also widely used by criminals, especially in drug crimes. The arms trade is discussed in chapter 13.

11

Heavy Conventional Weapons

TREATY ON CONVENTIONAL ARMED FORCES
IN EUROPE (CFE)

Introduction

By the end of the Second World War in Europe, the Allied victors were deploying large troops and holdings of conventional weapons and equipment. The arms build-up and the concentration of armed forces and weapons in Europe continued shortly after the end of the war and continued during the Cold War. It was only at the beginning of the 1970s that the tense security relationship between the two military blocs – NATO and the Warsaw Pact – improved somewhat, allowing the start of negotiations on limitations of conventional weapons in Europe.

In 1973, the first negotiations began in Vienna – the so-called Mutual and Balanced Force Reduction Talks or MBFR negotiations. The purpose of these negotiations was initially to reduce and control conventional weapons and military forces in Central Europe, i.e., on the NATO side in the former West Germany, the Netherlands, Belgium, and Luxembourg, and in the former East Germany, Czechoslovakia, and Poland on the Warsaw Pact side. Due to their forces stationed in Central Europe, the United States, the United Kingdom, Canada, and the former Soviet Union also participated in the negotiations. On grounds of principle, France refused to participate in the negotiations, because it was opposed to the block-to-block approach and to regional arms control in Europe. Denmark, Greece, Italy, Norway, Turkey, Bulgaria, Romania, and Hungary had a special status of "indirect" participants in the negotiations. From 1975 to 1979 the negotiations also included the issue of reductions of nuclear weapons and their means of delivery. Although the MBFR negotiations lasted for 15½ years, they did not lead to any concrete result in the form of an agreement on reductions to conventional forces and weapons. The main reason for this was that both sides disagreed on whether reductions of the military forces on both sides should be symmetrical, or whether larger (asymmetric) force reductions should be made by the member countries of the Warsaw Pact. The latter alternative was NATO's negotiating proposition, which was justified by the much larger conventional forces (especially ground forces and tanks) in the Warsaw Pact countries. NATO wanted these larger forces reduced to the same level as their own. The two sides also fundamentally disagreed about the method of calculating the numbers of personnel and equipment in the armed forces of the Warsaw Pact area and about verifying compliance with any agreement. The US's political motivation for participating in the MBFR negotiations was – in addition to seeking détente and to limiting the military confrontation in Europe through arms control – the desire to reduce the American military forces stationed in Western Europe. The Soviet Union considered the MBFR negotiations an opportunity to confirm the borders in Europe after the Second World War and at the same time reduce the US military presence in Europe. The latest negotiating proposals were submitted in 1985. The MBFR negotiations formally ended in 1989.

Despite the failure of the MBFR negotiations, they were an essential starting point and the basis for later negotiations on conventional armed forces in Europe. The background for the beginning of these new negotiations was a speech by Mikhail Gorbachev in Berlin in April 1986, in which he suggested that an agreement should be concluded to reduce all conventional land and air forces of the European countries and the American and Canadian forces stationed in Europe, with the area of the reductions covering the entire European continent from the Atlantic to the Urals. The initiative of taking new steps toward conventional disarmament and arms control was accepted and confirmed by NATO in a declaration by the North Atlantic Council in 1986. The Warsaw Pact countries collectively confirmed Gorbachev's proposal in a declaration in 1986.

CFE *Negotiations*

On this basis, informal discussions were initiated in 1987 between the then-sixteen NATO countries on the one hand and the seven former member states of the Warsaw Pact (WP) on the other. In 1989, the two parties agreed on a mandate for negotiations on conventional armed forces in Europe. The main elements of the mandate for the negotiations were as follows:

- The participants in the negotiations should be all twenty-three member countries of the two military alliances – NATO and WP.
- The negotiations should take place within the framework of the CSCE process.
- The aim of the negotiations should be to strengthen stability and security in Europe by establishing a secure and stable balance of conventional armed forces in Europe at lower levels, i.e., conventional weapon systems and equipment.
- Disparities prejudicial to stability and security should be eliminated.
- The capability for launching surprise attack and for initiating large-scale offensive action should be eliminated.
- The agreement should apply to all land territories of the participants on the European continent from the Atlantic Ocean to the Ural Mountains, and for the Soviet Union should include the entire Soviet territory west of the Ural River and the Caspian Sea.
- The negotiations should not include nuclear weapons, chemical weapons, or naval forces.
- Compliance with the agreement should be verified, including through the right of the participating states to on-site inspections and exchanges of sufficiently detailed information on the size of weapons holdings and geographical location.
- The agreement should be legally binding under international law.
- The venue for the negotiations should be in Vienna.
- All decisions in the negotiations should be taken by consensus.

CFE *Treaty*

The negotiations on the CFE Treaty started in Vienna in March 1989 at a time of political upheaval of historic significance and with new security challenges in Europe: the fall of the Berlin Wall on 9 November 1989 and the unification of the Federal Republic of Germany and the German Democratic Republic (GDR) on 3 October 1990. After the German unification, the final part of the CFE negotiations included the following twenty-two states: all the then-sixteen NATO countries: Belgium, Canada, Denmark, France, Germany, Greece, Iceland, Italy, Luxembourg, the Netherlands, Norway, Portugal, Spain, Turkey, the United Kingdom, and the United States, and the six WP countries: Bulgaria, Czechoslovakia, Hungary, Poland, Romania, and the Soviet Union.

After less than two years of intensive negotiations, agreement was reached on the Treaty on Conventional Armed Forces in Europe (CFE Treaty), which was signed in Paris on 19 November 1990, immediately before the summit of heads of state and government of the CSCE countries. The CFE Treaty entered into force in November 1992.

The CFE Treaty was the first – and probably the last – comprehensive international agreement on disarmament and arms control of major conventional weapons. The CFE no longer includes Russia because Russia has suspended its participation. In light of the historic significance of the agreement for understanding the actual security situation in Europe, the main contents of the Treaty are described below.

TREATY LIMITS

The treaty established a limit of 20,000 battle tanks, 30,000 armoured combat vehicles, 20,000 artillery pieces, 6,800 combat aircraft, and 2,000 attack helicopters for each of the two groups of parties, i.e., NATO and WP. The weapons categories and types of weapons that are limited by the treaty are enumerated in the treaty's Protocol on Existing Types of Conventional Armaments and Equipment. The CFE also established active unit limits for each weapon category and ceilings for the number of weapons that are allowed to be held in storage sites. Within the total group ceilings, the states in each group could decide how they would distribute the group's total holdings among themselves in maximum permitted national holdings. The treaty contains sub-regional ceilings for the maximum holdings of the first three weapon categories that may be located within each of the four zones stipulated by the treaty. The purpose of the division into four zones was to prevent concentrations of equipment, especially in Central Europe and in the European part of the Soviet

Union, and thereby ensure regional balance. The zones are concentric circles. The ceiling of the innermost zone was the lowest and the ceiling in the outer zone was the highest. The system of sub-ceilings for the zones made it possible to move equipment from the inside outward, but not in the opposite direction, toward the centre. To prevent equipment from being too concentrated in the outer zone, limitations were established for the maximum quantities of equipment that could be moved to the flank areas (in Norway and Turkey, on NATO's side).

TREATY REDUCTIONS

The ceilings were higher than the total inventories of the NATO countries, except for battle tanks and certain combat vehicles. The CFE Treaty committed the NATO countries to reducing their total holdings of battle tanks, with approximately 3,600 tanks. The holdings that exceeded the numerical limitations in the ceilings had to be reduced during a reduction period that did not exceed forty months from entry into force of the treaty. The reductions were to be carried out by destroying the equipment or removing it from the area of application, i.e., withdrawing American and Soviet forces in Europe.

TREATY VERIFICATION

The treaty contains comprehensive provisions on verification. By inspecting the territories of the other states parties it became possible to verify that the reductions of the excess equipment were actually carried out and that the limitations on the maximum allowed holdings were respected. More than 5,500 CFE inspections have been carried out. The treaty's Protocol on Inspection does not allow an unlimited number of inspections. Each state was assigned a certain number of active and passive quotas for how many inspections the state had the right to carry out and how many inspections it was required to receive. The basis for the inspections was an exchange of information in which each state party reported the amount and actual location of its holdings in each weapon category. This information was updated on 15 December each year. The treaty thus allowed for full transparency and predictability about military matters in all the other states parties. This was in itself confidence- and security-building. A JCG was established, in which the states parties could address questions about complying and implementing the treaty, resolving ambiguities and differences of interpretation, and updating the list of existing types of treaty limited equipment. The states parties are to meet every five years to review the operation of the treaty.

Comment

The military significance of the CFE Treaty was somewhat diminished by the Soviet withdrawal of its forces from Czechoslovakia and Hungary in 1990, the unification of the two German states later the same year, and the dissolution of the Warsaw Pact in 1991. After the dissolution of the Soviet Union on 31 December 1991, the number of states in the eastern group of countries increased by the following eight successor states: Armenia, Azerbaijan, Belarus, Georgia, Kazakhstan, Moldova, Russia, and Ukraine. After Czechoslovakia was partitioned into the Czech Republic and Slovakia in January 1993, the eastern group of countries expanded to fourteen states. The territories of Estonia, Latvia, and Lithuania were kept out of the treaty's area of application, and the Baltic ceilings transferred to the Kaliningrad area.

Despite the significant change in the security situation in Europe as a result of these events, the CFE Treaty had great importance for the disarmament of conventional weapons in Europe and thus for strengthening and continuing stability and security in Europe. The treaty was particularly important for the NATO countries because the CFE committed the Soviet Union and the Central and Eastern European countries to large reductions in all weapons categories (except attack helicopters) – a total of approximately 37,000 pieces of equipment. This eliminated the former Soviet advantage in conventional forces in Europe and established an equilibrium of forces at lower levels between the two military alliances. Between 1990 and 1995, the CFE parties reduced their total holdings by about 69,000 pieces of treaty limited equipment, including 26,100 battle tanks, 23,300 armoured combat vehicles, 16,700 pieces of artillery, 2,600 attack helicopters, and 300 combat aircraft. Since 1995, the holdings have been reduced further, by approximately 3,000 conventional weapons. The CFE arms control regime removed the ability to initiate both surprise attacks and major offensive operations, thereby significantly reducing the risk of a military conflict in Europe with conventional weapons. The CFE Treaty was also a prerequisite for further disarmament initiatives in areas other than conventional weapons.

It is possible that large reductions in conventional armed forces in Europe would have become a reality even without the CFE Treaty. This actually happened in several states that unilaterally reduced their conventional forces to levels below their limits under the CFE. But the CFE promoted the disarmament process and secured arms control and disarmament through legally binding commitments to reduce holdings of conventional armaments, exchange information, inspect, and destroy weapons, providing each state with a comprehensive, accurate, and unprecedented knowledge and insight into the weapons holdings and locations of the other states parties' conventional forces. Furthermore, the CFE ensured that the implementation of the reductions and of the destruction of large quantities of conventional military equipment were verified through inspections and, thus, made irreversible.

CFE-1A Personnel Agreement

The CFE Treaty does not contain provisions for limiting and controlling the personnel strength of conventional armed forces. However, the treaty does contain an article that commits the states parties, after signing the treaty, to continue negotiations to limit personnel strength.

The negotiations on personnel limitations and ceilings for military personnel were resumed in November 1990 in the CFE-1A negotiations. The agreement on personnel reductions – the Concluding Act of the Negotiation on Personnel Strength of Conventional Armed Forces in Europe (known as CFE-1A) – was signed at the OSCE Summit in Helsinki in July 1992 and took effect in November 1992. The agreement is not legally binding under international law. It is only politically binding. The agreement establishes national ceilings for land-based, military personnel forces in each of the participating states. Internal security forces, personnel in transit from a location outside the area of application to a final destination outside the area of application who are in the area of application for no longer than seven days, and personnel serving under United Nations command are not included within the personnel ceilings. In the agreement, Russia's national personnel limitation is 1,450,000. The personnel ceiling for US forces stationed in Europe is 250,000. The agreement provides for annual exchange of information, notifications of changes in personnel strengths (increases of more than 35,000 personnel from the reserve forces), and verification of compliance.

CFE Adaptation Agreement

After the dissolution of the Warsaw Pact and the Soviet Union, the end of the Cold War, and NATO's enlargement, it became evident that the basic structure of the CFE Treaty's group ceilings and division into zones, which had been based on adversaries in two military blocs, was out of date and no longer made sense. Inspections within each group's inspection quota could not be carried out as provided for in the treaty in the changing political and geographical situation, particularly for the successor states of the former Soviet Union. At the first CFE review conference in May 1996, the states parties recognized that it was time to revise and update the CFE to adjust the treaty to the new security situation in Europe. A new negotiation process for adaptation of the CFE Treaty was initiated in January 1997.

The Agreement on Adaptation of the Treaty on Conventional Armed Forces in Europe was signed by the heads of state and government of the thirty CFE states parties at the OSCE summit in Istanbul in November 1999. The adaptation agreement was concluded in order to replace the CFE Treaty. The agreement's most important change to the CFE Treaty is the abolition of the group ceilings and zones. These were replaced by national ceilings and territorial ceilings for each state's maximum equipment holdings in the five categories of conventional weapons.

The CFE Adaptation Agreement has only been ratified by Russia, Belarus, Kazakhstan, and Ukraine. The agreement has therefore not yet entered into force. The entry into force of the adaptation agreement requires all parties to ratify the agreement.

The Final Act of the Conference of the States Parties to the Treaty on Conventional Armed Forces in Europe was signed at the same time. The Final Act required that Russia withdraw its forces and equipment from Moldova and reduce its equipment in Georgia (battle tanks, armoured combat vehicles, and artillery systems) before 31 December 2000. Because Russia has not fulfilled these obligations in the Final Act (the "Istanbul commitments"), the NATO countries have refused to ratify the Adaptation Agreement.

CFE Treaty Suspension by Russia

Since the CFE Adaptation Agreement has not yet entered into force, it follows from the Law of Treaties that the original CFE Treaty formally remains in force.

However, Russia brought the continued validity and application of the CFE Treaty to an end, when it unilaterally suspended its implementation and compliance with the CFE Treaty in a statement of 14 July 2007, with effect 150 days later – i.e., from 12 December 2007. In a speech in the Russian Parliament (the Duma) in April, President Putin announced a moratorium on Russia's participation in and observance of its obligations under the CFE until all NATO countries had ratified the CFE Adaptation Agreement and had started to implement the agreement. Russia also announced that it would not participate in the CFE information exchanges, notifications, or inspections, and that it would no longer be bound by the limitations of the treaty. Putin's decree on the implementation of Russia's moratorium on the CFE Treaty was unanimously adopted by the Duma in November the same year. During the debate in the Duma, it was reiterated that the "Istanbul commitments" were not relevant or had no connection with the ratification of the CFE Adaptation Agreement. However, it was also emphasized that Russia wanted to continue the dialogue on the CFE regime's future and that Russia could resume its participation in the treaty as soon as all the Russian requirements had been met. Russia's main requirements were ratification of the Adaptation Agreement, concessions from the United States concerning the establishment of a missile defence in Europe, and removal of restrictions for the Russian forces in the flank areas – particularly in the southern part of North Caucasus.

Since December 2007, Russia has not exchanged information on the numbers, locations, and movements of its conventional weapons and equipment according to the terms of the CFE Treaty. Nor has Russia allowed any inspections on Russian territory. Russia justified its suspension of the CFE by arguing that the NATO countries had not ratified the CFE Adaptation Agreement and had made their ratification conditional on Russian troop withdrawals from Moldova and force reductions in Georgia. According to the Russian view, the withdrawal of those forces is a bilateral matter between the states concerned. Russia's decision to suspend its participation in the CFE was also based on Russia's opposition to American plans to deploy missile defence systems in Poland and the Czech Republic, which would change the security situation in Europe. Another factor was the admission of the Baltic countries in NATO. Russia demanded that Estonia, Latvia, and Lithuania become participants in the CFE and thus be imposed limits on their national and territorial weapons holdings. Putin repeatedly talked about the need for a new European security architecture – without giving details on the concrete content of such new arrangements.

The NATO countries tried to solve the problems caused by Russia's suspension by presenting a so-called parallel action plan which would require the two parties to have reciprocal and simultaneous obligations to promote adherence to the adapted CFE Treaty. According to this plan, the NATO countries would initiate their ratification processes concurrently with Russia's fulfillment of its "Istanbul commitments" to withdraw and reduce Russian forces and equipment from Moldova and Georgia. The crisis in Georgia in August 2008 put an end to the negotiations.

Comment

Seen from the perspective of international law, the Russian suspension of its participation in the CFE Treaty must be considered an unlawful cancellation. The CFE does not allow states to suspend their participation in the Treaty. If a state withdraws from the treaty, it withdraws from the cooperation under the treaty (see Article XIX of the CFE). The suspension is also a violation of Article 60 of the Vienna Convention on the Law of Treaties, which states that "A material breach of a multilateral treaty by one of the parties entitles the other parties by unanimous agreement to suspend the operation of the treaty in whole or in part or to terminate it either in the relations between themselves and the defaulting state, or as between all the parties." None of the other states parties has violated the CFE, and Russia has not raised this as an argument for its suspension of the treaty. The right to terminate, withdraw from, or suspend a treaty if a fundamental change of circumstances has occurred is regulated in Article 62 of the Convention on the Law of Treaties: "A fundamental change of circumstances may not be invoked as a ground for terminating or withdrawing from a treaty if the fundamental change is the result of a breach by the party invoking it either of an obligation under the treaty or of any other international obligation owed to any other party to the treaty."

Although negotiations on the dispute about the future CFE regime were resumed, they did not lead to any result and were stopped in 2011. The NATO countries therefore temporarily suspended their ratification processes. The negotiating positions seemed to be locked. Against this background, in November 2011 the United States ceased meeting some of its CFE obligations to Russia. The other NATO countries, as well as Georgia and Moldova, did the same. Thus, the CFE Treaty has ceased to have effect in relation to Russia. CFE cooperation without Russia's participation is of very limited significance, although inspections are still carried out between the other states parties. The unfortunate conclusion is that the main purpose of the CFE Treaty is no longer being fulfilled. According to repeated Russian statements, there are no prospects for reviving the treaty.[1]

It seems that the most promising way forward for creating a new conventional arms control regime in Europe would be to replace the CFE by a system of transparency measures only, without numerical or geographical limitations for the armed forces. Such a mechanism should be more comprehensive than the existing confidence- and security-building measures in the Vienna Document. The transparency would provide both the NATO member countries and Russia with actual information about the other side's military capabilities and early warning about increases and movements of their military forces, thus contributing to predictability and confidence in Europe.

The negative development in arms control of conventional armed forces in Europe is of continued concern. Today, the combined conventional forces in Europe of all the NATO countries are both numerically and technologically superior to the Russian conventional forces. As a result, there is a risk that Russia – because of this new inequality in conventional forces – will increasingly base its future defence on tactical nuclear weapons. Discontinuing the CFE could also lead to a renewed build-up of the conventional forces in Europe and weaken the trust between the West and Russia, which is already low because of Russia's illegal annexation of Crimea in March 2014 and the subsequent conflict in Ukraine.

VIENNA DOCUMENT ON CONFIDENCE- AND SECURITY-BUILDING MEASURES

The Vienna Document 1990 on the Negotiations on Confidence- and Security-Building Measures (Vienna Document) was signed by the (then) thirty-five CSCE member states on 19 November 1990. The Vienna Document contains a number of confidence- and security-building measures on the military activities of the CSCE countries. These include provisions on annual exchanges of information about military forces and equipment, notifications of military exercises of a certain size (more than 25,000 troops), exchange of observers, and mutual inspection and evaluation visits. The purpose of the Vienna Document is to strengthen security in Europe by providing greater openness and transparency between states, thereby increasing confidence and military stability in the European region. The Vienna Document is only politically binding – it is not a treaty.

Today the Vienna Document has been signed by all fifty-seven actual OSCE member states. The agreement is a further development of the principles of the Helsinki Final Act of 1975 and the Document of the Stockholm Conference on Confidence- and Security-Building Measures and Disarmament in Europe of 1986. The document has been modified and expanded several times (in 1992, 1994, and 1999) and was last updated in 2011. The Vienna Document is still being fully implemented by all the signatories as well as by Russia where observations and evaluation visits continue to be carried out. The implementation of the Document is discussed in the CSCE Forum for Security Co-operation (FSC), which meets in Vienna every week, and during annual review meetings.

OPEN SKIES TREATY

The initiative to establish an international regime for mutual air observations was originally put forward by President Dwight Eisenhower at a conference in 1955 between the United States, the Soviet Union, France, and the United Kingdom. However, the initiative was rejected by the Soviet Union. In 1989, President George H.W. Bush suggested that an "Open Skies" regime should be established as a confidence-building measure between East and West. It was proposed that the states participating in the Open Skies regime should allow overflights of each other's territories. The mutual observation flights should be carried out by unarmed aircraft equipped with cameras and other sensors.

The first round of talks between the twenty-three NATO and Warsaw Pact countries on the Open Skies regime began in Ottawa in 1990. After further rounds of negotiations in Vienna, agreement was reached on the Treaty on Open Skies, which was signed by the NATO countries and nine Eastern European countries, including Russia, at the opening of the CSCE follow-up meeting in Helsinki in March 1992. The Open Skies Treaty entered into force in 2002. The treaty currently has thirty-four states parties.

The purpose of the Open Skies Treaty is to promote openness and trust between the states parties and verify their compliance with arms control agreements, thus complementing the so-called national technical means of verification (satellite surveillance) in collecting military data. The treaty allows the parties to conduct reciprocal air observations, i.e., the right to fly over, observe, and photograph military activities, equipment, and installations in each other's territories. The treaty applies to all the territories of the states between Vancouver and Vladivostok. No areas are excluded from overflights. Each state party is required to accept a certain number of annual overflights (passive overflight quotas), depending on the size of the country. There are also fixed quotas for the states parties' own active overflights of the territories of the other states. More than 800 overflights have been completed under the Open Skies regime. The flights continue to be carried out, including over Russia. Under the treaty, an Open Skies Consultative Commission (OSCC) has been established in Vienna to deal with compliance issues.

12

Small Arms and Light Weapons, Inhumane Conventional Weapons, Anti-Personnel Mines, and Cluster Bombs

SMALL ARMS AND LIGHT WEAPONS

Introduction

Small arms and light weapons (SALW) include all firearms (and their ammunition) in the categories of pistols, revolvers, rifles, submachine guns, and light machine guns (all small arms), as well as heavy machine guns, mortars, rocket launchers (portable anti-tank weapons and MANPADS or light anti-aircraft missiles) of less than 100 millimetres calibre, hand grenades, anti-personnel mines (APM), and cluster munitions (bombs) (all light weapons).[1]

There is no universally agreed definition of small arms or light weapons. But it is widely recognized that both categories of weapons include both the weapons used by the military, security forces, and police, and the weapons that are commercially available in gun shops and purchased by civilians for personal protection or hunting. Small arms and light weapons may also be purchased or procured illegally and sold and used by irregular forces, terrorists, and criminal individuals or gangs.

At the request of the United Nations General Assembly, the secretary general, assisted by a panel of governmental experts, presented a report on small arms in 1997.[2] The report describes small arms as weapons manufactured for personal use and carried by one person as opposed to light weapons, which are used and transported by two or more persons or in a vehicle. The report concludes that there is a clear correlation between access to weapons and drugs- and arms smuggling and that the crimes and violence that are a result of the availability of small arms and light weapons inhibits development projects, economic assistance, and investment in developing countries.

The secretary general's report was the first to systematically map the types of small arms and light weapons that are actually being used in armed conflicts, and the nature and causes of the excessive and destabilizing accumulation and transfer of small arms and light weapons, including their illicit production and trade. Among the recommendations in the report was a call for the United Nations to consider the possibility of convening an international conference on all aspects of the illegal arms trade. The decision to convene the conference was taken by resolution 53/77 E, of 1998. The civil society organizations – in particular, the International Action Network on Small Arms (IANSA) – were critical to achieving consensus on convening the conference and played an important role in pushing the issue of SALW on the international agenda. The NGOs had pointed out the link between the small arms problem and human rights and development and humanitarian issues.[3]

Since 1995, the UN General Assembly has included the question of SALW on the agenda and adopted many resolutions on this item. The 70th General Assembly adopted resolution 70/49, The illicit trade in small arms and light weapons in all its aspects, which was adopted without a vote.

In recognition of the magnitude of the small arms problem and its negative consequences for maintaining international peace and security, the UN Security Council has since 1999 also included small arms and light weapons on its agenda every second year, when the Council holds a thematic discussion on SALW. In the chairman's statement from the first meeting in September 1999 the Security Council emphasized that the accumulation of small arms and light weapons poses a threat to international peace and security and contributes to causing and increasing the intensity and duration of armed conflicts. The Council called on member states to implement effective arms embargoes for countries that pose a threat to international peace and security or find themselves involved in an armed conflict, and recommended that peace agreements should contain guidelines to disarm, demobilize, and reintegrate former combatants. Resolution 2220 (2015) is the latest resolution of the Security Council on small arms and light weapons. The most recent report on small arms and light weapons from the secretary general to the Council is contained in document S/2015/289 of 2015.

The *Small Arms Survey Yearbook 2001: Profiling the Problem* sets the whole problem of small arms in perspective in the first sentence of the introduction: "At least 500,000 people are killed each year by small arms and light weapons. They die in an astonishingly diverse number of ways: as combatants in internal and inter-state wars; as participants in gang fights and criminal battles; as casualties of government-sponsored or condoned violence and terror; as innocent civilians trapped in deadly wars and social conflicts; and as victims of suicide, homicide, or random acts of violence." The number of deaths is 1,300 each day. The total number is higher than the number of deaths in almost all recent wars. Since 1990, approximately 4 million people have been killed by small arms and light weapons. It is therefore no exaggeration to call small arms and light weapons the real weapons of mass destruction. Most armed conflicts today are fought with small arms and light weapons: in civil wars, organized crime, including drug-related crime, gang violence, and terrorist attacks. In Mexico alone about 48,000 people have been killed over four years (2008–12) in drug-related violence in the war between the drug cartels and between these and the police and military – a war that is being fought mainly with small arms and light weapons.

Africa and Latin America are two regions where small arms and light weapons are widespread and have the greatest destabilizing effect. Economic and social development in many African countries has been impeded because of internal armed conflicts, to which the availability of small arms has contributed to flare up and continue the conflicts. In Latin America – and in particular in Colombia and Mexico and some of the Central American countries – drug-related crime is a serious social problem. The main concern in most Latin American countries is the rise in crime, particularly in major urban areas, which is mostly carried out with firearms.

Most small arms are owned by civilians. Most victims of small arms are civilians. The weapons are cheap to purchase and easy to operate, carry, and conceal. The widespread availability of small arms and light weapons and their ammunition in many countries is a key enabler of conflict. It is difficult to trace small arms, which are often transferred to criminals. According to the United Nations, around 8 million small arms are being produced each year. Today, the global number of small arms is about 875 million. The Small Arms Survey estimates that the value of the annual sales by authorized (legal) trade in small arms and light weapons is approximately US$7 billion. The United States is by far the largest import and export country of these weapons.

Comment

It is understandable and logical that the regulation of weapons in international law has been focused on introducing internationally applicable prohibitions and regulations of weapons of mass destruction. Obviously, these weapons have the potential to kill the biggest number of people. As a result of the prohibitions and regulations in the treaties and conventions on nuclear, biological, and chemical weapons, these weapons of mass destruction have been used very rarely. Nuclear weapons have not been used in more than seventy years.

The problem of small arms and light weapons and the many – mostly civilian – victims of small arms was first put on the international agenda after the end of the Cold War. In the beginning of the 1990s, the focus increased on small arms, which were increasingly spreading in large quantities to developing countries where internal conflicts had erupted. In recent decades, the light anti-aircraft missiles (MANPADS) have increasingly given rise to concern. About 500,000 of these weapons have been produced and many have been sold on the illicit arms market. The missiles, which are only about 1.8 metres long and weigh between 15 and 20 kilograms, are extremely effective because of their infrared (heat-seeking) targeting system and range: up to 6 kilometres in altitude, constituting a serious threat to low-flying helicopters and to both military and civilian aircraft during takeoff and landing.

United Nations Firearms Protocol

The international regulation of small arms and light weapons first began in 2001, when the United Nations General Assembly, by resolution 55/255, adopted the international, legally binding Protocol Against the Illicit Manufacturing of and Trafficking in Firearms, Their Parts and Components and Ammunition. The Protocol entered into force in 2005. The Protocol supplements the United Nations Convention against Transnational Organized Crime of 2008, whose purpose is to promote international cooperation on strengthening the prevention and combat of transnational organized crime.

Similarly, the purpose of the Firearms Protocol is to promote, facilitate, and strengthen cooperation between states to prevent, combat, and eradicate the illicit manufacture of and trafficking in firearms, and strengthen the prevention and control of transboundary organized crime. The parties to the protocol undertake to adopt laws that criminalize the illicit manufacture and trafficking of firearms and introduce rules on labelling and tracing firearms, and a licensing system for the export, import, and transit of firearms. The protocol has been ratified by 114 countries and signed by another 52 countries, including China, the United Kingdom, and Canada. The United States, Russia, France, Iran, Israel, and Pakistan are among the countries that have not signed.

United Nations Small Arms and Light Weapons Program of Action

The United Nations Conference on the Illicit Trade in Small Arms was held in July 2001 in New York, resulting in the unanimous adoption of the United Nations Programme of Action to Prevent, Combat and Eradicate the Illicit Trade in Small Arms and Light Weapons in All Its Aspects.[4] The Action Program is not legally binding under international law, only politically binding. The participating states in the Action Program agree to implement a wide range of measures at national, regional, and global levels to prevent, combat, and eradicate illicit trafficking of small arms and light weapons by monitoring the export, transit, and broking of transfers of small arms and light weapons. They must also promote the coordination of efforts and implement international measures to combat the illegal manufacture and transfer of small arms and light weapons.

To follow up on the decisions of the Conference, the participating states recommended that the United Nations General Assembly explore ways to adopt an international instrument to identify and trace illicit small arms, and consider further steps to enhance international cooperation to prevent, combat, and eradicate the illicit trade in small arms through professional arms brokers. They also recommended convening a review conference not later than 2006, and every six years thereafter, with follow-up meetings to be held every two years.

After the Action Program had been adopted, the president of the Conference made a final statement, expressing disappointment that, because of resistance from one country, the conference had failed to reach an agreement on the need to establish and maintain control of private possession of small arms by citizens and on preventing sales of small arms to non-state actors. This country was the United States.

United Nations Small Arms and Light Weapons International Tracing Instrument

Small arms tracing is "the systematic tracking of illicit small arms and light weapons found or seized on the territory of a state from the point of manufacture or the point of importation through the lines of supply to the point at which they became illicit." In December 2005, by a recorded vote of 151 in favour, none against, and with 25 abstentions (Latin American countries), the General Assembly adopted the International Instrument to Enable States to Identify and Trace, in a Timely and Reliable Manner, Illicit Small Arms and Light Weapons.[5] The International Tracing Instrument commits all United Nations member states to undertake measures to ensure specific marking and record-keeping standards for small arms and light weapons, and to use common rules to strengthen cooperation in tracing illicit firearms. However, it does not apply to ammunition, which still relies on an ineffective system of stamping and a patchwork of national regulations. The participating states report on a biennial basis to the secretary general on their implementation of the instrument, including their national experience in tracing illicit small arms and light weapons as well as the measures they take in the field of international cooperation and assistance. The states meet every two years to consider the national reports and review the implementation and future development of the Instrument.

Small Arms Policy in the United States

Opposition by the United States to the United Nations Program of Action for eradicating the illicit trade in small arms and light weapons was not unexpected. The American delegation made it clear on the first day of the United Nations Conference on the Illicit Trade in Small Arms in 2001 that it could not accept a ban on the right of citizens to possess small arms.

The background for the position of the United States on the right of private citizens to possess small arms, in particular handguns, is in the Second Amendment of the United States Constitution, adopted in 1791: "A well regulated militia, being necessary to the security of a free state, the right of the people to keep and bear arms, shall not be infringed." A militia is a group of non-professional soldiers, e.g., like the National Guard of the United States, which is the military reserve of the United States Armed Forces.[6]

This amendment may be interpreted as meaning that "in cases where a well-regulated militia is necessary for the security of a free state, the citizens' right to own and bear arms shall not be violated." This provision was included in the Constitution because small arms played an important role in colonizing America, especially for European immigrants' conquest of rural areas inhabited by the Indigenous populations. Arming citizens was also crucial during the fight for freedom against British forces during the American Revolutionary War (1775–83).

The interpretation of the Second Amendment in the United States Constitution and the very liberal arms legislation in most American states have been vigorously debated in American domestic politics and have been the subject of many analyses and judgments by courts in the United States. The controversial issue of American gun laws was demonstrated in the US Supreme Court's June 2008 decision in the District of Columbia v. Heller case. A majority of five judges confirmed a ruling by a district court that legislation banning handguns was unconstitutional because such legislation violated the Constitution's Second Amendment.

The majority ruled that Americans have an individual right to possess firearms, regardless of whether they are members of a militia, for traditionally lawful purposes, such as self-defence within the home. The majority of the judges in the Supreme Court rejected the argument by the four dissenting judges that the Second Amendment only secured the right to bear arms for members of a publicly regulated militia and did not restrict the legislature's right to regulate civil possession and use of firearms. In fifty American states it is legal to carry a firearm for protection and other lawful purposes. However, before a firearm may be purchased from a licensed dealer, manufacturer, or importer, a personal background check is required, according to the Brady Handgun Violence Prevention Act, signed into law by President Clinton in November 1993.

According to the 2008 majority ruling by the US Supreme Court, the right to private gun ownership in the home is not unlimited. It is still possible for individual states to regulate small arms by adopting legal provisions that may prohibit former convicted criminals or mentally disturbed individuals from possessing weapons, prohibit especially dangerous weapons, prohibit the presence of weapons in certain public places such as schools and government buildings, or introduce conditions and requirements for the commercial sale of arms to private citizens.

The discussion on regulating small arms for civilians has repeatedly flared up after major school shootings: In Littleton, Colorado, in April 1999, where twelve students and one teacher were killed; Blacksburg, Virginia, in April 2007, with thirty-two dead; and Newtown, Connecticut, in December 2012, with twenty-six victims, including twenty young children. Since 2013, there have been at least 150 school shootings in America – an average of nearly one per week. In President Obama's words, school shootings "have become routine."

According to "Gun Violence Archive,"[7] there were 330 mass shootings in the US in 2015. These are defined as incidents in which four or more people were shot and/or killed in a single event at the same time and location, not including the shooter. Gun violence caused 13,381 deaths in 2015 (an average of 36 per day) and almost 27,000 injuries. In 2015, there were five major mass shootings with more than eight casualties, the latest in Roseburg, Oregon, in October 2015, with ten killed and nine injured; and in San Bernardino, California, in December 2015, with sixteen killed and nineteen injured.

Comment

When will this gun madness stop?

There are more handguns per capita in the United States than any other country in the world – an estimated 300 million firearms – and one or more guns in forty per cent of all homes. Seventy million Americans own one or more guns.

The majority of the American population considers the right to own a firearm to defend themselves an inviolable right that is guaranteed in the Second Amendment, and there is a long and deep-rooted tradition of gun culture.

The most powerful American interest group of supporters of liberal arms legislation and defenders of the right of private citizens to own firearms is the National Rifle Association (NRA), which was founded in 1871. The NRA is a nonprofit organization that advocates for the right to own firearms. The Association has more than 5 million members and is considered one of the top three most influential lobbying groups in Washington. The NRA's yearly revenue exceeds US$250 million, roughly half of the income generated from fundraising. Millions of dollars are spent each year on lobbying to influence members of the US Congress to defend liberal arms legislation in the United States and to prevent any tightening of the legislation.

As established in the majority decision by the US Supreme Court in 2008, it would not be unconstitutional, as requested by President Obama in January 2013 and by many Democratic members of the US Congress, to ban certain types of particularly dangerous automatic weapons and large capacity magazines, and to also impose tighter controls of sales of firearms to former felons and mentally ill persons. In April 2013, an amendment bill (the Manchin-Toomey Bill) for tighter background checks fell short of the sixty votes required in the Senate by six votes.

As a first step, comprehensive, national background checks should be mandatory for all sales, including private sales on the Internet and sales at gun shows. Ninety per cent of the American population supports such background checks in order to prevent mentally disturbed and convicted persons from buying guns. Second, a nationwide ban on military assault weapons should be imposed to prevent private citizens from purchasing and possessing high-powered automatic assault rifles and submachine guns. Third, small arms with a large magazine capacity (more than ten rounds) should not be for sale to private persons. Moreover, gun-free zones should be established for schools, university campuses, shopping malls, and entertainment centres.

In order to reduce the numbers of killings by accidental shootings committed by children and by shootings with stolen guns, the new "smart pistol," produced by the German company Armatix, should be promoted in the United States and in other countries as well. This handgun, which is already on sale in California, is paired with a smart watch that, when worn, unlocks the pistol for use. To use the watch, the user must first enter a pin code, similar to unlocking a smart-phone. The gun cannot be fired without the watch.

Although the most recent polls show that 80 per cent of respondents are in favour of laws preventing the mentally ill from purchasing firearms, and 70 per cent are in favour of a national gun-sale database, there is, deplorably, still a majority of Republicans in the US Congress who are against tightening gun regulation.

At the global level, the United Nations Arms Trade Treaty of 2013 has made it illegal to sell small arms and light weapons to non-state actors (see chapter 13).

Regional Agreements on Small Arms and Light Weapons

EUROPEAN UNION JOINT ACTION

In December 1998, the Council of the European Union adopted Joint Action on the European Union's contribution to combating the destabilizing accumulation and spread of small arms and light weapons.[8] The Joint Action was updated in 2002[9] and has since been followed up in Council decisions on various implementation measures, including financial support to countries in Africa, Asia, Latin America, and the Balkans. In December 2005, the European Council adopted the EU Strategy to combat illicit accumulation and trafficking of SALW and their ammunition.[10] A Council Decision on EU action to counter the illicit trade of SALW by air was adopted in December 2010.[11]

OSCE DOCUMENT ON SMALL ARMS

In November 2000, the OSCE's Forum for Security Co-operation adopted the OSCE Document on Small Arms and Light Weapons.[12] The document contains concrete norms, principles, and measures to reduce the destabilizing accumulation and uncontrolled spread of small arms and light weapons and to combat the illicit trafficking of small arms and light weapons through national control measures for manufacturing, as well as the marking, registration, and export control of SALW. The OSCE document also contains rules for administering stocks, reducing surplus weapons, and destroying small arms. Since 2000, the OSCE has adopted a number of decisions on combating the illegal trafficking in small arms.

THE INTER-AMERICAN CONVENTION ON FIREARMS

In the Western Hemisphere, the member states of the Organization of American States (OAS), in 1997, adopted the Inter-American Convention Against the Illicit Manufacturing of and Trafficking in Firearms, Ammunition, Explosives and Other Related Materials.[13] The Convention entered into force in 1998 and has been ratified or agreed to by thirty-one Latin American countries. The United States, Canada, and Jamaica have signed but not ratified the Convention. The purpose of the Convention is to prevent, combat, and eradicate the illicit manufacturing of and trafficking in firearms, ammunition, explosives, and other related materials, and to promote and facilitate cooperation and exchange of information and experience between states parties. The participating states will adopt legislation that criminalizes illegal arms production and trafficking. There are also provisions on marking and licensing for the arms trade. However, the Convention has not been implemented as intended, since only five states parties are fulfilling their obligations to exchange information about authorized manufacturers, dealers, importers, exporters, and owners of weapons. This lack of implementation is probably due to the United States not ratifying the Convention.

ECOWAS CONVENTION ON SMALL ARMS

In West Africa, the fifteen member countries of the Economic Community of West African States (ECOWAS) signed the ECOWAS Convention on Small Arms and Light Weapons, their Ammunition and other Related Materials in 2006. The Convention entered into force in 2009. The Convention is based on ECOWAS's Political Declaration of 1998 on a Moratorium on the Importation, Exportation and Manufacture of Light Weapons in West Africa.

The purpose of the Convention is to prevent and combat the excessive and destabilizing accumulation of small arms and light weapons and to continue efforts to control small arms and light weapons within the ECOWAS region. The Convention contains detailed rules on transferring and manufacturing small arms and light weapons as well as transparency measures and exchange of information. Since most countries in the region do not manufacture weapons themselves, the weapons have to be imported from abroad. Therefore, there has been a particular need to regulate imports and to combat the illegal import of weapons to non-state groups.

CENTRAL AFRICAN CONVENTION ON SMALL ARMS
The Central African countries adopted the Central African Convention for the Control of Small Arms and Light Weapons, their Ammunition, Parts and Components that can be used for their Manufacture, Repair or Assembly – the so-called Kinshasa Convention, in April 2010. The Convention aims to regulate small arms and light weapons and to combat their illicit trade and trafficking in Central Africa. All eleven Central African states have signed the Convention, but it is not yet in force, because it has only been ratified by five countries. The convention must be ratified by one more state to enter into force.

INHUMANE CONVENTIONAL WEAPONS

Introduction

As mentioned in chapter 1, international humanitarian law includes rules on the methods and means (weapons) that may be used in armed conflicts. These rules are found in the Hague Conventions of 1907 and in the two Protocols of 1977 Additional to the 1949 Geneva Conventions. The conventions on biological and chemical weapons may also be classified as part of international humanitarian law, as well as the United Nations Convention on Certain Conventional Weapons of 1980.

Efforts to reduce human suffering during wars by prohibiting certain types of particularly inhumane weapons goes back to the Hague Conferences in 1899 and 1907, which established that warring parties do not have unlimited freedom in the weapons they choose to harm the enemy. This basic rule is stated in the Additional Protocol I, Article 35: "In any armed conflict, the right of the parties to the conflict to choose methods or means of warfare is not unlimited. It is prohibited to employ weapons, projectiles and material and methods of warfare of a nature to cause superfluous injury or unnecessary suffering." Another basic rule is Article 48, which states that "In order to ensure respect for and protection of the civilian population and civilian objects, the parties to the conflict shall at all times distinguish between the civilian population and combatants and between civilian objects and military objectives and accordingly shall direct their operations only against military objectives." According to Article 51 on protection of the civilian population, "indiscriminate attacks are prohibited." Indiscriminate attacks are:

a) those which are not directed at a specific military objective,
b) those which employ a method or means of combat which cannot be directed at a specific military objective,
c) those which employ a method or means of combat the effects of which cannot be limited as required by this Protocol, and consequently, in each such case, are of a nature to strike military objectives and civilians or civilian objects without distinction.

Some of the first weapons banned because of the unnecessary human suffering they caused were the expanding bullets – so-called dumdum bullets – which had already been banned in 1899. After the horrors of the First World War, the 1925 Protocol prohibiting the use in war of toxic gases and bacteriological weapons was signed in Geneva. The massive killings of civilians during the Second World War led to the Geneva Conventions of 1949, to protect civilians in time of war.

The increase in the numbers of civilian casualties and maiming of soldiers during later armed conflicts, including in the Vietnam War, made it increasingly obvious during the 1970s that the use of certain particularly harmful types of weapons needed to be further restricted or prohibited. Therefore, a diplomatic conference on international humanitarian law during armed conflicts was held in Geneva between 1974 and 1977, resulting in the two Additional Protocols of 1977 being adopted. As a follow-up to the diplomatic conference, the United Nations decided, by General Assembly resolution 32/152 of 1977, to convene a UN conference in 1979 to continue discussions and to possibly adopt prohibitions of or restrictions on the use of certain types of conventional weapons deemed to be excessively injurious or to have indiscriminate effects.

United Nations Convention on Certain Conventional Weapons

The United Nations conference on an additional weapons ban, held in Geneva in 1979–80, resulted in the adoption of the Convention on

Prohibitions or Restrictions on the Use of Certain Conventional Weapons Which may be Deemed to be Excessively Injurious or to Have Indiscriminate Effects. The Convention's long title is often abbreviated to the United Nations Convention on Certain Conventional Weapons (CCW), or Convention on Inhumane Conventional Weapons, or merely the 1980 Weapons Convention. The Convention was opened for signature in 1981 and entered into force in 1983. As of January 2016, the Convention had 121 states parties, including all five nuclear-weapon states. Five countries have signed but not yet ratified the Convention. Among the states that have not signed the Convention are Iran, North Korea, and Syria.

In December 2001, Article 1 of the Convention on the scope of application of the Convention and its additional protocols in international armed conflicts between two or more states was expanded to include armed conflicts that are not international, e.g., civil wars or internal armed conflicts. Eighty-two states have agreed to the amendment.

COMMENT

The Convention on Certain Conventional Weapons is a framework convention, which means that it does not contain specific rules on prohibitions of or restrictions on the use of certain weapons but establishes common general rules on applying and interpreting the additional protocols. Five protocols to the Convention establish the rules for the specific prohibitions and restrictions on the use of certain types of conventional weapons. The Convention on Inhumane Conventional Weapons and its Protocols constitute an important contribution to international efforts to further develop International Humanitarian Law, as it is applied in armed conflicts. Among the five protocols, Protocol II on Mines and Protocol V on Explosive Remnants of War are the most important.

The Convention has no provisions for verifying compliance. However, the third review conference of the Convention agreed to a CCW compliance mechanism, requiring all parties to submit annual information on

- disseminating information on the Convention and its annexed protocols to their armed forces and to the civilian population,
- steps they have taken to meet the relevant technical requirements of the Convention and its annexed protocols,

- legislation passed related to the Convention and its annexed protocols.

PROTOCOL I ON NON-DETECTABLE FRAGMENTS

Protocol I of 10 October 1980 on Non-detectable Fragments contains only one paragraph: "It is prohibited to use any weapon the primary effect of which is to injure by fragments which in the human body escape detection by X-rays." One hundred and sixteen states have consented to be bound by this protocol.

PROTOCOL II ON MINES

Protocol II of 1980 on the Prohibitions or Restrictions on the Use of Mines, Booby-Traps and Other Devices contains regulations on the use of land mines against personnel – anti-personnel mines (APM). A total prohibition of anti-personnel mines has been established in the Ottawa Anti-Personnel Mines Convention (see pages 198–202).

Landmines are explosive devices concealed under or on the ground and designed to destroy or disable enemy targets – either personnel, vehicles, or tanks as they pass over or near it. Landmines are typically detonated automatically when a target steps on them or drives over them, or through remote control. Modern landmines may be designed to be self-destructing or self-neutralizing after a certain period of time. Anti-tank mines were first used by the German army by the end of the First World War in 1918. During the Second World War, large numbers of landmines were laid out, especially in the Soviet Union, North Africa (particularly in Egypt), and at the Western Front in Europe. Ninety-four states have agreed to be bound by the Protocol, including China, India, Israel, Pakistan, Russia, and the United States.

AMENDED PROTOCOL II ON MINES

In light of the growing, unregulated, and irresponsible use of anti-personnel landmines in armed conflicts – particularly in internal conflicts in developing countries – and the resulting deaths and mutilations of ever more civilians, it became apparent during the 1980s that civilian populations were not being adequately protected and that there was a need to strengthen the rules in Protocol II. On France's initiative, protracted negotiations were held in 1994–95 to seek agreement on introducing new prohibitions and stricter conditions for the use of anti-personnel mines. The negotiations showed that there was insufficient support for entering into substantive negotiations on imposing a total ban on anti-personnel mines because military forces in many countries wished to continue to use anti-personnel mines as an inexpensive, easily deployable, and effective defence weapon. Instead, changes to the existing Protocol II were agreed upon in the Amended Protocol II of 1996, to improve the protection of civilians. The major improvements in the Amended Protocol II consist of

- extending the scope of the protocol to include internal armed conflicts,
- prohibiting the use of non-detectable anti-personnel mines; i.e., anti-personnel mines must be detectable by using mine detectors,
- making anti-personnel mines laid outside marked, fenced, and supervised areas self-destruct. Within 30 days after laying out, at least 90 per cent of the anti-personnel mines shall self-destruct, and after 120 days no more than one out of 1,000 deployed anti-personnel mines shall be able to function as a mine,
- not transferring anti-personnel mines that do not meet the new technical requirements for traceability, and prohibiting transfers to rebel movements and other non-state actors,
- introducing annual consultation conferences to review how rules and compliance are being applied on the basis of mandatory reports from states.

A few countries with large stockpiles of anti-personnel mines insisted on including transitional periods that give states the opportunity, when accepting the Amended Protocol, to declare that for a period of up to nine years, they will not be able to meet the requirements for traceability and self-destruction. The Amended Protocol II entered into force in 1999. One hundred and two states have agreed to be bound by the Amended Protocol, including China, India, Israel, Pakistan, Russia, and the United States.

PROTOCOL III ON INCENDIARY WEAPONS

Protocol III of 1980 on Prohibitions or Restrictions on the Use of Incendiary Weapons prohibits any attack against civilian populations, individual civilians, or civilian objects with incendiary weapons. They are defined as weapons or munitions primarily designed to set fire to objects or to cause injury to persons through the action of flames, heat, or a combination thereof. The protocol also prohibits airstrikes against military targets in residential areas. The main purpose of the Protocol is to prohibit the use of napalm and other incendiary weapons against the civilian population. The protocol does not prohibit the use of incendiary weapons against military targets. Napalm bombs were first used against Japanese cities during the Second World War and later by the United States during the Vietnam War. Vietnamese civilians were the primary victims of napalm bombing during the Vietnam War – in violation of the Fourth Geneva Convention on the Protection of Civilian Persons in Time of War. One hundred and twelve states have agreed to be bound by the protocol, including the United States. However, the US has made one reservation: that it "reserves the right to use incendiary weapons against military objectives located in concentrations of civilians where it is judged that such use would cause fewer casualties and/or less collateral damage than alternative weapons, but in so doing will take all feasible precautions with a view to limiting the incendiary effects to the military objective and to avoiding, and in any event to minimizing, incidental loss of civilian life, injury to civilians and damage to civilian objects."

PROTOCOL IV ON BLINDING LASER WEAPONS

Protocol IV on Blinding Laser Weapons prohibits the use of laser weapons specifically designed to cause permanent blindness of unprotected eyes. Protocol IV entered into force in 1998. One hundred and five states, including all five nuclear-weapon states, have agreed to be bound by Protocol IV.

PROTOCOL V ON EXPLOSIVE REMNANTS OF WAR

Protocol V on Explosive Remnants of War is the latest protocol, adopted in 2003 under the CCW. This protocol is the first multilateral agreement to address the issue of unexploded and abandoned ammunition, which – like landmines – causes many civilian casualties and continues to pose a daily danger for the populations of many former conflict zones and prevent habitation and development of, among others, agriculture in the affected areas. The protocol regulates the cleanup and destruction of unexploded and abandoned ammunition. A state that has been a party to an armed conflict is responsible for clearing, removing, and destroying all explosive remnants of war left on territories under its control (Article 3). Furthermore, the state must register and keep records on the use of the explosive weapons and the abandoned weapons (Article 4) and take all feasible precautionary measures in the controlled area with explosive remnants of war to protect the civilian population (Article 5). The states must cooperate and assist each other in marking, clearing, removing, and destroying all explosive remnants of war (Articles 7 and 8). Eighty-seven states have agreed to be bound by Protocol V, including China, France, Russia, and the United States. Israel, the United Kingdom, and Turkey have not agreed to the protocol.

ANTI-PERSONNEL MINES

Introduction

A number of countries had wanted the negotiations on strengthening Protocol II to result in a total prohibition of anti-personnel mines. But several of the major countries' military commanders argued strongly against a total ban on anti-personnel mines, which the military considered an indispensable defensive weapon.

Because of the many civilian victims of anti-personnel mines – 70 to 80 per cent of all mine victims are civilians – civil society organizations (NGOs) exerted an ever-stronger international pressure against governments for a total ban on anti-personnel mines. Among the most prominent organizations was the International Campaign to Ban Landmines (ICBL) – a global network established in 1993 of around 1,400 NGOs in nearly 100 countries, working for a world free of anti-personnel mines. In October 1997, the ICBL and the organization's American coordinator, Jody Williams, were awarded the Nobel Peace Prize in recognition of the tireless and decisive work of the organization, Williams in particular, for achieving the Ottawa Convention prohibiting anti-personnel mines. The organization's activities on promoting public awareness of the harmful effects of anti-personnel mines on civilian populations and rallying support to adopt a total ban, is one of the best examples of how civil society can play a crucial role in obtaining disarmament and arms control measures. The late Princess Diana's support for the landmine ban campaign was also instrumental in promoting the international campaign against landmines in the media and creating public and political awareness.

Anti-Personnel Mines Convention

Canada was one of the strongest advocates of a total ban. On Canada's initiative, the representatives of fifty countries supporting a total ban on landmines met in Ottawa in October 1996 to prepare the draft of a United Nations resolution and a plan of action to negotiate an international agreement on a total prohibition of anti-personnel mines. The draft resolution was adopted by the UN General Assembly in December 1996. Further negotiations took place in Vienna, Bonn, and Brussels in 1997, and were concluded in Oslo. The Ottawa process was remarkable because the countries that wanted a total ban on anti-personnel mines had given up on the UN system (the paralyzed Conference on Disarmament in Geneva) and instead established their own alternative negotiating forum. Governments and NGOs collaborated closely, starting with the ICBL and the ICRC. This cooperation strengthened the international campaign against landmines, which finally resulted in the Ottawa Anti-Personnel Mines Convention, which was adopted in Oslo in September 1997.

During the negotiations on the Convention, the United States proposed that the Convention should contain an exception clause to permit a minefield in South Korea at the border with North Korea to protect South Korea from invasion from the north. The other participants in the negotiations rejected such an exemption because they wanted to establish an exception-free total ban on anti-personnel mines. This was the main reason why the United States could not agree to the result of the negotiations. Another reason why the United States could not join the Ottawa Convention was that the US also wanted an exception for anti-personnel mines, which are laid out to protect anti-tank mines. This exception was also rejected by the other negotiating parties.

The Convention on the Prohibition of the Use, Stockpiling, Production and Transfer of Anti-Personnel Mines and on Their Destruction – the Ottawa APM Convention – established a total ban on anti-personnel mines. The Convention was opened for signature in Ottawa in December 1997 and immediately signed by 122 countries – an unusually large number, showing the broad international support for a total ban on anti-personnel mines. The entry into force was a reality in March 1999. The Convention has now been ratified by 162 countries. All the member states of the European Union and of NATO

– with the exception of the United States – are parties to the Convention. The US policy on anti-personnel mines is under review and influential political forces in the Senate support American adherence to the Ottawa Convention. The US has not used anti-personnel mines since 1991, has not exported mines since 1992, and has not produced them since 1997.

The most important Articles of the Ottawa Convention are:

- Article 1: States agree never under any circumstances to use, develop, produce, otherwise acquire, stockpile, retain, or transfer anti-personnel mines to anyone, directly or indirectly, nor to assist, encourage, or induce anyone to engage in any activity prohibited to a party under the Convention.
- Article 4: Each state party is committed to destroy or ensure the destruction of all anti-personnel mines, as well as all stockpiled anti-personnel mines owned or possessed by states, or that are under their jurisdiction or control, not later than four years after the entry into force of the Convention for that state. All anti-personnel mines in mined areas under its jurisdiction or control, must be destroyed as soon as possible but not later than ten years after the entry into force.
- Article 5: If a state is not able to destroy all its anti-personnel mines within the ten-year period, it may request an extension of the deadline up to an additional ten years.
- Article 6: Each state has the right to seek and receive assistance from other parties to the Convention, including assistance for clearing and destroying mines, as well as assistance to mine victims.
- Article 7: States must report annually to the secretary general of the United Nations on what they are doing to carry out the Convention.
- Article 11: States will meet regularly to consider how to apply and implement the Convention.
- Article 12: Conferences to review the operation and status of the Convention shall be convened every five years.
- Article 8: The Convention does not contain provisions on verification mechanisms, but states may establish a fact-finding mission to another party's territory to collect information on the spot or in other places directly related to alleged compliance issues.

The 70th General Assembly adopted resolution 70/55, Implementation of the Convention on the Prohibition of the Use, Stockpiling, Production and Transfer of Anti-personnel Mines and on Their Destruction, in which all states that have not signed the Convention are invited to agree to it without delay. The resolution was adopted by 168 votes in favour, none against, and 17 abstentions, including Egypt, India, Iran, Israel, North Korea, Pakistan, Russia, South Korea, Syria, and the United States.

Comment

The Ottawa Convention is probably the multilateral agreement that has been agreed to by the most countries within the shortest period of time, and that has entered into force most quickly after signing. More than three quarters of all countries are now parties to the Ottawa Convention. However, the Ottawa Convention's effect is limited by the fact that it only prohibits anti-personnel mines and not anti-vehicle mines (anti-tank mines), including remotely controlled roadside bombs, which have caused large numbers of casualties in Afghanistan and other war zones. Another major shortcoming is that several of the major mine-producing countries, such as China, Russia, and the United States, as well as countries that have tense relations with their neighbors, including India, Pakistan, North Korea, and South Korea, are not parties to the Convention, and therefore not formally bound by the mine ban. Israel and the majority of the Arab countries in the Middle East, including Egypt, Iran, Lebanon, Saudi Arabia, and Syria, are also not parties to the Convention. A total of thirty countries have still not adhered to the Convention. This, of course, weakens the ban against anti-personnel mines. However, China, Russia, and the United States, as well as India, Pakistan, South Korea, and Israel, have joined the Amended Protocol II to the 1980 Weapons Convention, so those countries are at least bound by the Amended Protocol II's restrictions on the use of anti-personnel mines (see pages 195–6).

Since the adoption of the Ottawa Convention, the number of land mine victims has fallen considerably, but there are still thousands of land mine victims every year, especially in Afghanistan, Pakistan, Colombia, and Myanmar. Most land mine victims are civilians – many of them children. More than 46 million anti-personnel mines have been destroyed. But it is estimated that approximately 110 million anti-personnel mines are still laid out in 68 countries, and about 10 million mines are stored in different states parties, which have not yet been destroyed. Furthermore, there are about 170 million anti-personnel mines stored in countries that are not parties to the Ottawa Convention.

The 1977 Additional Protocol I to the 1949 Geneva Conventions states that the parties to the conflict must always distinguish between the civilian population and combatants (i.e., soldiers and other military targets) and between civilian objects and military objectives and only direct their operations against military objectives (Article 48). Since an anti-personnel mine is not designed to distinguish between a combatant and a civilian who steps on the mine and thereby triggers an explosion, anti-personnel mines must be considered unlawful weapons, whose use violates the basic protection rules in international humanitarian law.

CLUSTER BOMBS

Introduction

Like anti-personnel mines, which continue to cause many casualties, especially civilian casualties, long after military operations have ended, cluster munitions – or cluster bombs – constitute a particular danger to civilians. Cluster munitions are small bombs that are dropped from aircraft in a bomb container, which is filled with up to several hundred pieces of so-called submunitions, i.e., small bomb shells. The bomb container opens above the target, spreading the small explosive shells over a large area. Sometimes the cluster bombs do not detonate when they hit the ground and lie unexploded. In many cases these unexploded bombs are picked up by children, killing or seriously injuring them. There are no exact data on the number of victims of cluster bombs, but various organizations estimate the number at between 60,000 and 85,000 people, 98 per cent of whom are civilians, and a third of these children. Cluster bombs have been used since the Second World War in thirty-six countries. Large areas are still contaminated with unexploded cluster bombs, especially in Laos, Cambodia, and Vietnam, but also in Lebanon, Kosovo, Afghanistan, Sudan, and Iraq.

Convention on Cluster Munitions

The question of prohibiting or regulating the use of cluster bombs was on the international agenda for several years. A number of countries wanted to regulate the use of cluster bombs, by banning all cluster bombs that do not self-destruct or self-deactivate. However, discussions within the auspices of the CCW failed to make progress on the regulation of cluster bombs and the negotiations stalled in November 2008 because of opposition from the biggest producers with the largest stocks of cluster bombs – the United States, Russia, China, India, Pakistan, Israel, and South Korea. The United States is estimated to have 700 million cluster bombs.

On the initiative of Norway, a few countries (Ireland, Mexico, New Zealand, Sweden, and Austria) initiated negotiations outside the UN negotiating machinery in the so-called Oslo process with a view to adopt an international, legally binding agreement on the total prohibition of the use, production, transfer, and stockpiling of cluster munitions. The negotiations in the Oslo process included representatives of both governments, the United Nations, the ICRC, and civil society organizations in the Cluster Munition Coalition. The first meeting was held in Oslo in February 2007, where the forty-six participating states agreed on a declaration that it was their intention before the end of 2008 to adopt a convention on prohibiting the use and storage of cluster bombs. Further meetings were held in Lima, Vienna, and Wellington. The text of the Convention was adopted in May 2008 at the final conference in Dublin. One hundred and seven countries participated in the conference. The Convention was adopted unanimously.

Ninety-four countries signed the Convention on Cluster Munitions (CCM) at a meeting in Oslo in December 2008. The Convention entered into force in August 2010. As of January 2016, the Convention has been ratified or agreed to by ninety-eight countries, including France and the United Kingdom, and twenty other countries have signed the Convention. Among the countries that have not signed the Convention are the United States, Russia, China, India, Pakistan, Israel, Egypt, Iran, and Syria.

The parties to the Convention on Cluster Munitions are committed never under any circumstances to use, develop, produce, otherwise acquire, stockpile, retain, or transfer cluster munitions to anyone, directly or indirectly (Article 1). The ban also applies to explosive bomblets that are specifically designed to be dispersed or released from containers on aircraft. For the purpose of the Convention, "cluster munition means a conventional munition that is designed to disperse or release explosive submunitions, each weighing less than 20 kilograms, and includes those explosive submunitions." The Convention does not apply to a munition that contains fewer than ten explosive submunitions or is equipped with an electronic self-destruction mechanism or an electronic self-deactivating feature. The Convention further obliges the states parties to destroy their stocks of cluster munitions as soon as possible and not later than eight years after the entry into force of the Convention. The deadline for destruction can be extended for a further maximum of four years (Article 3). The parties undertake to clear and destroy, or ensure the clearance and destruction of remnants of cluster munitions located in areas contaminated by cluster munitions, which are under their jurisdiction or control. The clearance and destruction shall be completed as soon as possible and not later than ten years after the end of the active hostilities (Article 4). The Convention also obliges the parties to provide assistance to victims of cluster munitions (Article 5) and gives parties the right to seek and receive assistance to implement the obligations of the Convention (Article 6). The states parties agree to meet once a year to consider how the Convention is being applied and implemented (Article 11) and to convene review conferences every five years (Article 12).

The 70th General Assembly adopted resolution 70/54, Implementation of the Convention on Cluster Munitions, urging all states outside the Convention on Cluster Munitions to join as soon as possible. The resolution was adopted by 139 votes in favour, 2 against (Russia and Zimbabwe), and 40 abstentions, including China, Egypt, India, Iran, Israel, Pakistan, South Korea, Syria, and the United States.

Comment

The Convention on Cluster Munitions is the most recently adopted international agreement to prohibit or regulate the use of a particular type of conventional weapon. Of course, the effect of the Convention is weakened by the fact that the countries who produce, store, and use the most cluster bombs (the United States, Russia, China, India, Pakistan, Israel, and Syria) are not parties to the CCM – nor are they like-

ly to accept joining the Convention in the foreseeable future. It is estimated that 85 per cent of the world's stocks of cluster bombs are
found in the above countries. Advocates of the Convention highlight
the fact that an international agreement banning the use of cluster
munitions has been signed and ratified or agreed to by almost half of
all the countries in the world. Cluster bombs thus belong to the same
category as anti-personnel mines: they are considered unacceptable
weapons according to prevailing international opinion.

13

Arms Trade, Export Control Regimes, and World Military Expenditure

ARMS TRADE

Introduction

In the Final Document of the First Special Session of the General Assembly devoted to Disarmament (SSOD-I) from in 1978, the General Assembly recommended to the major arms-supplier and recipient countries to consult among themselves "on the limitation of all types of international transfer of conventional weapons, based in particular on the principle of undiminished security of the parties with a view to promoting or enhancing stability at a lower military level."[1]

Efforts to regulate the international trade in conventional weapons only started seriously in 1995 when a group of Nobel Peace Prize recipients expressed concern about the unregulated arms trade and its destructive consequences and called on the international community to conclude an international agreement to prevent irresponsible transfers of conventional arms. This call was further developed in 2003 by a group of civil society organizations, which launched the Control Arms Campaign. The Campaign pointed out that the lack of control of international trade in arms was a contributing factor to continued armed conflicts, poverty, and human rights violations. It recommended a global, internationally binding agreement prohibiting the transfer of weapons to areas where the weapons would likely be used for serious violations of human rights. The purpose of such an agreement would be to stop widespread human suffering caused by the irresponsible transfers of conventional arms.

United Nations Arms Trade Treaty

Support for the Campaign's goal began to grow within the United Nations. In 2006, by an overwhelming majority, the General Assembly adopted a resolution 61/89 that called on member states to submit their views on the possibilities of concluding an arms trade agreement, and on its possible scope and content. There were 139 votes in favour and only one negative vote (the United States). Twenty-four countries, including Russia and China, abstained. The purpose of the agreement was to control the arms trade by establishing common international criteria and standards for the arms trade and creating an expert group of government representatives to continue working on the issue. In August 2008 the expert group presented its report, which recommended that an arms trade treaty, besides heavy conventional weapons, should also include small arms and light weapons. In December 2008, the General Assembly endorsed the report of the expert group and established a working group to analyze the proposals. In 2009, the assembly adopted a resolution 64/48 to convene a conference on an arms trade treaty in 2012. This was supported by 158 countries, including the United States. Further meetings were held during 2010 and 2011.

The Conference to negotiate and adopt an arms trade treaty was held in New York in July 2012. On the last day of the conference it became clear that it would not be possible to reach agreement on the draft treaty because the American delegation asked for more time to consider the draft treaty. A small group of other member countries were also not ready to accept the adoption of the treaty, which required unanimity. Against this background a group of more than ninety member states issued a joint statement expressing disappointment that it had not been possible to adopt the treaty and declaring that they were determined to conclude an arms trade treaty as soon as possible.

A final conference was convened by resolution 67/234A to adopt the arms trade treaty. The conference was held in March 2013. Because of opposition from Iran, Syria, and North Korea, the chairman of the conference noted that there was no consensus on adopting the treaty and the conference ended without result.

The draft treaty was then forwarded to the General Assembly, which – in an historic adoption, by an overwhelming majority of 154 votes in favour, 3 against, and 23 abstentions – adopted the Arms Trade Treaty (ATT) on 2 April 2013.[2] The three countries that voted against the treaty were Iran, North Korea, and Syria. The 23 countries that abstained included China, Russia, India, Bolivia, Cuba, Egypt, Belarus, Indonesia, Myanmar, Nicaragua, Saudi Arabia, Sri Lanka, Sudan, and Yemen. Contrary to the situation in the 2012 conference on the adoption of the treaty, the General Assembly could adopt the treaty by a two-thirds majority vote. The treaty was opened for signature in June 2013 (Article 21) and entered into force in December, 2014. As of January 2016, the treaty has been signed by 130 states, including the United States, and ratified by 80 states, including Argentina, Australia, Austria, Belgium, France, Germany, Ireland, Italy, Mexico, Netherlands, New Zealand, the Nordic countries, South Africa, and the United Kingdom. Canada has not yet signed the treaty.

The object of the Arms Trade Treaty is to establish the highest possible common international standards for regulating or improving the regulation of the international trade in conventional arms, and to prevent and eradicate the illegal trade in conventional arms and prevent their diversion.

Article 1: The treaty's overall purpose is to contribute to international and regional peace, security, and stability, reduce human suffering, and promote cooperation, transparency, and responsible action by parties in the international trade in conventional weapons and thereby build confidence among states. The treaty's introductory provisions stipulate the following eight principles, according to which all states shall:

1 Have an inherent right to individual or collective self-defence, as recognized in Article 51 of the Charter of the United Nations,
2 Settle international disputes by peaceful means in such a manner that international peace and security, and justice, are not endangered, in accordance with Article 2 (3) of the Charter,
3 Refrain in their international relations from threatening or using force against the territorial integrity or political independence of any state, or in any other manner inconsistent with the purposes of the United Nations, in accordance with Article 2 (4) of the Charter,
4 Not interfere in domestic matters, in accordance with Article 2 (7) of the Charter,

5 Respect international humanitarian law, in accordance with the Geneva Conventions of 1949; and respect for human rights in accordance with the Charter of the United Nations and the Universal Declaration of Human Rights,

6 Have the responsibility, in accordance with their respective international obligations, to effectively regulate the international trade in conventional arms, and to prevent their diversion, and to establish and implement their respective national control systems,

7 Have respect for the legitimate interests of states in acquiring conventional arms to exercise their right to self-defence and for peace-keeping operations, and to produce, export, import, and transfer conventional arms,

8 Implement the treaty consistently and objectively, and without discrimination.

The ATT also notes that certain conventional arms for recreational, cultural, historical, and sporting activities are permitted, when they are legal to trade, own, and use. Other aspects of the treaty are:

Article 2: The treaty applies to all conventional arms in the following categories: battle tanks, armoured combat vehicles, large-calibre artillery systems, combat aircraft, attack helicopters, warships, missiles and missile launchers, and small arms and light weapons.

Article 3: International trade activities, for the purposes of the treaty, comprise export, import, transit, trans-shipment, and brokering, referred to as "transfer." Each state party must establish and maintain a national control system to regulate exports of ammunition.

Article 4: The same applies to exports of parts and components that can be assembled as conventional weapons.

Article 5: Each state must establish and maintain a national control system, including a national control list, and provide its national control list to the Secretariat, which will make it available to other states parties. States parties are encouraged to make their control lists publicly available.

Article 6: Arms transfers are prohibited when:

- the transfer would violate the state's obligations under measures adopted by the United Nations Security Council under Chapter VII of the Charter, in particular, arms embargoes,
- the transfer would violate the state's relevant international obligations under international agreements to which it is a party, in particular the transfer of, or illicit trafficking in, conventional arms,
- a state knows that the arms or items would be used in acts of genocide, crimes against humanity, grave breaches of the Geneva Conventions of 1949, attacks directed against civilian objects or civilians protected as such, or other war crimes, as defined by international agreements to which it is a party.

Article 7: Before authorizing the export of conventional arms, each exporting state party shall objectively and without discrimination, taking into account relevant factors, including information provided by the importing state, assess the potential risk that the conventional arms or items would

- contribute to or undermine peace and security,
- be used to commit or facilitate a serious violation of international humanitarian law or international human rights or constitute an offence under international conventions or protocols on terrorism or transnational organized crime,
- be used to commit or facilitate serious gender-based violence or serious acts of violence against women and children.

Article 8: Regulates the obligations of the importing state in relation to the importing state.

Articles 9 and 10: Each state party shall take appropriate measures to regulate, where necessary and feasible, the transit or trans-shipment under its jurisdiction of conventional arms through its territory in accordance with relevant international law, and regulate brokering.

Articles 11 to 16: The treaty contains provisions on diverting arms, record-keeping, reporting, enforcement, international cooperation, and international assistance.

Article 17: Agrees to convene conferences.

Article 18: Establishes the Secretariat.

The First Conference of States Parties (CSP) to the Arms Trade Treaty took place in Cancun, in August 2015. According to the Control Arms Campaign, the conference was successful overall, and made decisions on various procedural issues, as well as agreeing on the location of the ATT Secretariat in Geneva. Disappointingly, however, the parties could not agree on which templates to use as the basis for their first annual reports, and some debates and decisions highlighted political tensions and a North–South divide in approaches and perspectives.

The 70th General Assembly adopted resolution 70/58, the Arms Trade Treaty, by which the General Assembly "calls upon all states that have not yet done so to ratify, accept, approve or accede to the Treaty, according to their respective constitutional processes." The resolution was adopted with 157 votes in favour, none against, and 26 abstentions, including Egypt, India, Iran, North Korea, Russia, Saudi Arabia, and Syria.

COMMENT

The Arms Trade Treaty is the first agreement to establish global regulation of the international trade in conventional weapons. The ATT is also the first international arms control agreement concluded under the auspices of the United Nations since the Comprehensive Nuclear-Test-Ban Treaty (CTBT) was adopted in 1996.

As described above, the ATT prohibits states from transferring conventional weapons to other countries, when the states know that the weapons will be used to commit or promote genocide, crimes against humanity, or war crimes. The overall objective of the treaty is to prevent conventional weapons from being sold or transferred to dictators, warlords, terrorists, and criminals who may use conventional weapons to kill civilians or commit gross human rights violations or crimes.

The ATT is a framework treaty, i.e., it contains only general principles for the international arms trade. It is the responsibility of individual states to implement the treaty and control compliance with its ban on the illegal arms trafficking at the national level. States thus retain their sovereign decision-making powers on the regulation of the arms deals. However, they must report on what steps they have taken to implement the treaty, including their legislation on national controls on arms trades. They must also report on how they apply the treaty, i.e., on the arms deals affected and permits issued for arms deals. The effectiveness of the ATT will depend to a large degree on the full national implementation by all its states parties.

The international human rights organizations, including Amnesty International, fully support the adoption of the Arms Trade Treaty, which Amnesty International calls a victory for human rights. One of the most positive elements in the ATT is the inclusion of small arms and light weapons, which is the largest category of conventional weapons traded illegally, mainly used by non-state actors, including terrorists, pirates, child soldiers, and criminals. The ATT makes it more difficult for illegal arms dealers to acquire conventional weapons and supply arms to the illegal market. The treaty does not affect the national trade of weapons within the borders of the states parties or the right to bear arms.

One of the shortcomings of the treaty is that it does not explicitly mention transfers of weapons when they are done as gifts, loans, or rents, allowing states to circumvent the provisions of the Treaty. Nor does the ATT contain specific rules on mechanisms to enforce the treaty's prohibitions. Another weakness is that large arms-exporting countries like Russia and China did not vote in favour of the resolution, and have not signed the treaty.

International Arms Trade

According to SIPRI, the volume of international transfers of major weapons grew by 16 per cent between 2010 and 2014. The five biggest exporters of major weapons from 2010 to 2014 were the United States (31 per cent), Russia (27 per cent), China, Germany, and France (5 per cent each), who account for approximately 74 per cent of the total global volume of the world's arms exports. The composition of the five largest exporters of arms changed between 2005 and 2014. While the United States and Russia remained by far the largest exporters (since 1950), China narrowly, but notably, replaced Germany and France between 2010 and 2014 as the third-largest supplier. The United Kingdom (4 per cent) dropped outside the top five exporters. Other major arms exporters were Spain, Italy, Ukraine (each 3 per cent), and Israel (2 per cent). The main recipient region in 2010–2014 was Asia and Oceania, accounting for 48 per cent of all imports of major weapons. Among the five largest importers of major weapons, three were Asian: India (15 per cent), China (5 per cent), and Pakistan (4 per cent). The Middle East accounted for the second largest amount of imports (22 per cent), Europe (12 per cent), the Americas (10 per cent), and Africa (9 per cent). Between 2005 and 2014, arms imports by states in Africa increased by 45 per cent, Asia and Oceania by 37 per cent, the Middle East by 25 per cent, and the Americas by 7 per cent. Imports by states in Europe decreased by 36 per cent.

The most significant change in exports was the increase in China's exports of major arms which increased by 143 per cent between 2005 and 2014. China's share of global arms exports increased from 3 to 5 per cent.

Between 2010 and 2014, the five largest importing countries were India (15 per cent), Saudi Arabia, and China (5 per cent each), the United Arab Emirates, and Pakistan (each 4 per cent). Together, these five countries received 33 per cent of all arms imports. Asia and Oceania accounted for nearly half of all imports between 2010 and 2014, followed by the Middle East, Europe, the Americas, and Africa.[3]

SIPRI's data on arms transfers do not represent their financial value, but most (90 per cent) of the arms-exporting states do publish figures on the financial value of their arms exports. Based on such data, SIPRI estimates that the total value of the global arms trade in 2013 – the latest year for which data are available – is at least US$76 billion. However, the true figure is likely to be higher. For 2012, this figure was estimated to be at least $58 billion.

COMMENT

It seems paradoxical that such a large share of arms transfers goes to developing countries. The main reason for this is that the tensions and conflicts in the world today mainly take place in developing countries. The developing countries' large share of international arms transfers is also due to the fact that many developing countries do not have the necessary technology and national capacity to manufacture modern weapons and have to import weapons from the outside – as opposed to many industrial countries that can produce most of their weapons themselves and therefore do not have as great a need for arms imports.

United Nations Register of Conventional Arms

The United Nations Register of Conventional Arms was established by resolution 46/36L, Transparency in armaments, of 1991, and made operational in 1992. The purpose of the register is to increase transparency for arms transfers and to register unusually large and possibly destabilizing accumulations of conventional arms. The exchange of information through the United Nations on arms transfers serves as a confidence-building measure.

The resolution requests member states to report annually before 30 April and submit information to the register on their import and export of weapons, as well as data on their military holdings, their nationally produced arms, and their defence policy. The reporting requirement is not an international legally binding obligation, but voluntary. The international transfers of weapons that the member states report to the register include the following seven categories of conventional weapons, which are defined in detail in the Annex to the resolution: battle tanks, armoured combat vehicles, large-calibre artillery systems (100 mm or more), combat aircraft, attack helicopters, warships, missiles, and missile launchers. The register was expanded in 2003 to include mortars of a certain calibre size and MANPADS. Small arms are not included in the register, but since 2004 a voluntary information exchange on all military small arms and light weapons has been introduced that member states are also encouraged to report to the register. Most countries also report on their transfers of small arms. The reports must contain information on the numbers and categories of the transferred weapons – exports and imports – from the previous year. The secretary general submits an annual report to the General Assembly on the recorded data, which is made available to all United Nations member states.

COMMENT

Since it was established, more than 170 countries have sent reports to the register, which is administered by the UNODA. However, the number of countries that report on their arms transfers fell from eighty-six countries in 2011 to a record low of fifty-two in 2012.

As the Arms Trade Treaty is implemented, the United Nations Register will most likely become less important. However, the weapons register remains relevant for countries that have not agreed to the ATT.

EXPORT CONTROL REGIMES

Introduction

The purpose of control regimes for arms exports is to control the international arms trade and to prevent the uncontrolled and illegal proliferation of conventional weapons, as well as products, materials, and technologies that can be used to develop or produce weapons of mass destruction. The export control regimes thus contribute to the maintenance of international peace and security.

The permanent export control measures can be found in international guidelines and export control commitments in the following export control regimes: the Australia Group (chemical and biological weapons), the MTCR, the Nuclear Suppliers Group (NSG), the Wassenaar Arrangement (conventional weapons and dual use items), and the Proliferation Security Initiative (PSI).

Temporary export control measures may be imposed by the United Nations Security Council "to give effect to its decisions, and it may call upon the member nations to apply such measures. These may include complete or partial interruption of economic relations" (Article 41 of the Charter). The interruption of economic relations may include trade sanctions or embargoes of arms exports.

Australia Group

The Australia Group, established in 1985, is an informal forum for cooperation between the forty-one participating countries, plus the European Union. All the participants are western countries. Argentina, Mexico, and Ukraine are also participating. The Australia Group countries seek to prevent the spread of chemical and biological weapons by harmonizing their national export control measures to ensure that their exports do not contribute to the development of these weapons of mass destruction.[4]

The Australia Group was formed when an investigation by a United Nations team in 1984 in Iraq found that chemical weapons had been used in the war between Iran and Iraq. Iraq had obtained some of the chemicals and materials through legitimate trade channels. This led to several countries introducing export controls on chemicals that could be used to manufacture chemical weapons. But these control measures were not uniform and attempts were made to circumvent them. Australia took the initiative of proposing a meeting of countries that had export controls with the goal of harmonizing their national licensing measures and enhancing cooperation between them.

The Group has met regularly since 1985, and the annual meetings are now held in Paris. Members of the Group exchange information on their exports and on other issues of common interest. Because the cooperation is informal, decisions on specific export applications are made by the individual participating countries.

Evidence of attempts in the early 1990s to divert dual-use materials to biological weapons has also led to the adoption of export controls on specific biological agents. These are included in a common list of products subject to export controls.

The Australia Group complements the conventions prohibiting chemical and biological weapons. Its control lists differ somewhat from the CWC lists and also include technologies and production equipment.

Missile Technology Control Regime

The MTCR is an informal and voluntary association of countries that share the goals of non-proliferation of unmanned delivery systems capable of delivering weapons of mass destruction, and that seek to coordinate national export licensing efforts aimed at preventing the proliferation of missiles and missile technology. The MTCR was originally established in 1987 by Canada, France, Germany, Italy, Japan, the United Kingdom, and the United States. Since then, the number of MTCR partners has increased to a total of thirty-four western countries. The MTCR now includes Argentina, Brazil, Russia, South Africa, and Ukraine.[5]

The MTCR was initiated partly in response to the increasing proliferation of weapons of mass destruction. After the terrorist attacks on America on 11 September 2001, it became evident that more had to be done to decrease the risk of WMD delivery systems falling into the hands of terrorist groups and individuals, by maintaining vigilance over the transfers of missile equipment, material, and related technologies that can be used for systems capable of delivering WMD.

The participating countries have committed themselves to controlling their export of missiles and missile-related technology that can be used to deliver a payload of 500 kilograms or more over a distance of more than 300 kilometres. The participants are required to follow common export policy guidelines for issuing export permits, which apply to a common list of controlled items (equipment, software, and technology). As a result of MTCR cooperation, all participating countries have voluntarily introduced export licensing measures on rocket and other unmanned air vehicle delivery systems or related equipment, material, and technology. All decisions are taken by consensus, and MTCR partners regularly exchange information about relevant national export licensing issues (see also pages 161–2).

Nuclear Suppliers Group

The NSG, created in 1974, is a group of countries that seeks to contribute to reducing the spread of nuclear weapons by implementing two sets of guidelines for nuclear exports and for nuclear-related (dual use products) exports. The NSG comprises forty-eight western participating governments, plus Argentina, Belarus, Brazil, China, Kazakhstan, Mexico, Russia, Serbia, South Africa, and Ukraine.[6]

According to NSG guidelines, a supplier may only authorize a transfer of nuclear materials, equipment, and technology when it has been assured that the transfer would not contribute to the proliferation of nuclear weapons. Each participating government implements the NSG guidelines in accordance with its national laws and practices and exchanges information on its exports of nuclear-related products and other issues of common interest. The cooperation is informal and decisions on specific export applications are taken at the national level in accordance with national export licensing requirements. The NSG is an important complement to the Treaty on Non-Proliferation of Nuclear Weapons (NPT) and to the global efforts of the IAEA to prevent the spread of nuclear weapons.

Wassenaar Arrangement

The purpose of the Wassenaar Arrangement on Export Controls for Conventional Arms and Dual-Use Goods and Technologies, created in 1996, is to contribute to regional and international security and stability, by promoting transparency and greater responsibility in transferring conventional arms and dual use goods and technologies that can be used for both civilian and military purposes, thus preventing destabilizing accumulations of such goods and technologies. Participating countries, through their national policies, seek to ensure that transfers of these items do not contribute to the development or enhancement of military capabilities and are not diverted to support such capabilities. The Wassenaar Arrangement has forty-one participating western countries, plus Argentina, Mexico, Russia, South Africa, and Ukraine. Representatives of the participating countries meet regularly in Vienna, home of the Wassenaar Secretariat.[7]

The participants have drawn up a common list of weapons and dual-use products that are the subject of export control and have adopted specific guidelines for exports of small arms and light weapons and MANPADS. Members exchange information on their exports of arms and dual-use products as well as on other issues of common interest. The cooperation is informal, and decisions about specific export applications are taken by each individual country. Decisions on concrete export applications are taken in accordance with national legislation and are implemented at each country's discretion.

Comment

All four export control regimes are informal arrangements with parallel contents. The participants in the regimes are also largely identical, and consist mainly of western countries. The three western permanent members of the Security Council – France, the United Kingdom, and the United Sates – participate in all four export control regimes. Russia is a member of the NSG, MTCR, and the Wassenaar Arrangement. China is only a member of the NSG. Of the two other BRIC countries, Brazil is a member of the NSG and MTCR. India does not participate in any of the export control associations.

Unfortunately, the export control regimes have not been fully effective in preventing illegal transfers and diversions of conventional weapons, missiles, and materials and technologies for producing weapons of mass destruction. Alarmingly, there have been many cases of attempts to smuggle nuclear materials – including to terrorist organizations – which have only been prevented at the last minute by effective international cooperation between law enforcement agencies.

EU *Common Position Governing Exports of Military Technology and Equipment*

In 1998, the Council of Foreign Ministers of the European Union adopted the European Union Code of Conduct on Arms Exports (doc. 8675/2/98 Rev. 2). The Code is a politically binding agreement under which the EU member states agree to abide by certain criteria when granting arms export licenses. The aim of the Code is to set "high common standards for the management of and restraint in arms exports from the EU" and to increase transparency among EU states on arms exports.

The code contains eight criteria that the member states have to take into account when granting arms export licenses. These criteria include:

1 respect for member states' international obligations and commitments, in particular the sanctions adopted by the UN Security Council or the European Union, and agreements on non-proliferation and other subjects;
2 respect for human rights in the country of final destination as well as respect for international humanitarian law by that country;
3 evaluation of the internal situation in the country of final destination; member states will not allow exports that would provoke or prolong armed conflicts or aggravate existing tensions or conflicts in the country of final destination;
4 maintenance of regional peace, security, and stability;
5 behaviour of the buyer country with regard to the international community, in particular its attitude in relation to terrorism, the nature of its alliances, and respect for international law;
6 existence of a risk that the military technology or equipment may be diverted within the buyer country for other purposes or re-exported under undesirable conditions;
7 compatibility of the arms exports with the technical and economic capacity of the recipient country, taking into account that it is desirable for states to meet their legitimate security and defence

needs, diverting as few as possible of their human and economic resources for armaments.

These criteria of the Code of Conduct are complemented by provisions that oblige the member states to inform each other of any licenses they have refused, along with an explanation, and require member states to circulate an annual report on their defence exports and on the implementation of the Code.

The Code of Conduct was supplemented in 2008 when the Council adopted Common Position 2008/944/CFSP. Both the Code and the Common Position aim to harmonize EU member states' arms export policies in line with agreed minimum standards.

According to these standards, the EU states pledge not to approve arms exports in cases where

- the sale would violate the exporting state's commitments under the UN Charter or specific arms control agreements,
- the sale could provoke or prolong armed conflict,
- a "clear risk" exists that the weapons will be used for internal repression or that the arms would be used aggressively against another country.

The EU has also adopted Regulation (EU) No. 1232/2011 of the European Parliament and of the Council, of 2011, amending Council Regulation (EC) No 428/2009. These regulations establish the Community regime to control the export, transfer, brokering, and transit of dual use items. The Common Position establishes provisions to be implemented through national legislation. This requires member states to regulate brokering activities on their territory or carried out by their nationals, in particular subjecting brokering transactions to license applications, establishing a system for exchange of information on brokering activities, and establishing adequate sanctions for effective enforcement.

WORLD MILITARY EXPENDITURE

According to SIPRI, global military expenditure in 2014 was an estimated US$1.776 billion (at current prices and exchange rates), equivalent to 2.3 per cent of global gross domestic product (GDP). The global military expenditure in 2014 was equivalent to approximately US$4.7 billion per day and $234 per person yearly (the world's total population as of July 2015 was estimated at 7.3 billion people). The expenditure in 2014 represents a fall of about 0.4 per cent in real terms compared with 2013.[8] This is the third consecutive year that total global military expenditure has decreased. However, the decreases during the previous two years were comparatively small. World military expenditure is still only 1.7 per cent below its 2011 peak, and it remains significantly above the levels of the late 1980s.

Overall military spending decreased in North America, Western and Central Europe, and Latin America and the Caribbean, but rose in Asia and Oceania, the Middle East, Eastern Europe, and Africa. While the United States remains clearly the world's largest military spender, at nearly three times the level of second-place China, its expenditure dropped by 6.5 per cent, to $610 billion in 2014, equivalent to 3.5 per cent of US GDP, largely as a result of budget deficit control measures. Since reaching its highest recorded peak in 2010, US military expenditure has decreased by 19.8 per cent in real terms. The US's share of world military expenditure remains the highest at 34 per cent.

The military defence budget for the United States in 2016 is $585 billion – an increase of $25 billion as compared with 2015. According to the Arms Control Association, the US Congressional Budget Office released a report in January 2015 showing that current plans to maintain and eventually rebuild all three legs of the US nuclear triad (i.e., strategic bombers, intercontinental ballistic missiles (ICBMs), and SLBMs) and its associated warheads will cost American taxpayers roughly $35 billion per year over the next decade, or 5 to 6 per cent of the planned overall budget for national defence spending. Over the next thirty years, the bill could add up to $1 trillion, according to a recent report of the National Defence Panel Review of the 2014 Quadrennial Defence Review.

Spending in Central Europe broke with recent trends and began to rise again following the large decreases in previous years as a result of the global financial crisis that began in 2008. The five biggest spenders in 2014 were the United States, China, Russia, Saudi Arabia, and France. In 2014, China, Russia, and Saudi Arabia were the second-, third-, and fourth-highest military spenders, respectively. China's expenditure rose by 9.7 per cent to an estimated spending of $216 billion, Russia's spending was up 8.1 per cent to an estimated $84.5 billion, and Saudi Arabia's by 17 per cent to $80.8 billion. From 2005 to 2014, China's military expenditures increased by 167 per cent.

Comment

In his article "The World Is Over-armed and Peace Is Underfunded," the United Nations secretary general Ban Ki-moon notes that global daily military expenditure is almost twice as much as the UN budget for a whole year.

The world's exorbitant military expenditure appears to be out of proportion to countries' real needs for military forces to defend their sovereignty and national independence. This has been the case ever since the Cold War.

The threats to national security have changed significantly in recent years. Today, a country's security is not only maintained by the military defence of national borders. Increasingly, security threats arise as a result of demographic changes, e.g., large uncontrolled refugee and immigration flows, poverty and economic inequality, climate change, environmental pollution, global infectious diseases, organized crime, and oppressive regimes. No country can control or defend itself alone against these threats, and no military power – not even by using nuclear weapons – can defeat these new security challenges. What is needed to cope with actual and future security threats is a greater and more effective use of preventive diplomacy and of measures to prevent new international crises and conflicts and to contain them before they develop into armed conflicts, in other words, soft power. Obviously, conventional military forces will continue to be needed for securing national defence, deployment in peacekeeping, or peacemaking missions, and for ensuring the reconstruction of war-torn countries.

Another major obstacle to greater reductions in military expenditure is the strong position and influence of the military industrial complex in many of the major countries. In the United States especially, the "military establishment" and the military industry represent a significant factor of power – both in domestic policies and economically. Significant reductions in US military forces and the US arms industry would result in the loss of hundreds of thousands of jobs in the armed forces, the military industry, and jobs in related research institutes.

The member states of the United Nations should make greater use of the UN's possibilities to mediate when international conflicts are emerging, and to launch conflict prevention measures, such as deploying UN peacemaking and peacekeeping forces. Member states should demonstrate greater political will to implement and comply with the resolutions adopted by the UN Security Council and General Assembly.

Recommendations for Further Development of International Law on Disarmament, Arms Control, and Non-Proliferation

14

Recommendations for Further Development of International Law on Disarmament, Arms Control, and Non-Proliferation

INTRODUCTION

Which tasks should be given priority in future work to promote the international legal regulation of disarmament, arms control, and non-proliferation?

Several disarmament and arms control civil society organizations and individual experts have made recommendations on the next steps to take in the disarmament and arms control process. The recommendations are contained in various reports, including the following:

- *Report of the Canberra Commission on the Elimination of Nuclear Weapons*, August 1996;
- *Protecting against the Spread of Nuclear, Biological and Chemical Weapons: An Action Agenda for the Global Partnership, Center for Strategic and International Studies*, January 2003;
- *Weapons of Terror: Freeing the World of Nuclear, Biological, and Chemical Arms*, Weapons of Mass Destruction Commission, June 2006;[1]
- *Abolishing Nuclear Weapons*, International Institute for Strategic Studies, 2008.

A number of civil society organizations, including NTI[2] and the Nuclear Security Project (NSP), have also presented many recommendations for further disarmament and arms control steps. The recommendations by the NTI are presented in the DVD *Nuclear Tipping Point*, produced by the Nuclear Security Project to raise awareness about

nuclear threats and to help build support for the urgent actions needed to reduce nuclear dangers.

Some of the most important recommendations in these reports are
reproduced below. The list of recommendations for the next disarmament steps also contains the author's own suggestions. The order in
which the recommendations are mentioned does not reflect any priority, but follows the methodology in the book.

GENERAL RECOMMENDATIONS

- Encourage states to adhere to existing treaties and conventions, so
  that the treaty regimes become universal with the participation of
  all states.
- Ensure that the existing treaties and conventions are implemented
  and made more effective to fulfill the purposes of the treaties and
  conventions.
- Promote compliance with the existing treaties and conventions so
  that all countries fully comply with the rules.
- Strengthen verification of compliance with the existing treaties
  and conventions so that states that do not comply with the rules
  are quickly exposed and held accountable for their violations of
  the agreements.
- Strengthen sanctions for violations of the existing treaties and conventions to deter potential violators of the rules from committing
  breaches of the agreements.

RECOMMENDATIONS
FOR WEAPONS OF MASS DESTRUCTION

Nuclear Weapons

GENERAL RECOMMENDATIONS[3]

The five nuclear-weapon states recognized in the NPT – the United
States, Russia, the United Kingdom, France, and China – should initiate real negotiations on practical steps that can lead to a gradual reduction of their nuclear weapons with total elimination of all nuclear
weapons as the ultimate goal. The nuclear-weapon states should take
the following initial steps:

- The United States and Russia should remove their nuclear weapons from high-operational-readiness status (i.e., high alert, ready to launch within minutes) and establish increased warning and decision time to reduce the risk of an accidental launch. The United Kingdom and France should take their nuclear weapons out of operational readiness.[4]
- Remove nuclear weapons from deployment.
- Remove the nuclear warheads from their delivery vehicles (missiles) and keep them in separate storage.
- Withdraw without delay all tactical nuclear weapons from deployment on the territory of other states (US tactical nuclear weapons in Europe).
- Stop modernizing existing nuclear weapons and developing new types of nuclear weapons.
- Initiate negotiations on additional verifiable and irreversible reductions by destroying both strategic and tactical nuclear weapons.
- Initiate complete openness, greater cooperation, and enhanced confidence through increased transparency and effective verification of the numbers of nuclear weapons and stocks of fissile materials for military purposes.
- Change nuclear doctrines and strategies, i.e., conclude legally binding international agreements on mutual obligations between the nuclear-weapon states on no-first-use of nuclear weapons against each other and on negative security assurances for non-use or threat of use of nuclear weapons against non-nuclear-weapon states.
- Strengthen cooperation to prevent the proliferation of nuclear weapons and the know-how, technology, equipment, and materials for the manufacture of nuclear weapons.
- Stop the production of fissile material for use in nuclear weapons and establish international control of existing stocks of fissile material for nuclear weapons.
- Promote information, education, and awareness about the alarming dangers of nuclear weapons, especially to young people.

SPECIFIC RECOMMENDATIONS

- Promote universal adherence to the Nuclear NPT by integrating or associating Israel, India, and Pakistan in the non-proliferation regime, possibly by separate agreements or protocols to the NPT.
- Promote adherence – in particular of the key states listed in Annex 2, whose adherence is necessary for its entry into force – to the Comprehensive Test Ban Treaty (CTBT) with a view to the Treaty's early entry into force.
- Initiate negotiations in the CD on a treaty banning the production of fissile material for nuclear weapons (Fissile Material Cut-off Treaty).
- Promote adherence to IAEA's comprehensive safeguards system by concluding additional protocols to the safeguards agreements and make transfers of fissile materials (uranium and plutonium) and equipment for non-nuclear weapons states subject to the acceptance of IAEA's comprehensive safeguards system, and to the obligation not to acquire nuclear weapons.
- Initiate negotiations on an International Convention on Nuclear Security.
- Increase the efforts to establish a weapons of mass destruction–free zone (WMDFZ) in the Middle East.
- Establish a NWFZ in South Asia.
- Initiate negotiations on an international agreement on limitation and control of missiles, particularly of cruise missiles and medium-range missiles, preferably by extending the INF Treaty's ban globally.
- Promote efforts to strengthen the international control of the production of and trade in uranium.
- Develop a protocol to the Outer Space Treaty to prohibit the placement of any kind of weapons in outer space.

Biological Weapons

- Adopt rules on effective verification of compliance with the Biological Weapons Convention (BWC).

without nuclear weapons, the risk of a nuclear detonation caused by accident, misperception, miscalculation, or terrorist act must be diminished and the security of nuclear materials must be strengthened to prevent theft and sabotage.

Since the late 1990s, global limitations of nuclear weapons have no longer been in the forefront of international security politics, and negotiations on further reductions of nuclear weapons have stalled. Local and regional conflicts – such as the conflict in Ukraine and the wars in the Middle East – international terrorist attacks, and concerns about nuclear proliferation – rather than the nuclear weapons themselves – have taken over the security agenda, both nationally and internationally. Technological developments and the proliferation of new delivery systems (cruise missiles) and ballistic missile defences have complicated efforts to promote disarmament and control of nuclear weapons. Since 2011, there has been renewed confrontation and reduced cooperation between the United States and Russia, undermining progress in arms control. The two major nuclear-weapon states must renew their efforts and cooperate to ensure that existing treaties continue to be fully implemented, and to start new negotiations on further reducing and controlling nuclear weapons (see the recommendations in Part III, pages 228–31).

Why do people – in particular politicians – not realize that today we all continue to live in constant danger of total annihilation as long as nuclear weapons exist? If these weapons fall into the wrong hands through theft, smuggling, or other illicit transfers, they may be used by rogue states, extremist religious groups, militants, or terrorist organizations. Nuclear weapons in the arsenals of the nuclear-weapon states or possessed by the nuclear-armed states could also be launched as a result of misunderstandings, miscalculations, human mistakes, technical malfunction, accidents, sabotage, unauthorized launch, or cyberattacks causing false alerts – and possibly counterattacks, with catastrophic health and environmental consequences for humanity.[1] Why this indifference to the potential catastrophe of an unprecedented dimension? Is it because of lack of information or understanding of the problem?[2] Or is it because people today are more concerned with other global dangers, caused by climate change, our continued destructive treatment of the environment, irresponsible exploitation of the earth's natural resources, or uncontrollable flows of refugees and immigrants?

In January 2007, four senior US statesmen and "cold warriors" –
George Shultz, William Perry, Henry Kissinger, and Sam Nunn – presented their vision of "A World Free of Nuclear Weapons," in an article in the *Wall Street Journal*. They elaborated on this theme in four
later articles in the *Journal* over the next six years. In an effort to promote global action, the four dignitaries joined together to form the
Nuclear Security Project, to reduce urgent nuclear dangers and build
support for reducing reliance on nuclear weapons. The project links
the vision of a world free of nuclear weapons with urgent steps that
can be taken immediately to reduce nuclear dangers. The NTI is the
coordinator of the project. The Nuclear Security Project has produced
a very thought-provoking documentary film, *Nuclear Tipping Point*, to
deepen awareness of the growing nuclear dangers and build support
for the project goals.[3]

As the film shows, we are at a critical turning point today: either we
start an irreversible and internationally controlled process that will
lead to a gradual reduction and ultimately to the total elimination of
all nuclear weapons, or else nuclear weapons can be expected to
spread to more countries and – still worse – to rogue states and terrorist organizations. The threat of nuclear terrorism is real and growing. As long as there are stockpiles of nuclear weapons, the possibility of nuclear terrorism remains. Al-Qaeda has publicly stated that it
intends to acquire nuclear weapons to use against the United States
and its allies. The only way to completely eliminate the risk of sabotage or theft by terrorists is to abolish all nuclear weapons and to keep
all fissile materials usable for nuclear weapons under strict international control. The risk of a disaster as a result of a nuclear weapon or
radiological bomb has been confirmed by military intelligence ser-
vices in several countries.

The world has been very close to nuclear war at least five times,
which could have resulted in the total annihilation of humanity and
destruction of all life on earth. The first four serious incidents happened during the Cold War: On 27 October 1962, during the Cuban
missile crisis, the captain of a nuclear-armed Soviet submarine intended to launch a nuclear torpedo. But the commander of the Soviet fleet
in the area, who was on-board the submarine, prevented the launch
and, most probably, prevented a nuclear war with the United States.
On 3 June 1980, a computer chip malfunction in an American command centre indicated that a massive Soviet nuclear attack had been
launched. A retaliatory nuclear strike was avoided when it became

clear that it was a false alarm. On 26 September 1983, the command-
ing officer of a Soviet missile control centre chose to ignore the false
alarm from the Russian satellite warning system showing that an
American missile attack had been launched against the Soviet Union,
thus avoiding a massive Russian nuclear retaliation attack on the
United States at the last minute.[4] Less than two months later, at the
beginning of November 1983, NATO conducted a large exercise that
the Soviet political and military leadership believed was preparation
for a nuclear first strike. The Soviet nuclear forces were put on high
alert until the exercise ended. The fifth close call to the brink of
nuclear war happened on 25 January 1995 when a US scientific rocket was launched from a Norwegian island near the coast of northern
Russia. Although the proper Russian authorities had been notified
about the launch, this information had not been transmitted to the
Russian early warning centre, where the scientific rocket launch was
mistakenly believed to be an initial American attack with a ballistic
missile. Once again, a Russian nuclear counterattack was avoided at
the last moment.

There have been several nuclear weapon accidents. Among the
most notable and scary are the crash of a B-52 plane in 1961 in North
Carolina. Two nuclear bombs fell off the plane, but did not explode
when they hit the ground because of one single safety switch, which
prevented a nuclear catastrophe. In 1966, two military aircraft collid-
ed off the coast of Spain. The B-52 involved in the crash was carrying
four nuclear bombs. Three of the bombs fell on land and the non-
nuclear explosives in two of them detonated, resulting in radioactive
plutonium contamination of the area. Another crash happened two
years later when a B-52 caught fire and crashed onto sea ice in Greenland. The four nuclear bombs onboard ruptured and were dispersed,
resulting in widespread radioactive contamination. In 1980, an American missile carrying a 9-megaton nuclear warhead exploded in its silo
in Arkansas when a maintenance worker accidentally dropped a sock-
et wrench. It fell into the silo, hit the missile, and opened a leak, fill-
ing the silo with rocket fuel. The fuel leak caused the missile to
explode. The nuclear warhead was thrown 180 metres away, but did
not detonate.[5]

A disturbing incident of negligence in the handling of nuclear
weapons happened in 2007 when six nuclear warheads went missing
for thirty-six hours. Six nuclear-armed cruise missiles were mistakenly
mounted onto the wings of a B-52 and flown from an air force base

in North Dakota, by pilots who did not know they were carrying nuclear weapons, to an airbase in Louisiana where nobody knew the missiles were coming. The aircraft was parked and left overnight unguarded. The next day a maintenance crew discovered the mistake.

How long will we continue to rely on luck?

The new global non-military threats, such as climate change and environmental disasters, may help to raise public and political awareness about the urgent need to promote disarmament, arms control, and non-proliferation – in particular of nuclear weapons and other weapons of mass destruction. In addition to the benefits of reducing or even eliminating the dangers of attacks with weapons of mass destruction, a significant part of the current exorbitant military expenditures in the world could be used to avert the threats to our climate and environment and to improve people's living conditions, particularly in developing countries.

Since the end of the Cold War, the arsenals of both conventional arms and nuclear weapons have been significantly reduced. However, the hope and optimism of the 1990s for a more peaceful world with fewer weapons have faded away and have been replaced by a climate of tension, mistrust, and lack of dialogue on further common steps to reduce armaments – in particular between the western countries and Russia. According to the Nuclear Threat Initiative,

> the risk of nuclear weapons use in the Euro-Atlantic region is on the rise and it is higher today than it has been since the end of the Cold War. The significant deterioration in relations between the United States and Russia has led to dangerous conditions that make nuclear weapons use more likely – although the probability remains low. The United States and Russia are on an increasingly dangerous path. Weak channels of communication, close military encounters, and other factors have increased the likelihood of misunderstanding and the possibility that a significant escalation in tensions could lead to catastrophe.[6]

The pace of reducing American and Russian nuclear weapons has slowed down in recent years. The excessive stockpiles of spare nuclear weapons held in reserve could be significantly reduced without negatively affecting national security or decreasing the deterrent effect of the deployed nuclear weapons. Such reductions could be made unilaterally without concluding further arms control agreements. The two major possessor states and all the other nuclear-weapon states and nuclear-armed states are modernizing and upgrading their nuclear weapons, making them more effective. Both the United States and Russia continue to implement their reduction obligations under the New START Treaty, but there are currently no serious talks between them on further reductions of their nuclear weapons after the New START Treaty expires in 2020. Both the United States and Russia still deploy about 1,500 strategic warheads on several hundred missiles and bombers. This "overkill capacity" for "mutual assured destruction" or "MAD" is far more than necessary to deter a nuclear attack from the other side. In addition, the deliberate use of nuclear weapons by the United States and Russia against each other in a full-scale nuclear war must be considered a very remote possibility, because such attacks would be suicidal. The proper functioning of the nuclear command and control centres in both countries, mutual restraint, and transparency and continued effective dialogue and communication between the two major nuclear powers are vital for avoiding nuclear war. Although the likelihood of a nuclear war between the United States and Russia has decreased significantly, the continued presence of large numbers of deployed and stockpiled nuclear weapons makes the accidental or unauthorized use of such weapons a real and constant risk.

China, India, and Pakistan continue to improve their nuclear capabilities and are developing new ballistic missiles, cruise missiles, and sea-based nuclear weapon delivery systems. This development is dangerous and destabilizing for regional security in southern Asia, and makes a regional nuclear war a possibility. Pakistan has developed tactical nuclear weapons to counter perceived Indian conventional military threats and superiority, and Pakistan's nuclear doctrine is based on possible first use.

Under current security policy conditions, it has been argued that the threats – even use of nuclear weapons – from Russia after its illegal annexation of the Crimea, Russia's military involvement in the hostilities in Eastern Ukraine, and the war in Syria, call for increases in military budgets and the rearmament of the armed forces of NATO's member states, not for disarmament. However, increases in conventional armed forces do not exclude the simultaneous disarmament of nuclear weapons. Indirectly, the rearmament of conventional forces may even be conducive to further disarmament of nuclear weapons that a possessor state will no longer need, or be less inclined to use as a last resort when that state is confident that it has sufficient conventional forces to defeat the enemy or deter a potential enemy from attacking.

The fact that the nuclear-weapon states and nuclear-armed states are voting against UN General Assembly resolutions calling for disarmament and control of nuclear weapons clearly demonstrates that none of them appears to be willing to give up their nuclear weapons in the foreseeable future. These states continue to modernize their nuclear arsenals, developing new types of nuclear weapons and delivery systems, and maintaining nuclear deterrence in their security doctrines and military strategies. The United States plans to spend $355 billion over the next decade – or $35 billion per year – to maintain and modernize its nuclear forces. The costs of simply maintaining their actual nuclear weapons and facilities are about $8 billion per year. Russia is also significantly modernizing its nuclear weapons. It is planning to spend $54 billion over the next ten years. The deal made in the Nuclear Non-Proliferation Treaty was not to grant the five nuclear-weapon states a "licence to keep" their nuclear arsenals indefinitely. The understanding was, and continues to be, that the nuclear weapon states could keep their nuclear weapons temporarily, but that they were committing themselves to a negotiation process in good faith, which ultimately would lead to the total elimination of these weapons.

How can this obstacle to disarmament, and ultimately the abolition of nuclear weapons, be overcome so that the process of obtaining a world free of nuclear weapons can be advanced and the vision for this ultimately realized? The Marshall Islands' case before the International Court of Justice may lead to a judgment declaring the nuclear-weapon states and the nuclear-armed states in breach of the NPT and of customary international law because they refuse to initiate and pursue negotiations until they are successfully concluded, as stated in Article 6 of the NPT obligation "to pursue negotiations in good faith on effective measures relating to ... nuclear disarmament, and on a treaty on general and complete disarmament under strict and effective international control." However, such a judgment will not be enforceable through sanctions imposed by the United Nations Security Council. Proposals for sanctions will, of course, be blocked by vetoes from the five permanent members of the Security Council and nuclear-weapon states.

The only possible way ahead to promote disarmament of nuclear weapons seems to be increased engagement and pressure from civil society organizations and the public in general. Such pressure could involve voting for political leaders and candidates to parliaments that support disarmament, and promotion of media campaigns, and public debates. There is a clear need for the public to become much more informed about the continued – and in many experts' view – increasing dangers and risks of use of nuclear weapons, either deliberate or accidental. The NGOs, think tanks, and research institutions have an important role to play here. Broad public awareness, active support, and political pressure for abolition of nuclear weapons is necessary to reach the goal of a safer world, free of nuclear weapons. Reaching this goal will, undoubtedly, be a very, very long process, but not only can we do it – we must do it, before it is too late.

The Doomsday Clock remains at three minutes to midnight – the closest we have been to nuclear destruction in twenty years! Let us all unite against the insanity of nuclear weapons. We must now demand that our political leaders embark on the long and arduous journey to abolish all these inhumane weapons, the use of which must generally be considered unlawful.

List of Agreements

The agreements on disarmament, arms control, and non-proliferation discussed in this book are listed below.

The texts of the treaties and conventions can be found by searching on the full titles or abbreviations on the relevant websites. See the website list below.

WEAPONS OF MASS DESTRUCTION

Nuclear Weapons

Treaty on the Non-Proliferation of Nuclear Weapons (NPT), of 1 July 1968, p. 66

Treaty on the Prohibition of the Emplacement of Nuclear Weapons and Other Weapons of Mass Destruction on the Seabed and the Ocean Floor and in the Subsoil Thereof, of 11 February 1971, p. 100

Treaty on Measures for the Further Reduction and Limitation of Strategic Offensive Arms (New START or Prague Treaty), of 8 April 2010, p. 58, 60

Missiles

Treaty between the United States of America and the Union of Soviet Socialist Republics on the Limitation of Anti-Ballistic Missile Systems (ABM), of 26 May 1972, p. 164

Treaty between the United States of America and the Union of Soviet Socialist Republics on the Elimination of Their Intermediate-Range and Shorter-Range Missiles (INF), of 8 December 1967, p. 61

International (Hague) Code of Conduct against Ballistic Missile Proliferation (HCOC), of 25 November 2002, p. 162–3

Test Ban Treaties

Treaty Banning Nuclear Weapon Tests in the Atmosphere, in Outer Space and Under Water (Partial Test Ban Treaty – PTBT), of 5 August 1963, p. 81

Treaty between the United States of America and the Union of Soviet Socialist Republics on the Limitation of Underground Nuclear Weapon Tests (Threshold Test Ban Treaty – TTBT), of 3 July 1974, p. 81

Treaty between the United States of America and the Union of Soviet Socialist Republics on Underground Nuclear Explosions for Peaceful Purposes (Peaceful Nuclear Explosions Treaty – PNET), of 28 May 1976, p. 81

The Comprehensive Nuclear-Test-Ban Treaty (CTBT), of 24 September 1996, p. 81–4

Nuclear-Weapon-Free Zones

The Antarctic Treaty, of 1 December 1959, p. 92–3

Treaty for the Prohibition of Nuclear Weapons in Latin America (Treaty of Tlatelolco), of 14 February 1967, p. 89–90

South Pacific Nuclear Weapon Free Zone Treaty (Treaty of Rarotonga), of 6 August 1985, p. 90

Treaty on the Southeast Asia Nuclear Weapon-Free Zone (Treaty of Bangkok), of 15 December 1995, p. 90

African Nuclear-Weapon-Free-Zone Treaty (Treaty of Pelindaba), of 11 April 1996, p. 91

Treaty on a Nuclear-Weapon-Free-Zone in Central Asia (Treaty of Semipalatinsk), of 8 September 2006, p. 91

Biological Weapons

Protocol for the Prohibition of the Use in War of Asphyxiating, Poisonous or Other Gases, and of Bacteriological Methods of Warfare
(1925 Geneva Protocol), of 17 June 1925, p. 129–30
Convention on the Prohibition of the Development, Production and
Stockpiling of Bacteriological (Biological) and Toxin Weapons and
on Their Destruction (Biological Weapons Convention – BWC), of
10 April 1972, p. 131–4

Chemical Weapons

Protocol for the Prohibition of the Use in War of Asphyxiating, Poi-
sonous or Other Gases, and of Bacteriological Methods of Warfare
(1925 Geneva Protocol), of 17 June 1925, p. 129–30
Convention on the Prohibition of Military or Any Other Hostile
Use of Environmental Modification Techniques (ENMOD), of 18
May 1977, p. 137
Convention on the Prohibition of the Development, Production,
Stockpiling and Use of Chemical Weapons and on Their Des-
truction (Chemical Weapons Convention – CWC), of 13 January
1993, p. 137–44

Outer Space

Treaty on Principles Governing the Activities of States in the
Exploration and Use of Outer Space, Including the Moon and
Other Celestial Bodies (Outer Space Treaty), of 27 January
1967, p. 150–1
Agreement Governing the Activities of States on the Moon and
Other Celestial Bodies (Moon Agreement), of 5 December 1979,
p. 152
Convention on Registration of Objects Launched into Outer Space
(Registration Convention), of 14 January 1975, p. 152

CONVENTIONAL WEAPONS

Heavy Conventional Weapons

Treaty on Conventional Armed Forces in Europe (CFE), of 19 November 1990, p. 170–4

Concluding Act of the Negotiation on Personnel Strength of Conventional Armed Forces in Europe (CFE-1A Agreement), of 10 July 1992, p. 174–5

Agreement on Adaptation of the Treaty on Conventional Armed Forces in Europe (Agreement on CFE adaptation), of 19 November 1999, p. 175

Vienna Document 1990 of the Negotiations on Confidence- and Security-Building Measures (Vienna CSBM Document), of 17 November 1990, p. 179

Vienna Document 2011 of the Negotiations on Confidence- and Security-Building Measures (Vienna CSBM Document), of 30 November 2011, p. 179

Treaty on Open Skies (Open Skies), of 24 March 1992, p. 179–80

Small Arms and Light Weapons

Protocol against the Illicit Manufacturing of and Trafficking in Firearms, Their Parts and Components and Ammunition (Firearms Protocol), of 31 May 2001, p. 184–5

Programme of Action to Prevent, Combat and Eradicate the Illicit Trade in Small Arms and Light Weapons in All Its Aspects (UN SALW Program of Action), of 21 July 2001, p. 185–6

Council Joint Action on the European Union's Contribution to Combating the Destabilising Accumulation and Spread of Small Arms and Light Weapons (EU Joint Action on SALW), of 12 July 2002, p. 190

EU Strategy to Combat Illicit Accumulation and Trafficking of SALW and their Ammunition (EU Strategy on SALW), of 13 January 2006, p. 190

Council Decision on EU Action to Counter the Illicit Trade of Small Arms and Light Weapons By Air (EU Council Decision on SALW), of 2 December 2010, p. 190

OSCE Document on Small Arms and Light Weapons (OSCE SALW Document), of 24 November 2000, p. 190

Inter-American Convention Against the Illicit Manufacturing of and Trafficking in Firearms, Ammunition, Explosives and Other Related Materials (Inter-American SALW Convention), of 14 November 1997, p. 191

ECOWAS Convention on Small Arms and Light Weapons, their Ammunition and other Related Materials (ECOWAS SALW Convention), of 14 June 2006, p. 191–2

Central African Convention for the Control of Small Arms and Light Weapons, their Ammunition, Parts and Components that can be used for their Manufacture, Repair and Assembly (Central African SALW Convention), of 30 April 2010, p. 192

Inhumane Conventional Weapons

Geneva Conventions for the Amelioration of the Conditions of the Wounded and Sick in Armed Forces in the Field, and of Shipwrecked Members of Armed Forces at Sea, relative to the Treatment of Prisoners of War, and relative to the Protection of Civilian Persons in Time of War (1949 Geneva Conventions), of 12 August 1949, p. 16

Protocols Additional to the Geneva Conventions relating to the Protection of Victims of International Armed Conflicts and of Non-International Armed Conflicts (1977 Additional Protocols), of 8 June 1977, p. 16, 22, 111, 160, 192–3, 202

Convention on Prohibitions or Restrictions on the Use of Certain Conventional Weapons which may be deemed to be Excessively Injurious or to have Indiscriminate Effects (Certain Conventional Weapons – CCW), of 10 October 1980, p. 193–5

Protocol I on Non-detectable Fragments, of 10 October 1980, p. 195

Protocol II on Prohibitions or Restrictions on the Use of Mines, Booby-Traps and Other Devices (APM Protocol), of 10 October 1980, p. 195–6

Protocol III on Prohibitions or Restrictions on the Use of Incendiary Weapons, of 10 October 1980, p. 196–7

Protocol IV on Blinding Laser Weapons, of 13 October 1980, p. 197

Protocol V on Explosive Remnants of War (ERW Protocol), of 28 November 2003, p. 197–8

Convention on Cluster Munitions (CCM), of 30 May 2008, p. 202–5

Anti-Personnel Mines

Protocol II on Prohibitions or Restrictions on the Use of Mines,
  Booby-Traps and Other Devices (APM Protocol), of 10 October
  1980, p. 195–6
Convention on the Prohibition of the Use, Stockpiling, Production
  and Transfer of Anti-Personnel Mines and on Their Destruction
  (Ottawa APM Convention), of 18 September 1997, p. 199–202

Arms Trade

The Arms Trade Treaty (ATT), of 2 April 2013, p. 207–12

Classification of Agreements

The existing disarmament and arms control agreements can be divided into the following main categories:

- Disarmament agreements
- Arms control agreements
- Preventive arms control agreements

DISARMAMENT AGREEMENTS CONTAINING A TOTAL PROHIBITION OF CERTAIN TYPES OF WEAPONS:

- Convention on the Prohibition of Biological Weapons of 1972 (BWC)
- Convention on the Prohibition of Military or Any Other Hostile Use of Environmental Modification Techniques of 1977 (ENMOD)
- Treaty on the Elimination of Intermediate-Range and Shorter-Range Missiles of 1987 (INF)
- Convention on the Prohibition of Chemical Weapons of 1993 (CWC)
- Convention on the Prohibition of Anti-Personnel Mines of 1997 (APM)
- Convention on Cluster Munitions of 2008 (CCM)

ARMS CONTROL AGREEMENTS LIMITING OR REGULATING
THE NUMBER, CAPABILITY, DEPLOYMENT, USE, AND TRADE
OF CERTAIN TYPES OF WEAPONS:

- Treaty between the United States and the Soviet Union on the
  Limitation of Anti-Ballistic Missile Systems (anti-missile defence
  systems) of 1972 (ABM)
- Interim Agreement between the United States and the Soviet
  Union on Certain Measures with Respect to the Limitation of
  Strategic Offensive Arms of 1972 (SALT I)
- Treaty between the United States and the Soviet Union on the
  Limitation of Strategic Offensive Arms of 1979 (SALT II)
- Treaty between the United States and the Soviet Union on the
  Reduction and Limitation of Strategic Offensive Arms of 1991
  (START I) and on Further Reduction and Limitation of Strategic
  Offensive Arms of 1993 (START II)
- Treaty on Conventional Armed Forces in Europe of 1990 (CFE)
- Protocol II on Prohibitions or Restrictions on the Use of Mines,
  Booby-Traps and Other Devices of 1980 (APM Protocol) and Proto-
  col V on Explosive Remnants of War of 2003 (ERW Protocol) –
  both under the Convention on Certain Conventional Weapons of
  1980 (CCW)
- Treaty between the United States and Russia on Strategic Offen-
  sive Reductions of 2002 (SORT or Moscow Treaty)
- Treaty between the United States and Russia on Measures for the
  Further Reduction and Limitation of Strategic Offensive Arms of
  2010 (New START or Prague Treaty)
- Arms Trade Treaty of 2013 (ATT)

PREVENTIVE ARMS CONTROL AGREEMENTS PROHIBITING
PLACEMENT AND PROLIFERATION OF NUCLEAR WEAPONS,
WITHIN CERTAIN GEOGRAPHICAL AREAS (OR CONTINENTS)
AND TO NON-NUCLEAR-WEAPON STATES:

- Antarctic Treaty of 1959
- Outer Space Treaty of 1967
- Treaty for the Prohibition of Nuclear Weapons in Latin America
  of 1967

- Treaty on the Non-Proliferation of Nuclear Weapons of 1968 (NPT)
- Agreement Governing the Activities of States on the Moon and Other Celestial Bodies of 1979 (Moon Agreement)
- South Pacific Nuclear Weapon Free Zone Treaty of 1985
- Treaty on the Southeast Asia Nuclear-Weapon-Free Zone of Bangkok of 1995
- African Nuclear-Weapon-Free-Zone Treaty of 1996
- Treaty on a Nuclear-Weapon-Free Zone in Central Asia of 2006
- Comprehensive Nuclear-Test-Ban Treaty of 1996 (CTBT)

Notes

CHAPTER ONE

1 International Court of Justice. www.icj-cij.org.
2 See http://www.icrc.org/.
3 The presentations at the symposium are published in the United Nations
publication *The International Law of Arms Control and Disarmament –
Proceedings of the Symposium Geneva, 28 February–2 March 1991*, Dahlitz and
Dicke, eds., New York.

CHAPTER TWO

1 See Jozef Goldblat, *Arms Control* (2002), 285.

CHAPTER THREE

1 See UN doc. A/S-10/4.
2 Pakistan was the only country to vote against resolution 70/39, treaty banning the production of fissile material for nuclear weapons or other
nuclear explosive devices, adopted by the 70th General Assembly by 179
votes in favour, 1 against (Pakistan), and 5 abstentions (Egypt, Iran, Israel,
North Korea, and Syria). In the resolution the General Assembly urges the
Conference on Disarmament to agree on and implement a program of
work that includes immediately starting negotiations on a treaty banning
the production of fissile material for nuclear weapons or other nuclear
explosive devices.

3 The texts of all the resolutions adopted during the latest (the 70th General Assembly in 2015), and all earlier general assemblies, can be found at www.un.org/en/ga/70/resolutions.shtml – which also contains references to documents with information on the results of the voting. See also explanations of votes in which states explain the reasons for their voting.

4 See also http://eu-un.europe.eu.

CHAPTER FOUR

1 There is no universally accepted definition of verification. Canada has been a pioneer in studies of the issue of verification and, in partnership with The Verification, Research, Training and Information Centre (VERTIC – www.vertic.org), presented the report WMD *Verification and Compliance: The State of Play* of 2004.

2 Doc. A/RES/S-10/2.

3 Doc. A/45/372 of 28 August 1990.

4 The reports of the expert groups are contained in doc. A/50/377 (1995) and A/61/1028 (2007).

5 A detailed examination of verification provisions in key disarmament, arms control, and non-proliferation treaties and examples of cases of violations is contained in Jozef Goldblat's *Arms Control* (2002).

6 An overview of compliance provisions in the main multilateral treaties is contained in UNIDIR's publication *Coming to Terms with Security: A Handbook on Verification and Compliance*.

7 See www.icj-cij.org.

8 See *Nuclear Tests (Australia v. France), Judgment, ICJ Reports 1974*, 253–455 and *Nuclear Tests (New Zealand v. France), Judgment, ICJ Reports 1974*, 457–528.

9 See www.icc-cpi.int/ and the Rome Statute of 17 July 1998, adhered to by 123 states parties, including France and the United Kingdom, but none of the other nuclear-weapon states and nuclear-armed states.

CHAPTER FIVE

1 See an explanation of the difference between nuclear-weapon states and nuclear-armed states in the section below on the Nuclear Non-Proliferation Treaty, p. 66–8.

2 The strategic US-deployed nuclear weapon systems include approximately 450 ICBMs armed with 470 warheads, 288 SLBMs on board 12 nuclear-

powered ballistic missile submarines with 1,150 warheads, and 60 strategic bombers with 300 warheads.

3 See http://armscontrolcenter.org/factsheet-implementation-of-iran-nuclear-deal/.

4 See doc. NPT/CONF.2000/28 (Parts I and II). http://www.un.org/disarmament/WMD/Nuclear/2000-NPT/pdf/FD-Part1and2.pdf.

5 See resolution A/70/33, Taking forward multilateral nuclear disarmament negotiations.

6 Russia's membership in the G8 was suspended in March 2014 because of the Crimean crisis.

7 See Security Council resolution 2094 (2013) and 1929 (2010).

8 See also statements from the meeting. http://www.un.org/en/ga/68/meetings/nucleardisarmament/statements.shtml.

9 See *Bridging the Military Nuclear Materials Gap*, November 2015, Nuclear Threat Initiative. http://www.nti.org/media/pdfs/NTI_report_2015_e_version.pdf?_=1447091315.

10 See the comprehensive examination of the nuclear security problem *Nuclear Weapons: The State of Play 2015* by Gareth Evans, Tanya Ogilvie-White, and Ramesh Thakur, Australian National University.

11 See US Department of State, Nuclear Security Summits. http://www.state.gov/t/isn/nuclearsecuritysummit/.

12 See *International Convention on Nuclear Security* by John Bernhard, Kenneth C. Brill, Anita Nilsson, and Shin Chang-Hoon, Nuclear Security Governance Experts Group, http://www.nsgeg.org/ICNSReport315.pdf.

13 See also "A Convention on Nuclear Security: A Needed Step against Nuclear Terrorism," published in *Arms Control Today*, June 2015. http://www.armscontrol.org/ACT/2015_06/Features/A-Convention-on-Nuclear-Security-A-Needed-Step-Against-Nuclear-Terrorism.

14 See https://ola.iaea.org/ola/treaties/multi.html.

15 See www.psi-onli.info.

16 See www.ctbto.org/nuclear-testing.

17 See Statement of 8 January, "Fourth North Korean Nuclear Weapons Test," by The Center for Arms Control and Non-Proliferation.

18 Resolution 50/245, The text of the Comprehensive Nuclear Test-Ban Treaty is contained in document A/50/102.

19 See a thorough examination of test ban history, CTBT negotiation history, and the treaty's contents in *Unfinished Business: The Negotiation of the CTBT and the End of Nuclear Testing*, by Rebecca Johnson, UNIDIR.

20 Doc. A/54/42 (1999).

21 See the United Nations Convention on the Law of the Sea, Article 55 and 57.

22 Internal waters are defined in Article 8 of the Convention on the Law of the Sea as the waters on the landward side of the baseline of the territorial sea.

23 Doc. NPT/CONF.1995/32 (Part I), Annex.

24 Former Israeli nuclear technician Mordechai Vanunu revealed details of Israel's nuclear weapons program to the British press in 1986. Vanunu was sentenced for revealing Israeli nuclear secrets and spent eighteen years in prison.

25 See resolution 70/70 of 7 December 2015, The risk of nuclear proliferation in the Middle East, by which the General Assembly called upon Israel to accede to the NPT without further delay, not to develop, produce, test, or otherwise acquire nuclear weapons, to renounce possession of nuclear weapons, and to place all its unsafeguarded nuclear facilities under comprehensive IAEA safeguards. The resolution was adopted by 157 votes in favour, 5 against (including Israel, the United States, and Canada) and 20 abstentions (including France, the United Kingdom, and India). In another resolution, 70/24, Establishment of a nuclear-weapon-free zone in the region of the Middle East, the General Assembly "urges all parties directly concerned seriously to consider taking the practical and urgent steps required for the implementation of the proposal to establish a nuclear-weapon-free zone in the region of the Middle East in accordance with the relevant resolutions of the General Assembly." Resolution 70/24 was adopted without a vote.

26 Doc. A/45/435, 1991.

27 In the article "A Chemical Weapons-Free Middle East," Cindy Vestergaard, visiting fellow at the Center for Strategic & International Studies, proposes first to establish a chemical-weapons-free zone in the Middle East – see also http://csis.org/files/publication/130521_Vestergaard_ChemicalWeaponsFree MidEast.pdf.

28 See "Conference on an Arctic Nuclear-Weapon-Free Zone, Copenhagen, 10–11 August, 2009," by Cindy Vestergaard, ed., DIIS report, 2010:03.

29 See also one of the most comprehensive and recent books describing and assessing the issue: Nuclear Weapons under International Law (503 pages), 2014, by Gro Nystuen, Stuart Casey-Maslen, and Annie Golden Bersagel, eds., Cambridge.

30 See also www.icj-cij.org.

31 See also The (Il)legality of Threat or Use of Nuclear Weapons – A Guide to the

Historic Opinion of the ICJ, by John Burroughs, International Association of Lawyers Against Nuclear Arms.

32 See also Article 36 of the Statute of the ICJ.

33 See also *The Marshall Islands' Nuclear Zero Cases in the International Court of Justice* at www.lcnp.org/RMI/ and http://www.nuclearzero.org/in-the-courts – with Applications and other Court documents, the Lawyers Committee on Nuclear Policy.

34 Doc. A/62/650 of 18 January 2008.

35 See also *Nuclear Disarmament: The Road Ahead*, 2015. http://lcnp.org/pubs/Nuclear-Disarmament-The-Road-Ahead.pdf, International Association of Lawyers Against Nuclear Arms.

36 See *A Treaty Banning Nuclear Weapons* by Ray Acheson, Thomas Nash, and Richard Moyes, Article 36 and Reaching Critical Will. http://www.article36 .org/wp-content/uploads/2014/04/AR06_TREATY_REPORT_27.4.14.pdf. Article 36 is a UK-based not-for-profit organization working to prevent the unintended, unnecessary, or unacceptable harm caused by certain weapons. The name refers to Article 36 of the 1977 Additional Protocol I of the Geneva Conventions that requires states to review new weapons, means, and methods of warfare in order to determine whether their employment would, in some or all circumstances, be prohibited by the Protocol or by any other rule of international law applicable to the High Contracting Party.

37 ECOSOC doc. E/CN.4/Sub.2/2002/38 of 27 June 2002.

38 www.hsrgroup.org

39 A more detailed analysis of the relationship between human security and human rights lies outside the scope of this book. Reference is made to the reports *Human Security* in doc. A/64/701 of 8 March 2010, *A More Secure World: Our Shared Responsibility* in doc. A/59/565 of 2 December 2004, *In Larger Freedom: Towards Development, Security and Human Rights for All* in doc. A/59/2005 of 21 March 2005, *Report by the secretary general on Human Security* in doc. A/66/763 of 5 April 2012 and *General Assembly resolution 66/290* of 10 September 2012.

40 See also Chair's Summary, "Austrian Pledge," statements and presentations from the Vienna Conference on the Humanitarian Impact of Nuclear Weapons, 8–9 December 2014. http://www.bmeia.gv.at/en/european-foreign-policy/disarmament/weapons-of-mass-destruction/nuclear-weapons-and-nuclear-terrorism/vienna-conference-on-the-humanitarian-impact-of-nuclear-weapons/.

41 See also Council of Delegates of the International Red Cross and Red Cres-
    cent Movement, Geneva, Switzerland, 26 November 2011, resolution 1
    Working towards the elimination of nuclear weapons.
    https://www.icrc.org/eng/resources/documents/resolution/council-delegates-
    resolution-1-2011.htm.

CHAPTER SIX

1 See also report no. 18 from the Henry L. Stimson Center, *Biological Weapons
   Proliferation: Reasons for Concern, Courses of Action*, January 1998.

CHAPTER EIGHT

1 In 2001, the Council of Europe adopted the Convention on Cybercrime, also
   known as the Budapest Convention on Cybercrime or the Budapest Convention. The convention entered into force on 1 July 2004 and has been ratified by 47 states, including non-Council of Europe states, including Canada,
   Japan, and the United States. It is the first international treaty seeking to
   address Internet and computer crime by harmonizing national laws, improving investigative techniques, and increasing cooperation among states.

CHAPTER ELEVEN

1 Such statements have been made by former Lieutenant-General Yevgeny P.
   Buzhinsky, consultant and vice president of The Russian Center for Policy
   Studies (PIR Center in Moscow), since 2010. Previously, Lt. Gen. Buzhinsky
   served in the Russian General Staff and in Russia's Defence Ministry as
   head of treaties and international military cooperation. During an interview
   with the author on 5 June 2013 in Moscow, Buzhinsky stated that the CFE
   Treaty was obsolete because the purpose of the treaty to limit and regulate
   conventional forces in Europe was aimed at a now-terminated block-to-
   block situation. From a security policy view, there was no longer any need
   for the CFE, since there was no risk of an armed conflict in Europe. The
   holdings of conventional weapons of the CFE countries had been reduced
   considerably below the treaty's reduction commitments, and today, there
   was no longer any need to further reduce holdings of conventional
   weapons. According to the Russian defence chiefs, the Adaptation Agreement was also outdated. A possible new arms control agreement on conven-

tional forces in Europe could, according to Buzhinsky, be worked out in the form of a radically expanded Vienna Document which would also cover the three Baltic countries and confidence- and security-building measures (CSBMs) for naval forces. Any new agreement should not contain reduction commitments and did not need to be a legally binding treaty. Russia wanted a politically binding document like the current Vienna Document. The OSCE would be the appropriate forum for negotiations on a possible new agreement to replace the agreement on conventional forces in Europe, and for new measures (CSBMs) on naval forces. Furthermore, the future control and regulation of conventional forces in Europe could not be determined in isolation, but had to be dealt with in connection with missile defence and the role of nuclear weapons – including, in particular, the role of tactical nuclear weapons.

CHAPTER TWELVE

1 For a detailed description of the categories of small arms and light weapons and presentation of all small arms issues, see the handbook *A Diplomat's Guide to the UN Small Arms Process*, released in August 2012 by the Small Arms Survey, an independent research project established in 1999 and located at the Graduate Institute of International Studies in Geneva. Also see the Small Arms Survey's first edition *Profiling the Problem* – 2001. www.smallarmssurvey.org.

2 UN doc. A/52/298 of 27 August 1997.

3 See *The Geneva Declaration on Armed Violence and Development* of 7 June 2006 and the secretary general's report *Promoting Development through the Reduction and Prevention of Armed Violence* (doc. A/64/228 of 5 August 2009).

4 See doc. A/CONF.192/15. The Conference and the Action Program is described and analyzed in the Small Arms Survey's yearbook for 2002.

5 See General Assembly decision 60/519, adopted in December 2005.

6 The National Guard was originally organized as a militia force in each of the states and territories of the United States. Local militias were formed from the earliest English colonization of the Americas in 1607. The first colony-wide militia was formed by Massachusetts in 1636.

7 www.gunviolencearchive.org

8 Doc. 1999/34/CFSP.

9 Doc. 2002/589/CFSP.

10 Doc. 5319/06.
11 Doc. 2010/765/CFSP.
12 FSC.DOC/1/00/Rev.1.
13 Organization of American States. www.oas.org/juridico/english/treaties/a-63.html.

CHAPTER THIRTEEN

1 Doc. A/S-10/2, paragraph 85.
2 Resolution 67/234B.
3 See also Stockholm International Peace Research Institute, http://www.sipri.org/yearbook/2015/10, and SIPRI Fact Sheet *Trends in International Arms Transfers, 2014*, 2015, by Pieter D. Wezeman and Siemon T. Wezeman, http://books.sipri.org/files/FS/SIPRIFS1503.pdf.
4 www.australiagroup.net.
5 www.mtcr.info.
6 www.nuclearsuppliersgroup.org.
7 www.wassenaar.org.
8 See also Stockholm International Peace Research Institute (SIPRI) Fact Sheet *Trends in World Military Expenditure, 2014*, 2015, by Sam Perlo-Freeman, Aude Fleurant, Pieter D. Wezeman, and Siemon T. Wezeman. http://books.sipri.org/files/FS/SIPRIFS1504.pdf.

CHAPTER FOURTEEN

1 The Weapons of Mass Destruction Commission's report contains sixty concrete recommendations. www.wmdcommission.org and UN doc. A/60/934.
2 See "Toward a World without Nuclear Weapons" – an op-ed series of five articles published in the *Wall Street Journal* between January 2007 and March 2013, written by George P. Shultz, William J. Perry, Henry A. Kissinger, and Sam Nunn. www.nti.org.
3 See the thirteen Practical Steps for the Systematic and Progressive Efforts for the Implementation of Article VI of the Treaty on the Non-Proliferation of Nuclear Weapons, adopted at the Non-Proliferation Treaty (NPT) review conference in 2000 and the 1995 Decision on Principles and Objectives for Nuclear Non-Proliferation and Disarmament, in the NPT Briefing Book (2008 ed.), published by Mountbatten Centre for International Studies.
4 According to *Reducing Alert Rates of Nuclear Weapons*, published by UNIDIR, the nuclear weapons of China, India, Pakistan, and Israel are normally not deployed in operational readiness.

EPILOGUE

1 See *The Humanitarian Consequences of Nuclear War* by Ira Helfand, Arms Control Association. www.armscontrol.org/act/2013_11/The-Humanitarian-Consequences-Of-Nuclear-War. The horrors of a nuclear attack on the United States are depicted in the movie *The Day After* (1983).

2 See the easily read and thought-provoking presentation of the problem in the book *Common Sense on Weapons of Mass Destruction*, by arms control veteran Ambassador Thomas Graham.

3 See Nuclear Security Project.
http://www.nuclearsecurityproject.org/uploads/publications/NS P_brochure.pdf. All five articles are available at http://www.nuclearsecurity project.org/publications/wall-street-journal-op-eds.
The documentary film *Nuclear Tipping Point* can be downloaded at http://www.nucleartippingpoint.org/film/film.html.

4 Both incidents have been turned into movies, both entitled *The Man Who Saved the World*.

5 See the detailed and well documented account of nuclear accidents in the United States in the (632-page) book *Command and Control* by Eric Schlosser.

6 See also The Nuclear Threat Initiative, NTI's report *Rising Nuclear Dangers: Assessing the Risk of Nuclear Use in the Euro-Atlantic Region*, 2015.
http://www.nti.org/media/pdfs/NTI_Rising_Nuclear_Dangers_Paper_FINA L.pdf?_=1443443566.

Bibliography

The selected bibliography does not include books and articles in Danish on international law, humanitarian international law, security policy, United Nations, NATO, peace, and war.

Acheson, Ray, eds. 2013. *Still Assuring Destruction Forever.* New York: Reaching Critical Will.

Arbatov, Alexei, and Vladimir Dvorkin, eds. 2013. *Missile Defence: Confrontation and Cooperation.* Moscow: Carnegie Moscow Center.

– eds. 2012. *Nuclear Reset: Arms Reduction and Nonproliferation.* Moscow: Carnegie Moscow Center.

– eds. 2009. *Nuclear Proliferation: New Technologies, Weapons, Treaties.* Moscow: Carnegie Moscow Center.

Arbatov, Alexei, Vladimir Dvorkin, Sergey Oznobishchev, and Alexander Pikaev. 2010. *NATO-Russia Relations.* Moscow: Institute of World Economy and International Relations and the Nuclear Threat Initiative.

Athanasopulos, Haralambos. 2000. *Nuclear Disarmament in International Law.* Jefferson, NC, and London: McFarland & Company, Inc., Publishers.

Barnaby, Frank. 2003. *How to Build a Nuclear Bomb.* London: Granta Books.

Berry, Ken, Patricia Lewis, Benoît Pélopidas, Nikolai Sokov, and Ward Wilson. 2010. *Delegitimizing Nuclear Weapons: Examining the Validity of Nuclear Deterrence.* Monterey, CA: James Martin Center for Nonproliferation Studies, Monterey Institute of International Studies.

Beukel, Erik. 2012. *The Last Living Fossil of the Cold War.* Copenhagen: Danish Institute for International Studies.

Blackaby, Frank, Jozef Goldblat, and Sverre Lodgaard, eds. 1984. *No-First-Use.* London: Taylor & Francis.

Blix, Hans. 2005. *Disarming Iraq.* London: Bloomsbury Publishing.

Borrie, John, and Tim Caughley. 2013. *Viewing Nuclear Weapons through a Humanitarian Lens.* New York and Geneva: UNIDIR.

Burroughs John. 1997. *The (Il)legality of Threat or Use of Nuclear Weapons.* Münster: Lit Verlag.

Busch, Nathan E., and Daniel H. Joyner, eds. 2009. *Combating Weapons of Mass Destruction – The Future of International Nonproliferation Policy.* Athens: University of Georgia Press.

Canberra Commission. 1996. *Report of the Canberra Commission on the Elimination of Nuclear Weapons.* Canberra.

Center for Strategic and International Studies. 2003. *Protecting against the Spread of Nuclear, Biological and Chemical Weapons – Volume 1: An Agenda for Action.* Washington: Nuclear Threat Initiative.

Chilaty, Dariush. 1978. *Disarmament – A Historical Review of Negotiations and Treaties.* Iran National University.

Cirincione, Joseph, Jon B. Wolfsthal, and Miriam Rajkumar. 2005. *Deadly Arsenals – Nuclear, Biological, and Chemical Threats.* Washington: Carnegie Endowment for International Peace.

– 2013. *Nuclear Nightmares – Securing the World before It is Too Late.* New York: Columbia University Press.

Clarke, Richard A., and Robert K. Knake. 2010. *Cyber War – The Next Threat to National Security and What to Do about It.* New York: HarperCollins Publishers.

Dahlitz, Julie, 1996. *Future Legal Restraints on Arms Proliferation.* New York and Geneva: United Nations.

– ed. 1994. *Avoidance and Settlement of Arms Control Disputes.* New York and Geneva: United Nations.

Dahlitz, Julie, and Detlev Dicke, eds. 1991. *The International Law of Arms Control and Disarmament.* New York: United Nations.

De Gruyter, Walter. 1982. *Disarmament Terminology.* Berlin and New York: Walter de Gruyter & Co.

Evans, Gareth, Tanya Ogilvie-White, and Ramesh Thakur. 2015. *Nuclear Weapons: The State of Play.* Canberra: Centre for Nuclear Non-Proliferation and Disarmament.

Goldblat, Jozef. 2002. *Arms Control – The New Guide to Negotiations and Agreements,* including new CD-ROM Documentation Supplement. Oslo and London: International Peace Research Institute and Stockholm International Peace Research Institute.

– 1996. *Arms Control – A Guide to Negotiations and Agreements.* Oslo and London: International Peace Research Institute and SAGA Publications.

Gormley, Dennis M. 2001. *Dealing with the Threat of Cruise Missiles*. Oxford: Oxford University Press.

Graham, Thomas, Jr. 2004. *Commonsense on Weapons of Mass Destruction*. Washington: University of Washington Press.

Graham, Thomas, Jr, and Damien J. LaVera. 2003. *Cornerstones of Security*. Seattle and London: University of Washington Press.

Gray, Colin S. 1993. *Weapons Don't Make War*. Kansas: University Press of Kansas.

Gripstad, Birger. 1986. *Biological Warfare Agents*. Stockholm: The Swedish National Defence Research Institute.

Hamel-Green, Michael. 2005. *Regional Initiatives on Nuclear- and WMD-Free Zones*. Geneva: UNIDIR.

Hutchinson, Robert. 2004. *Weapons of Mass Destruction*. London: Cassell.

International Association of Lawyers Against Nuclear Arms and International Human Rights Clinic. 2009. *Good Faith Negotiations Leading to the Total Elimination of Nuclear Weapons*. Cambridge, MA: Harvard Law School.

International Court of Justice. 1996. *Legality of the Use by a State of Nuclear Weapons in Armed Conflict, Advisory Opinion, 8 July 1996*. The Hague.

– 1996. *Legality of the Threat or Use of Nuclear Weapons, Advisory Opinion, 8 July 1996*. The Hague.

Johnson, Rebecca. 2009. *Unfinished Business – The Negotiation of the CTBT and the End of Nuclear Testing*. New York and Geneva: UNIDIR.

Kissinger, Henry. 2014. *World Order*. New York: Penguin Press.

– 1994. *Diplomacy*. New York: Simon & Schuster.

Krieger, David. 2013. *Zero – The Case for Nuclear Weapons Abolition*. A Nuclear Age Peace Foundation Book.

Kristensen, Hans M., and Matthew McKinzie. 2012. *Reducing Alert Rates of Nuclear Weapons*. New York and Geneva: UNIDIR.

Larsen, Jeffrey A., and Kerry M. Kartchner, eds. 2014. *On Limited Nuclear War in the 21st Century*. Stanford: Stanford University Press.

Larsen, Jeffrey A., and Gregory J. Rattray, eds. 1996. *Arms Control toward the 21st Century*. Boulder, CO, and London: Lynne Rienner Publishers.

Lindstrom, Gustav, and Burkard Schmitt. 2003. *Fighting Proliferation – European Perspectives*. Paris: Institute for Security Studies.

Lysén, Göran. 1990. *The International Regulation of Armaments: The Law of Disarmament*. Uppsala: Iustus Förlag.

Mazarr, Michael J., and Alexander T. Lennon, eds. 1994. *Toward a Nuclear Peace*. Hampshire and London: The Macmillan Press.

Melzer, Nils. 2011. *Cyberwarfare and International Law*. Geneva: UNIDIR.

Minot, Sarah, ed. 2015. *Nuclear Scholars Initiative*. Washington: Center for Strategic and International Studies and Rowman & Littlefield.

Narang, Vipin. 2014. *Nuclear Strategy in the Modern Era*. Princeton: Princeton University Press.

New Zealand Ministry of Foreign Affairs & Trade. 2015. *United Nations Handbook 2015–16*. Wellington, New Zealand.

Nuclear Security Governance Experts Group. 2015. *International Convention on Nuclear Security*. Washington: Asian Institute for Policy Studies, Partnership for Global Security, and the Stanley Foundation.

Nystuen, Gro, Stuart Casey-Maslen, and Annie Golden Bersagel, eds. 2014. *Nuclear Weapon under International Law*. Cambridge: Cambridge University Press.

Parker, Sarah, and Marcus Wilson. 2014. *A Diplomat's Guide to the UN Small Arms Process*. Geneva: Small Arms Survey.

Perkovich, George, and James M. Acton. 2008. *Abolishing Nuclear Weapons*. London: International Institute for Strategic Studies.

Podvig, Pavel. 2011. *Global Nuclear Security – Building Greater Accountability and Cooperation*. New York and Geneva: UNIDIR.

Ringsmose, Jens, and Sten Rynning, eds. 2011. *NATO's New Strategic Concept: A Comprehensive Assessment*. Copenhagen: Danish Institute for International Studies.

Rosamond, Annika Bergman. 2011. *Perspectives on Security in the Arctic Area*. Copenhagen: Danish Institute for International Studies.

Schlosser, Eric. 2013. *Command and Control – Nuclear Weapons, the Damascus Accident, and the Illusion of Safety*. New York: The Penguin Press.

Schmitt, Burkard, ed. 2001. *Nuclear Weapons: A New Great Debate*. Paris: Institute for Security Studies of Western European Studies.

Sinclair, Sir Ian McTaggart. 1984. *The Vienna Convention on the Law of Treaties*. Manchester: Manchester University Press.

Siracusa, Joseph M. 2008. *Nuclear Weapons – A Very Short Introduction*. Oxford: Oxford University Press.

Small Arms Survey. 2013. *Small Arms Survey 2013 – Everyday Dangers*. Cambridge: Cambridge University Press.

– 2002. *Small Arms Survey 2002 – Counting the Human Cost*. Oxford: Oxford University Press.

– 2001. *Small Arms Survey 2001 – Profiling the Problem*. Oxford: Oxford University Press.

Spies, Michael, and John Burroughs, eds. 2007. *Nuclear Disorder or Cooperative Security?* New York: Lawyers' Committee on Nuclear Policy.

Staur, Carsten. 2014. *Shared Responsibility – The United Nations in the Age of Globalization*, Montreal and Copenhagen: McGill-Queen's University Press and Djoef Publishing.

Stockholm International Peace Research Institute. *Yearbook 2012, 2013, 2014 and 2015*. Oxford: Oxford University Press.

Sur, Serge, ed. 1991. *Verification of Current Disarmament and Arms Limitation Agreements Ways, Means and Practices*. UK: Dartmouth Publishing Company and UNIDIR.

Tulliu, Steve, and Thomas Schmalberger. 2003. *Coming to Terms with Security: A Lexicon for Arms Control, Disarmament and Confidence Building*. Geneva: UNIDIR.

UNIDIR. 2004. *Building a Weapons of Mass Destruction Free Zone in the Middle East.* Geneva.

– 2003. *Outer Space and Global Security.* Geneva: UNIDIR, Project Ploughshares Canada, and The Simons Centre for Peace and Disarmament Studies.

– 2002. *Missile Defence, Deterrence and Arms Control: Contradictory Aims or Compatible Goals?* Geneva.

– 1991. *Verification of Current Disarmament and Arms Limitation Agreements: Ways, Means and Practices.*

UNIDIR and VERTIC. 2003. *Coming to Terms with Security: A Handbook on Verification and Compliance.* Geneva.

United Nations. 2015. *The United Nations Disarmament Yearbook 2014.* New York.

– 2008. *Small Arms and Light Weapons – Selected United Nations Documents.* New York.

– 1995. *The United Nations and Nuclear Non-Proliferation.* New York.

– 1978. *Final Document of the Special Session of the General Assembly on Disarmament 1978.* New York.

Vestergaard, Cindy. 2009. *Modern Non-proliferation and Disarmament: Denmark and the G8 Global Partnership.* Copenhagen: Danish Institute for International Studies.

– 2010. *The Disarmament Factor: Toward a Typological Theory of WMD Disarmament.* Copenhagen: Department of Political Science, University of Copenhagen.

– ed. 2010. *Conference on the Arctic Nuclear-Weapon-Free Zone, Copenhagen 2009.* Copenhagen: Danish Institute for International Studies.

Vignard, Kerstin, ed. 2012. *Agent of Change? The CW Regime.* Geneva: UNIDIR disarmament forum.

– ed. 2011. *Confronting Cyberconflict.* Geneva: UNIDIR disarmament forum.

– ed. 2004. *Weapons of Mass Destruction and Human Rights.* Geneva: UNIDIR.

Weapons of Mass Destruction Commission. 2006. *Weapons of Terror – Freeing the World of Nuclear, Biological, and Chemical Arms.* Stockholm.

Wilson, Ward. 2014. *Five Myths About Nuclear Weapons.* New York: First Mariner Books.

Websites

Acronym Institute for Disarmament Diplomacy: www.acronym.org.uk
Arms Control Association (ACA): www.armscontrol.org
Carnegie Endowment for International Peace:
    www.carnegieendowment.org
Center for Arms Control and Non-Proliferation:
    www.armscontrolcenter.org
Center for Strategic and International Studies (CSIS): www.csis.org
Comprehensive Nuclear-Test-Ban Treaty Organization (CTBTO):
    www.ctbto.org
Conference on Disarmament (CD): www.unog.ch/cd
Control Arms: www.controlarms.org
European Leadership Network: www.europeanleadershipnetwork.org
Federation of American Scientists (FAS): www.fas.org
Global Zero: www.globalzero.org
International Atomic Energy Agency (IAEA): www.iaea.org
International Campaign to Abolish Nuclear Weapons (ICAN):
    www.icanw.org
International Committee of the Red Cross (ICRC): www.icrc.org
International Institute for Strategic Studies (IISS): www.iiss.org
James Martin Center for Nonproliferation Studies: cns.miis.edu
Nuclear Abolition Forum: www.abolitionforum.org
Nuclear Security Project: www.nuclearsecurityproject.org
Nuclear Threat Initiative (NTI): www.nti.org
Nuclear Zero: www.nuclearzero.org
Organization for Security and Co-operation in Europe (OSCE):
    www.osce.org

Organization for the Prohibition of Chemical Weapons (OPCW):
www.opcw.org
Pugwash Conferences on Science and World Affairs: www.pugwash.org
Reaching Critical Will: www.reachingcriticalwill.org
Stimson Center: www.stimson.org
Stockholm International Peace Research Institute (SIPRI): www.sipri.org
United Nations (UN): www.un.org
UN Institute for Disarmament Research (UNIDIR): www.unidir.org
UN website on the status of treaties: disarmament.un.org/treaties/
UN Disarmament Commission (UNDC):
www.un.org/Depts/ddar/discomm/undc.html
UN Disarmament Fact Sheets on Disarmament Issues:
www.un.org/disarmament/factsheets/
UN Disarmament Yearbook:
www.un.org/disarmament/publications/yearbook/volume-39-2014/
United Nations Office for Disarmament Affairs (UNODA):
www.un.org/disarmament/
Nuclear weapons: www.un.org/disarmament/wmd/Nuclear/
Biological weapons: www.un.org/disarmament/wmd/bio/
Chemical weapons: www.un.org/disarmament/wmd/chemical/
Missiles: www.un.org/disarmament/wmd/Missiles/
Small Arms and Light Weapons:
www.un.org/disarmament/convarms/salw/
Landmines: www.un.org/disarmament/convarms/landmines
Arms Trade Treaty: www.un.org/disarmament/convarms/att/
Conventional Weapons Register:
www.un.org/disarmament/convarms/Register/
UN General Assembly (UNGA): www.un.org/en/ga
UN General Assembly Resolutions (UNGA res.):
www.un.org/en/sections/documents/general-assembly-resolutions
/index.html
UN Security Council (UNSC): www.un.org/en/sc
UN Security Council Resolutions (UNSC res.):
www.un.org/en/sc/documents/resolutions/

Index